CAPITAL GAINS

minimal taxes

Also by the Author

For general readers

Go Roth!
Your Guide to Roth Retirement Accounts

Consider Your Options
Get the Most from Your Equity Compensation

That Thing Rich People Do
Required Reading for Investors

For professionals

Equity Compensation Strategies
A Guide for Professional Advisors

Capital Gains, Minimal Taxes

The Essential Guide for Investors and Traders

2023 Edition

Kaye A. Thomas

A Plain Language Guide From

FAIRMARK PRESS

Capital Gains, Minimal Taxes

The Essential Guide for Investors and Traders

This edition of *Capital Gains, Minimal Taxes* reflects relevant legal authorities as of April 30, 2023.

Publisher:
Fairmark Press
Fairmark.com
(630) 728-3835

Print edition ISBN-13: 978-1-938797-19-4
Kindle edition ISBN-13: 978-1-938797-20-0

Printed in the United States of America

Table of Contents

About the Author

Kaye Thomas spent over 30 years as a tax lawyer dealing with matters relating to business transactions, finance and compensation. His writings include technical works for tax and finance professionals as well as publications like this book, designed for the general public. His books have sold over 70,000 copies.

Kaye maintains **Fairmark.com**, a free website that provides news, reference materials, tools and hundreds of pages of plain language guidance on matters related to investment and taxation.

Kaye's law degree is from Harvard Law School, where he served on the Harvard Law Review and graduated *cum laude* in 1980.

About this edition

This is the seventh edition of *CGMT*. It has been updated to reflect changes in the tax law through April 30, 2023.

> A 2017 law known as the Tax Cuts and Jobs Act made many changes affecting individuals that are effective for years 2018 through 2025, after which they revert to prior law. This edition, like the previous one, ignores the sunset provision. In a world where Congress so frequently makes major changes in the tax law, there's little practical difference between an eight-year provision that may later be made permanent, and a permanent provision that may end up being altered or repealed.

The previous (2019) edition of this book reflected changes made by the 2017 tax law. There have been relatively few significant developments affecting the topics covered here since then. A notable addition is new material in chapter 11 concerning cryptocurrencies and other digital assets. Chapter 32 describes how Form W-4 has changed, making it easier to adjust withholding. After the 2017 tax law changed the "kiddie tax," Congress backtracked on that change. Chapter 33 reflects the return to using parents' tax rates to tax investment income of their children.

Part I
Laying the Foundation

1

The Big Picture

Tax compliance and planning for stocks, mutual funds and options in taxable investment accounts.

OUR PURPOSE IS TO UNDERSTAND taxation of investments held in regular investment accounts. We'll learn what's needed for accurate compliance with the rules, and seek to identify strategies that minimize the tax cost of investing.

To stay within bounds of the reader's patience and the author's endurance, we restrict our attention almost entirely to stocks, mutual funds and options. We won't explore the distinct and often complicated tax treatment of other investments such as bonds, annuities and partnerships. Likewise, rules for retirement accounts and other tax-exempt or tax-deferred accounts are beyond the scope of this book. We aim to do one thing well: learn how to handle U.S. federal income tax for someone who buys and sells these investments in a taxable account.

Overview

We'll tackle these issues under nine main headings:

- Part I (where you are now) provides background on taxes and investing in general.
- Part II covers the rules for capital gains and losses the typical investor is most likely to encounter, from the capital loss limitation to the infamous wash sale rule.
- Part III explains how to deal with dividends, investment interest expense, and other investment expenses.
- Part IV is for investors who pursue advanced strategies such as short sales and trading in stock options.
- Part V summarizes rules for gifts, including custodial accounts for minors and charitable gifts of stock.
- Part VI tells how to determine if you're a *trader* as defined in the tax law, and how that status affects your taxes.
- Part VII explains two other taxes you may encounter as an investor: alternative minimum tax (AMT) and net investment income tax.
- Part VIII provides help with issues related to filing returns and paying taxes.
- Part IX brings together tax planning ideas that can reduce your taxes.

2

The Investment Context

A tax strategy for investments must be considered within the context of a sound investment strategy.

IT'S OFTEN SAID, AND UNDENIABLY TRUE, that you shouldn't pursue a tax strategy if it's a bad investment strategy. So, what's a good investment strategy? Experts haven't settled on a single approach that's best for everyone. Most would agree on three key principles, however.

An appropriate mix

Financial markets offer various types of investments that can be broadly classified into four categories: stocks, bonds, cash and other. In this brief discussion we'll focus on the first three, which typically make up most if not all of an investment account, either directly or through mutual funds that invest in these assets. They have three distinctly different risk/reward profiles:

Cash. In connection with investments, this term refers to extremely low-risk, short-term investments. Generally you're free to add to them or take money out any time you want, so they function pretty much like cash except they earn interest. Complete liquidity and close to zero risk make these investments suitable for money you'll need in the near future, perhaps to pay taxes or a tuition bill. You can also use cash as a reserve fund for emergencies, a temporary place for money to be deployed in other investments later, or simply an investment that dampens the overall risk of your portfolio.

Yet one of the biggest mistakes an investor can make is putting too much money in cash for an extended period of time. These nearly riskless investments produce minimal returns, usually barely above the rate of inflation and sometimes below that rate. In "real" terms (that is, after taking inflation into account), cash investments produce little or no growth over the long term. Cash is an indispensable tool for investors but can prevent you from reaching your goals if overused.

Bonds. The next step up the ladder of risk and reward is bonds. Like cash investments, bonds produce interest income, but they represent a longer-term commitment, exposing you to risk of default by the company or government responsible for repaying the debt. You can suffer a loss even without a default if interest rates rise. The bond you bought when 5% was reasonable becomes unattractive, and therefore has a lower value, when similar bonds paying 7% are available.

> An increase in interest rates sounds like something that would be good for bondholders, but it's an advantage only to new investors, not to those who already own bonds paying lower rates.

Bonds compensate their holders for these risks by paying higher rates of interest than you can expect from cash investments. The potential for faster growth makes bonds suitable for a significant portion of a typical investment portfolio.

Stocks. Although bonds typically produce returns above the rate of inflation, most investors need a more potent source of growth to reach their goals. There's no getting around this iron rule of investing: to obtain more generous rewards, investors have to accept greater risk. Typically this means investing in stocks. Investing too little in stocks has the same effect as investing too much in cash, stunting the growth of your portfolio.

How much is enough? That varies by individual circumstances. Your investment goals and time horizon can point toward an appropriate range, but an elusive, subjective factor known as risk tolerance may be of even greater importance. How much loss are you able to stomach before you bail out? Nothing is more damaging to investment success than abandoning stocks after a steep slide, yet millions of investors do this in every bear market, selling at low prices and buying later when stocks are higher, the exact opposite of the formula for success.

> It's all but impossible to know in advance how much loss you can bear when you have real money at risk. Yet this is one of the keys to success: invest enough in stocks to produce the growth you need for the long-term, but not so much that you'll be unable to weather the bad times.

Diversification

Second in our list of key investment principles is *diversification.* The term is sometimes applied to the subject discussed above, creating a good mix of different types of investments. We use it here in a narrower sense. Within each category of investment, especially stocks, money should be divided among many different items that may perform differently.

Many investors resist diversification with the view that they can make their money grow faster by concentrating their money in a few stocks, or even just one. To be sure, an investment in one stock, or a few, that perform well above average will produce more growth than a widely diversified portfolio. Yet the inherent difficulty of selecting stocks that will outperform others is such that even the most astute stock pickers fail much of the time. The highly efficient auction mechanism of the stock market makes it impossible for investors to know in advance which stocks will prevail.

The most powerful reason for diversification stems from basic mathematics. We might be presented with a choice of several stocks that all have the same expected return—say, 10%. We can choose one of them, or divide our money among all of them. Either way, the expected return of our portfolio remains 10%, because all the investments have the same expected return. Yet the risk of investing in just one of the stocks is much higher than if we divide the money among all of them. Price variations for the diversified portfolio are smaller because during any given period some of the stocks will perform better than others, eliminating the widest swings.

The upshot is that diversification can have the effect of reducing risk without reducing expected return. This is contrary to the general rule of investing that associates lower risk with lower returns. Investors who fail to diversify make the fundamental error of taking greater risk with no additional reward.

Expenses

The third and last in our list of key investment principles is to minimize expenses. Over a lifetime of investing, an investor who minimizes expenses may end up with more than twice as much wealth as another whose savings and pre-expense earnings are similar. Our main concern in this book will be to minimize taxes, often the largest single expense.

Investors must of course be cognizant of other expenses. A review of all the expenses that may be incurred in buying, holding and selling stocks, mutual funds and other investments is beyond the scope of this brief summary. Those needing a primer—people buying and selling stocks without understanding how the bid-ask spread is costing them money, for example—may wish to consider the small investment of time and money necessary to read my book *That Thing Rich People Do.*

Stock selection and market timing

We've covered all the key principles of investing without mentioning stock selection or market timing. These are the topics that receive the most attention in the financial press and in many books, yet they are not essential elements of a good strategy.

Stock selection. During any given period some stocks will perform far better than others. Plainly it would be an advantage to hold stocks that will outperform and exclude the laggards. The problem is that all investors have this same desire, and they can't all perform above average. Every dollar of superior performance comes at the expense of some other investor. Competition among investors to buy underpriced stocks and sell the others causes prices to gravitate toward levels where it's difficult for even the most perceptive professionals to determine which stocks will outperform.

As a result, studies have found that skillful stock selection is of relatively little importance in determining the performance of a portfolio. Superior results that appear to indicate outstanding skill typically involve a large component of luck and fail to replicate. It is not unusual to see one year's star investment managers appear among the poorer performers in a later year.

Market timing. The same forces that make superior stock selection so difficult prevent us from earning easy profits by choosing when to move money into and out of the stock market. You can only sell your stocks at a price some other investor is willing to pay, and as a result we are never in a situation where investors in general know which direction the market is going to move in the near future. At any given time we have experts predicting strong performance and others forecasting a decline. Given that no one truly knows which way stocks are going to move, attempts to time the market are as likely to damage your returns as they are to enhance them.

Tax planning and investment strategy

Tax planning principles are often, but not always, consistent with a sound investment strategy. When a conflict occurs it should not automatically be resolved on one side or the other, but evaluated to determine how to produce the best balance of risk and reward on an after-tax basis.

A large position in the stock of a single company, for example, may cry out for diversification. Continued holding of those shares may expose you to excessive risk without enhancing your expected return. Yet concentrated positions often result from appreciation in value, so that a sale of the shares would result in a taxable gain. Typically we would expect to find that the benefit of diversification outweighs the detriment of reporting capital gain on a sale, though we might reach a different conclusion in some cases.

Tax loss harvesting offers a different dynamic. A sale of shares that have declined in value produces a capital loss that will yield immediate tax savings or contribute to a capital loss carryover that may be used to shelter capital gains in later years. The wash sale rule, covered in detail later, prevents you from claiming this loss if you buy identical shares within 30 days before or after the date of sale. To many investors, the idea of altering their stock selections, even for a period of 31 days, is distasteful, but given the small role stock selection plays in producing superior performance, the detriment of doing so may be small in relation to the tax benefit of securing a deductible capital loss.

In short, investment strategies don't always overrule tax strategies, nor is the reverse true. Each must be evaluated in the context of the other to determine an approach that produces an appropriate balance of all relevant considerations.

3

Structure of the Income Tax

Tax rules, techniques and strategies for investments apply within the framework of the federal income tax.

THE OVERALL STRUCTURE of the federal income tax is mirrored in Form 1040. Briefly, the form reports your *total income*, then a group of deductions known as *adjustments* that lead to *adjusted gross income*, followed by more deductions that allow you to show a smaller amount as *taxable income*. Tax rates applied to your taxable income determine the amount of tax, which is reduced by any credits to which you are entitled.

Filing status

Your *filing status* determines the size of your standard deduction (described later) and the tax rate schedule that applies to your income, and may affect other tax benefits. There are four possibilities:

- married filing jointly
- head of household
- single
- married filing separately

In each of the last three categories the tax return reports income of one individual. Given all the same income and deductions, the tax will generally be lowest on a return for a head of household and highest for married individuals filing separately.

The return for a married couple filing jointly combines the income of two individuals. At low to moderate income levels the tax is likely to be equal to or less than the combined total if the individuals were single. At higher income levels the tax on a joint return may be higher than if the individuals were single, especially if the income is divided roughly equally between the spouses.

> For up to two years after the death of a spouse, a widow or widower meeting certain requirements can file using the rate table for couples that are married filing jointly.

Total income

The first part of the tax return (after preliminary information) tallies your *total income.* Here you must report, in the famous words of the tax law, "all income from whatever source derived." Among the items appearing here are all the familiar types of investment income: interest, dividends, capital gains and so forth. A few points worth noting:

- Exempt interest is reported here even though it is not included in your total income. This item can affect the amount of social security income that's included in your taxable income.

- Capital gains are included here even though (as explained in a later chapter) they are not considered "ordinary income" and get a special tax calculation.
- Although many deductions (notably, most deductions associated with investment expenses) appear later, some deductions are claimed as part of the calculation of total income. If you engage in business as an individual, for example, you generally claim your business deductions on the same form where you report the income (Schedule C), and only the net amount appears as part of your total income.

Adjusted gross income

Deductions that fall into a category known as *adjustments* have a kind of exalted status. They're used in calculating your *adjusted gross income*, or *AGI*. Roughly speaking, AGI is conceived as a measure of how much income you have at your disposal. The deductions allowed here include items such as contributions to retirement plans and health savings accounts, penalty for early withdrawal of savings, and student loan interest payments. Deductions allowed later as *itemized deductions* (see below) relate, again roughly speaking, to how you used the income rather than how much you had available in the first place. As a result, *modified AGI*, often abbreviated *MAGI*, is used in a wide variety of contexts to determine whether you qualify for tax benefits and, if so, in what amount.

> In most cases, exclusions related to foreign earned income are added back in arriving at MAGI, so that AGI and MAGI are often the same for taxpayers without this type of income. Other modifications are used in connection with some tax benefits, however.

An increase in your MAGI may reduce or eliminate various credits, and affect your tax bill in other ways.

- An increase in total income (including a capital gain) will increase your MAGI, possibly resulting in a decrease in other tax benefits.
- An increase in the deductions you claim in this section of your tax return (such as a deductible contribution to an IRA) will reduce your MAGI, perhaps allowing you to qualify for an increase in other tax benefits.

> Beginning in 2018, a redesigned Form 1040 requires adjustments to be listed on Schedule 1, then subtracted from total income to produce AGI.

Personal exemptions

The Tax Cuts and Jobs Act eliminated the familiar deduction for personal exemptions beginning in 2018, giving us instead a larger standard deduction and an enhanced child credit.

Itemized deductions and standard deduction

Unless you claim the standard deduction (see below) you're allowed to claim *itemized deductions*. The main categories are medical and dental expenses, state and local taxes, interest you paid, and charitable gifts. The Tax Cuts and Jobs Act wiped out a category known as *miscellaneous deductions subject to the 2% floor*, preventing us from claiming such items as tax return preparation costs, safe deposit box rental, and certain investment expenses.

> Some itemized deductions are reduced based on the size of your modified AGI.

Keeping track of all those items can involve a fair amount of paperwork. Taxpayers can eliminate that effort if they instead claim the *standard deduction*. This deduction varies depending on your filing status and is adjusted for inflation each year. A majority of taxpayers claim the standard deduction rather than itemizing, often because they find that the standard deduction is larger.

The Tax Cuts and Jobs Act greatly increased the size of the standard deduction beginning in 2018. As a result, the number of itemizers is now much smaller than in previous years.

Taxable income and tax rates

The result after claiming all deductions (including personal exemptions) is *taxable income*. Special tax rates apply to the portion consisting of long-term capital gain and qualifying dividends. The remainder is taxed at regular rates based on your filing status (such as single or married filing jointly).

Other taxes

Form 1040 is used to report other taxes in addition to the income tax. Two are of particular importance to investors.

Alternative minimum tax (AMT). The name of this tax comes from the concept of using an alternative set of rules to calculate the minimum amount of tax someone with your income is required to pay. If your regular income tax falls below this minimum, you have to pay additional tax to make up the difference. The number of individuals paying AMT decreased dramatically following changes made by a 2017 tax law. Yet a large long-term capital gain can still bring an unwelcome surprise. See Chapter 29.

Net investment income tax. Since 2013, a 3.8% net investment income tax applies to taxpayers in the higher tax brackets. See Chapter 30 for details.

Credits

Tax credits of various kinds can reduce the amount you owe or increase your refund. Credits differ from deductions in that they apply against your tax rather than your income.

> **Example:** You are in the 25% tax bracket and a preliminary calculation indicates you will owe $1,200 when you file your tax return. If you identify a $400 deduction you can claim, it will reduce your tax by $100 ($400 times 25%). If you identify a $400 *credit* you can claim, it will reduce your tax by $400.

Credits are classified as refundable or nonrefundable. You can claim a *refundable* credit even if it reduces your tax below zero, causing the government to send you a refund that exceeds the amount you paid through withholding or otherwise. *Nonrefundable* credits can reduce your tax to zero but no further.

> **Example:** In a preliminary calculation, your tax is $800 and you paid $1,200 through withholding, so you're entitled to a refund of $400. You discover you're entitled to an additional credit of $1,000. If the credit is refundable, you can claim the entire amount, producing a refund of $1,400, which is more than the amount of tax you paid through withholding. If it's a nonrefundable credit, you can claim only $800, the amount that reduces your tax to $0.

> Note that a nonrefundable credit can increase the amount of your refund. It's called nonrefundable because it can't increase the amount of your refund above the amount you paid.

4

Tax Brackets

Your tax bracket can be an important factor in deciding whether to adopt a particular strategy.

A CLEAR PICTURE OF HOW TAX BRACKETS WORK can help you select a more tax-efficient strategy.

Progressive rates

Income tax rates are *progressive*, which is to say the rates become higher as income increases. We might say the lowest rate is 0%, as the standard deduction establishes an amount of income you can earn without paying any tax at all. We then move up the ladder, with rates ranging from 10% to 37%.

It is often said that tax rates differ according to your filing status. To be more precise, each filing status has the same tax rates but the *amount of income* subject to each rate differs according to your filing status. The following table shows the income levels where each tax rate begins in the year 2023 for taxpayers in each filing status:

married filing jointly, head of household, single, and married filing separately.

Tax Bracket Beginning Points 2023				
	MFJ	HH	Single	MFS
10%	0	0	0	0
12%	22,000	15,700	11,000	11,000
22%	89,450	59,850	44,725	44,725
24%	190,750	95,350	95,375	95,375
32%	364,200	182,100	182,100	182,100
35%	462,500	231,250	231,250	231,250
37%	693,750	578,100	578,125	346,875

Note that these are dollar amounts of *taxable* income—that is, after taking into account deductions and exemptions. The standard deduction can remove over $13,000 of income from the return of a single taxpayer who is not a dependent, and over $27,000 from the return of a couple filing jointly.

Note also the unevenness of the increments between tax rates. The move from 12% to 22% is particularly significant. This is an increase of 10 percentage points, the largest gap in the table. From another perspective, the amount you get to retain out of $100 goes from $88 to $78, a decrease of more than 11%. And from yet another, the amount of tax you pay on each additional $100 of income goes from $12 to $22, an increase of 83%.

> Tax planning near the boundary between the 12% and 22% brackets can be especially beneficial.

Net investment income tax. High-income taxpayers pay a 3.8% surtax on their net investment income. Although this is a separate tax, rather than part of the income tax, it has the effect of raising the tax rate on investment income if your total income is above the threshold where it applies.

Moving to a higher tax bracket

People sometimes worry that a small increase in income will have a dramatic impact on their tax liability if it moves them into a higher tax bracket. This is a mistaken notion: the lower tax rate continues to apply to income up to the level where the tax rate changes, and the higher rate applies only to the increment above that level.

> **Example:** Your income is $100 below the level where the 22% tax bracket begins before you receive $500 in additional income. The first $100 falls into the 12% bracket, requiring you to pay $12. Then you have no more room in the 12% bracket, so the remaining $400 falls into the 22% bracket, requiring you to pay $88. The amount of tax you pay on the income you had before receiving this additional $500 is unchanged. Overall your tax will increase $100 ($12 plus $88) as a result of adding this income.

Withholding rates distinguished

Many workers mistakenly equate their withholding rate with their tax bracket. For most people, these two rates are not even close.

Withholding rates are designed to make the total amount withheld for the year be roughly equal to the amount of tax owed on that amount of income. As a result, your withholding rate can be far lower than the tax rate that applies in your current tax bracket.

> **Example:** If you earn enough to make your taxable income just a few thousand dollars above the top of the 12% bracket, you are in the 22% bracket where a $1,000 deduction will save you $220. Yet if you check your paystub you'll likely find that federal income tax is being withheld at a rate below 12%. Your withholding rate takes into account income taxed

at 0% (because of the standard deduction) as well as income taxed at 10% and 12%. If your pay stub shows tax being withheld at 11%, it may seem that a $1,000 contribution to your 401k account would save you only $110, but this contribution will actually reduce your tax by $220. You'll avoid $110 in withholding and save another $110 in the form of a smaller amount owed, or larger amount refunded, when you file your income tax return.

Finding your tax bracket

Since you can't find your tax bracket by looking at your paystub you need a different way. Normally we begin with your taxable income on your most recent tax return.

Recall that this is the amount of income remaining after you claim all allowable deductions, so it's generally quite a bit lower than your total income. Compare that income with the tax brackets for your filing status to see where it falls.

> Tax rate schedules are available in the Reference Room on Fairmark.com.

Adjustments. For tax planning purposes we're usually interested in your tax bracket for the current year (or next year) rather than for a previous year. If your income, deductions or filing status are likely to be different from the previous year you should make appropriate adjustments.

Distance from boundaries

For planning purposes it isn't always enough to know which tax bracket you currently occupy. Your tax bracket is dynamic, meaning it can change if your income or deductions change. If you're close to one of the boundaries, a choice based on your current tax bracket could produce unexpected results.

> **Example:** Your income happens to be just $1,000 below the level where the 22% rate begins to apply, so you are in the 12% tax bracket. If you adopt a strategy that adds $10,000 to your income, your added tax will be $2,100, not $1,200, because most of this added income will fall into the 22% bracket.

Occasionally we hear from someone who believes his tax bracket is established by his salary level and will be unaffected by tax planning he undertakes with his investments. This is incorrect. Investment strategies generally won't affect rates of withholding on earned income, but as noted earlier, withholding rates are not the same as tax brackets.

Planning with tax brackets

Investors are often faced with a choice that may produce additional income or a deduction that will reduce income. Your tax bracket determines the size of the effect on your tax bill.

> **Example:** You're considering increasing your 401k contribution by $4,000. If you're in the 12% tax bracket, this choice will reduce your tax by $480. In the 22% bracket your tax will go down by $880.

You save money with this 401k contribution in either case, but the savings are larger in the 22% bracket. The difference may prompt a change in strategy. For example, if you're in the 12% bracket you might save instead in a Roth account, which produces no deduction but makes subsequent investment earnings tax-free.

Capital gain tax rates

Income is divided between ordinary income and capital gains, which are further divided between short-term and long-term capital gains. (These terms will be defined in a later chapter.) The tax rates set forth above apply to ordinary income and short-term capital gains. Long-term capital gains are taxed at lower rates. As in the case of rates for ordinary income, the capital gains rates increase as your income rises. At the lowest levels of income, the rate on long-term capital gain is zero. The rate changes to 15% at about the same level where ordinary income begins to be taxed at 22%, and a 20% capital gains rate clicks in at a much higher level of income.

> Certain types of long-term capital gain are taxed at special rates that are higher than the rates indicated here.

In determining tax rates for capital gains, tax brackets are filled first with ordinary income and subsequently with long-term capital gain.

> **Example:** Your ordinary income is $1,000 below the level where the 15% capital gains rate begins to apply, and you have a $3,000 long-term capital gain. The rate is zero for the first $1,000 of this capital gain, and the remaining $2,000 is taxed at the 15% rate.

5

Investment Income

This chapter provides a brief overview of the main types of investment income covered by this book.

IN THIS BOOK WE'LL BE DEALING PRIMARILY WITH three types of investment income: interest, dividends and capital gains.

Interest income

The most familiar sources of interest income are savings accounts and interest-bearing checking accounts, but many other investments produce interest income, including certificates of deposit, savings bonds, and Treasury notes, among others. When taxable, interest bears the same tax rates as other forms of ordinary income, such as wages and pension income.

Normally we think of this income as being taxed at the highest rate that applies to your income. In other words, if you earn wages, we think of the wage income as coming first, so that it fills up the lower tax brackets, and the interest income as coming last. Wages and interest income are both equally eligible for the lower tax brackets, but we usually have more flexibility in planning for investment income, so we take the wage income (and any other fixed income, such as annual pension payments) as a given, and treat the interest income (and any other investment income) as something extra that's tacked on (and taxed) at the end.

> **Example:** Your wage income puts you in the 22% bracket. You're considering an investment that will produce interest income. As part of your thought process you should keep in mind that the interest income will be taxed at a rate of 22%.

Interest income from government obligations may receive special tax treatment. Generally, interest earned on state and local bonds (often called *municipal bonds*, or simply *municipals*) is exempt from federal income tax. Conversely, interest earned on debt obligations of the federal government is exempt from income taxes imposed by state and local governments.

Capital gains

Broadly speaking, capital gain is profit you have when you sell an investment at a higher price than you paid. We'll be mainly concerned with capital gain from selling stocks, mutual fund shares and options, but you can have capital gain when selling other assets, including your home. When you lose money on the sale of an investment you have a capital loss.

> For this purpose, your home is not considered an investment because you use it as a residence. That means you can't claim a capital loss if you lose money when selling your home, even though you may have to report a capital gain if you have a profit.

The tax law favors capital gains. Profit from selling an asset you've held more than a year is *long-term capital gain*, which qualifies for lower tax rates than ordinary income. We'll see later that you can effectively lower the rate even further by postponing the gain, either by continuing to hold profitable assets or by strategically harvesting capital losses.

Investments that have the potential to produce capital gain can also produce capital loss, and here the tax law taketh away. You can't deduct a capital loss from *personal use property*, such as your home. Furthermore, capital losses can be disallowed under various rules we'll discuss later, such as the wash sale rule. If you get past these hurdles, you still have the problem that the losses go into a separate calculation where they're paired up with capital gains, possibly reducing the amount that qualifies for favorable tax rates. Finally, if capital losses exceed capital gains, the amount you can deduct against ordinary income is limited to $3,000 per year.

Reporting capital gain and loss. The special tax rules for capital gains require a unique manner of reporting. We begin by separating capital gains and losses from all other income, and working through some calculations that involve only these items to determine whether you have an overall gain or loss, and how that gain or loss is divided between long-term and short-term. Then this income (or loss, to the extent allowed as a deduction) goes into the calculation of *total income*. As part of your total income, capital gain will be included in your adjusted gross income, the number that's used (with various modifications) to determine whether you qualify for various tax benefits.

> This point is worth noting because people sometimes contrast capital gains with "income," leading to the mistaken impression that capital gains are not included in total income or adjusted gross income.

Having been included in total income, capital gains take part in other tax calculations until very near the end, when we apply the tax rates to taxable income. At this point any long-term capital gain must be separated from other income so that the special tax rates can be applied. Your total tax will include the tax on ordinary income and the tax on long-term capital gain.

> **Example:** For a particular year you have $70,000 of wage income, $4,000 of interest income, $3,000 of short-term capital gain, and $8,000 of long-term capital gain. You also have itemized deductions adding up to $20,000.

In this example your total income and adjusted gross income are the same: $85,000. After subtracting the deductions you have $65,000 of taxable income. Before applying the tax rates we have to divide this between ordinary income and long-term capital gain. Your total tax will be the sum of (a) the tax on $57,000 of ordinary income, and (b) the tax on $8,000 of long-term capital gain. The amount of tax you actually pay on these amounts will depend on your filing status (married filing jointly, single, etc.).

Dividends

For many years, dividend income was treated the same as interest income, being taxed at the same rates as other forms of ordinary income such as wages. We now have rules that apply lower tax rates to *qualifying dividends*. Nonqualifying dividends are taxed at the same rates as interest and other forms of ordinary income.

The tax rates that apply to qualifying dividends are the same as the rates that apply to long-term capital gain. They aren't treated exactly the same as capital gain, however. They're not included in the special calculation that's used to determine the net amount of capital gain or loss that's included in total income. Instead, they're included in total income directly, without going through that calculation. When we reach the point where we apply the tax rates, these dividends are separated from ordinary income in the same way as long-term capital gain.

Example: In the previous example, you ended up paying tax on $57,000 of ordinary income and $8,000 of long-term capital gain. The results would change if you also had $6,000 of dividend income, with $5,000 of that amount being qualified dividends. Now you have $58,000 being taxed at the rates that apply to ordinary income (adding the $1,000 of dividends that were not qualifying) and $13,000 being taxed at the rates that apply to long-term capital gain (including the actual long-term gain and the qualifying dividends).

Other investment income

You may receive other types of investment income, including annuity income, rents, or royalties. Generally these are treated as ordinary income, though special rules may apply. Specifics on the tax treatment of these other kinds of investment income are beyond the scope of this book.

Part II
Capital Gains and Losses

6

Capital Gain Basics

MOST SUCCESSFUL INVESTMENT PROGRAMS rely at least in part on the growth in wealth that comes from owning assets that increase in value over a period of time—typically offset in part by shrinkage produced when the opposite occurs. This chapter covers the most basic tax rules that apply when these changes in value find their way onto your tax return as capital gains and losses. You'll learn the answers to the following questions:

- How do *capital gain* and *capital loss* differ from *ordinary income* and *ordinary deductions*?
- At what point does a capital gain become taxable?
- How do you measure capital gain and loss? What are the meanings of the terms *basis* and *amount realized*?
- How long before a capital gain is *long-term*? How do you measure the *holding period* of an asset?

Capital gain and ordinary income

In the simplest terms, capital gain is profit from selling an asset that has gone up in value. If you buy something for $30 and sell it for $40, you have a capital gain of $10. In this book we're mainly concerned with capital gains from buying and selling stocks and mutual funds, but the same idea applies to gains from almost any kind of asset, from fine art to real estate to cryptocurrency and other digital assets.

Some investments can produce capital gain without a sale. You may invest in a mutual fund that makes a capital gain distribution, for example. Typically this means the mutual fund itself sold assets at a profit, and a share of that profit has been passed along to you.

If you happen to be in a business that sells goods to customers, you should be aware that these sales do not produce capital gains or losses. The tax law specifies that inventory held for sale to customers in the ordinary course of business is not a capital asset.

Ordinary income. We use the term "ordinary income" for any type of taxable income other than capital gain. This category includes items that are genuinely ordinary (such as wages and interest income) and some that are not (your prize money for winning the British Open). The term simply means income other than capital gain.

Occasionally we see people omit the word "ordinary" and contrast capital gain with "income." Lurking within this choice of words is the potential for confusion as it may produce the mistaken impression that for purposes of the income tax, capital gain isn't income. It is! In particular, capital gain is included in *adjusted gross income*, which is used (often with certain modifications) to determine your eligibility for various tax benefits. A capital gain, like any other form of income, may affect your ability to claim a medical expense deduction, a child care credit, or any of countless other tax benefits.

Deductions. We also distinguish capital losses from ordinary deductions. Generally you have a *capital loss* when you sell an investment asset that declined in value while you held it. All other deductions, from the most commonplace to the casualty loss you had when an asteroid destroyed your '65 Corvette, are considered *ordinary deductions.*

Note that capital loss generally relates to sale of an *investment* asset such as stock. A loss from selling a *business* asset (for example, equipment used in your profession) is generally an ordinary loss. Also, you aren't allowed to claim a deduction for a loss from selling a *personal use* asset such as your home.

	Ordinary Items	**Capital Items**
Income	Ordinary income	Capital gain
Loss	Ordinary deduction	Capital loss

When capital gains are reported

Once in a while, someone who's new to investing asks a question something like this:

> **Q:** *I bought stock last May, and by the end of December it was up $3,000. When do I have to report this on my taxes?*

That's a legitimate question. When your investments go up in value, your wealth increases. The money is there for the taking: all you have to do is sell the stock. Yet the tax law says you don't have income until you make the sale. You can continue to hold the stock for years while it increases in value many times over without paying a dime of income tax. This is one of the reasons long-term investing in stock is a great way to build wealth.

To be a little more precise, you don't report capital gain or loss until you have a *sale or exchange.* If you exchange one asset for another, you may have to report capital gain even though you didn't receive any cash in the transaction. Not all exchanges are taxable, though. In fact, not all *sales* result in capital gain or loss. In later chapters we'll look at various rules that postpone or eliminate capital gain or loss incurred in a sale or exchange. An example is the wash sale rule (Chapter 10), which says you can't claim a deduction if you sell stock at a loss and buy it back right away.

Conversely, in some special situations you can be treated as if you sold your stock even though you still hold it. For example, you're treated as if you sold stock at the end of the year in which it becomes worthless (Chapter 11). Also, traders who elect to use the mark-to-market method of accounting (Chapter 28) are treated as if they sold all their stock at the end of the year.

Terminology: When you make a sale or exchange, a tax pro would say you *realized* a gain or loss (in other words, turned it from a "paper" gain or loss to a "real" one). A gain or loss affects your tax if it is *recognized.* A gain or loss that does not affect your tax (as in the case of a wash sale described above) is *realized but not recognized.*

These terms tend to cause confusion, so I avoid them whenever possible. We'll see below, though, that the term used for the precise measure of what you received in a sale is the *amount realized.*

The rule that ties capital gains and losses to sales and exchanges may seem like a big yawn, but it's the key to powerful tax savings. Other forms of income—wages, interest, dividends—arrive according to someone else's schedule. When it comes to capital gains and losses, you're in the driver's seat. Using principles we'll explain in Chapter 34, you can use your control over the timing of sales to take gains and losses when they produce the most favorable tax consequences.

Q&A about capital gain timing

Q: *I sold stock at a profit but used the money right away to buy more stock. Do I have to report a capital gain?*

A: Yes. With very limited exceptions, you have to report the gain. It doesn't matter that you reinvested the proceeds—even if you bought more stock in the same company.

Q: *I moved money from one mutual fund to a different one in the same family. Do I have to report capital gain?*

A: Yes. The mutual fund company may refer to this transaction as an "exchange," but as far as the tax law is concerned you're selling one asset and making a new investment in a different one.

Q: *I didn't want to sell my stock, but was forced into a sale when another corporation bought the company. Do I still have to report the gain?*

A: Most capital gains come from voluntary sales, but the fact that a sale is involuntary doesn't excuse you from reporting gain or loss. A merger in which you receive stock may be partly or completely tax-free (see Chapter 11), but there's no deferral rule for forced sales that result from a taxable merger.

Q: *For tax purposes, when does a sale of stock occur?*

A: As explained in Chapter 8, stock purchases and sales occur on the *trade date.*

Measuring capital gains and losses

The size of your capital gains and losses affects the amount of income tax you have to pay, so it's important to have a precise way of measuring these gains and losses. The basic idea is to determine how much you invested in the relevant asset, and then compare the amount you received when you sold it.

Under the tax law, the term used for the amount of your investment in an asset is *adjusted basis.* Typically this is determined by the amount you paid for the asset, so people sometimes refer to it as *cost basis.* The term *adjusted basis* reminds us that the basis of an asset may change from its original cost. We'll look at adjusted basis in a moment.

The tax law also gives us a term for the amount you receive when you sell an asset. This is called the *amount realized.* It may seem obvious that the amount realized is the cash you receive when you sell an asset, but there are a few potential points of confusion we'll cover below.

With these terms in hand, we're ready to state more precisely how to measure capital gain or loss:

> The amount of a capital gain or loss is the difference between the amount realized and the adjusted basis of the asset you sold.

Adjusted basis

The rules for determining adjusted basis are a precise way of measuring the amount you have invested in a capital asset. The normal starting point is the amount you paid to acquire the asset, including any expenses you incurred in making the purchase. When you buy stock, for example, you may pay a brokerage commission. If so, that becomes part of your basis in addition to the actual price paid for the stock.

> **Example:** You bought 50 shares of XYZ at $30 per share, paying a $20 brokerage commission. Your basis in the stock is $1,520, or $30.40 per share.

After you've bought an asset, it's possible that something will happen to change its basis. For example, the company may declare a stock split. You started out with 50 shares, but now you have 100. When this happens, your basis splits, too. If you had a basis of $30.40 per share before the split, your new basis is $15.20 per share. The total amount of basis remains the same, but the basis per share has been adjusted.

Suppose you sell stock before there have been any adjustments to basis. It may seem that the term *adjusted basis* can't apply here because there haven't been any adjustments. Yet the tax law uses this term to refer to your basis with relevant adjustments, *if any*. If there haven't been any adjustments, your adjusted basis is the same as your initial basis.

> **Basis.** In the rest of this book, unless otherwise specified, the word "basis" by itself will mean the same thing as "adjusted basis."

In Chapter 11 we'll go over many of the situations that may cause adjustments to basis in stock. For now you may want to note that there are some general principles that usually make it easy to guess what the result will be in most situations. One is that your basis goes up if you report income or gain. For example, when you exercise a nonqualified stock option, you report compensation income equal to the bargain element in the option. This income gets included in your basis for the stock, together with the amount you actually paid to exercise the option. That way you won't be taxed on the same income again when you sell the stock.

Conversely, in a situation where no gain or income is reported, generally the basis of the stock remains the same. For example, if you receive stock as a gift from your spouse, your initial basis for the stock will be the same as your spouse's adjusted basis at the time of the gift. That's because your spouse didn't report gain or loss at the time of the gift.

Amount realized

At first glance it may seem obvious how much you received in a sale. There are three points of potential confusion, though: costs of selling, treatment of debt, and property received in an exchange.

Costs of selling. Your amount realized on a sale is reduced by any costs directly related to the sale. The most obvious cost in a typical stock transaction is the commission charged by the broker. If you sell stock for $2,400 and pay a commission of $30 on the sale, the amount realized is $2,370. Brokers are now required to report the net figure in their tax reports, so you should not claim this as a deduction. (Similarly, if the broker reports basis in the transaction, the broker will include any commission charged on the purchase.)

There's another cost of selling that's so small you may not notice it: the *SEC fee.* You may see this after a stock sale if you scrutinize your brokerage statement carefully. The broker is passing through a fee that provides funding for SEC supervision of the securities markets. The rate is low enough to make it a trivial expense, but it's another cost that reduces your amount realized on a sale.

The main thing to keep in mind about these expenses is this: *you aren't allowed to claim them as a separate deduction.* They're always part of calculating your capital gain or loss.

Commission rebates. Some brokers provide a partial rebate of their brokerage commissions in certain situations. For example, you might receive a credit against your commissions if you have a minimum number of transactions per month. Strictly speaking, this rebate reduces the cost of sale for every sale that occurred during the month. As a practical matter, it should normally be acceptable to handle this type of rebate by showing it as a short-term capital gain.

Treatment of debt. Some people get confused about the amount realized on a sale if they had debt on the property they sold. The rule here is to include the debt as part of the amount realized.

Example: You bought stock for $12,000. Its value rose to $18,000 and you took a margin loan of $5,000 against this stock. Later, you sold the stock for $20,000, receiving $15,000 after paying the $5,000 margin loan. If you compare the $15,000 you received in the sale with the $12,000 you paid to buy the stock, it looks like a $3,000 gain. But your amount realized includes the $5,000 loan that was paid off when you sold the stock. You actually have a gain of $8,000.

Capital Gain Calculation	
Net sale proceeds	$15,000
Debt repaid	5,000
Amount realized	*20,000*
Basis	(12,000)
Capital Gain	**$ 8,000**

It may seem unfair that you have to report $8,000 of gain when you ended up with only $3,000 more than the $12,000 you originally used to buy the stock. Yet you received another $5,000 in the form of a loan. Even if you no longer have that $5,000—perhaps you spent it before you sold the stock—it's part of your profit from the purchase and sale of this stock.

Gain greater than net proceeds. It's worth noting that you can end up with *gain* that's greater than the amount of *money* you receive in a sale. That's one reason to plan carefully when you use debt to acquire investment assets. You may have to come up with money from other sources to pay the tax on your gain.

> **Example:** You bought stock for $12,000. Its value went sky high and you were able to take a margin loan of $15,000 against this stock. Then the value of the stock dropped and you sold it for $20,000, receiving $5,000 after paying the $15,000 margin loan. This time your cash proceeds are only $5,000, but you still have to report gain of $8,000 because you bought the stock for $12,000 and sold it for $20,000.

Capital Gain Calculation	
Net sale proceeds	$5,000
Debt repaid	15,000
Amount realized	*20,000*
Basis	(12,000)
Capital Gain	**$ 8,000**

There's only one thing worse than having to report gain that's greater than your net sale proceeds, and that's having *the tax itself* be greater than the net sale proceeds. In fact, you can have a gain even with no net sale proceeds at all! In the example above, the stock could have dropped all the way to $15,000 before you sold. That's just enough to pay off the margin debt, leaving you with no sale proceeds. Yet you still have a gain of $3,000, because you bought the stock for $12,000 and sold it for $15,000.

Whether you have a problem in this situation depends on what you did with the money you borrowed when you took out the margin loan. If that money is gone, you need to come up with cash from some other source to pay tax on your gain.

Property received in an exchange. If you receive something other than cash in exchange for stock or another capital asset, the amount realized includes the fair market value of the other property. For example, if you exchange shares of one company for $10,000 in cash plus $6,000 worth of shares of another company, your amount realized is $16,000, just as if you received that much cash. That's true even if you haven't sold the property you received—and even if for some reason you *can't* sell it.

As mentioned earlier, not all exchanges are taxable. You may exchange shares as a result of a tax-free merger, for example. We'll look at the tax rules for this type of transaction in Chapter 11. Even when dealing with those rules, though, you may need to know the amount realized, and that figure includes the value of shares or other property received in the exchange.

Holding period

You're only partway home when you know the amount of gain or loss on a sale. You also need to know the *holding period* of the asset you sold, to determine whether your gain or loss is short-term or long-term.

Year and a day. To have a long-term capital gain or loss, your holding period has to be at least a year and a day. Exactly one year is not enough. To be more precise, if you sell stock on the anniversary of the date you bought it, your gain or loss will be short-term. The first day you can have a long-term gain is the anniversary of *the day after* the date of purchase.

Some people figure this has to be wrong. If you sell on the anniversary, you've held the stock on 366 days (or 367, if you held the stock on February 29 in a leap year), and that should be enough. That's not the way the rules work, though. When you figure your holding period, you count the date of sale but not the date of purchase. As a technical matter, your holding period begins the day after the date of purchase, and that's why you have to wait until the anniversary of the day after the date of purchase if you want a long-term capital gain.

> **Trick question:** You bought shares on February 28. The following year is a leap year. Which is the first day you can sell for a long-term capital gain or loss?
>
> (a) February 27
>
> (b) February 28
>
> (c) February 29
>
> (d) March 1

Many people are inclined to choose (c), because it seems you've held the stock "a year and a day" by February 29. Pat yourself on the back if you selected (d). Your holding period *began* the day after the date of purchase—March 1. You must hold until March 1 of the following year to have a long-term gain or loss.

Flip side. What if you *bought* in a leap year? If you bought on February 29, your holding period began on March 1, so you have to wait until March 1 of the following year to sell for a long-term gain. But you also have to wait until March 1 of the following year if you bought on February *28* of a leap year. Your holding period began the day after your purchase, on February 29. To sell *more than one year* later, you have to wait until March 1 of the following year.

Special holding periods. Your holding period for an asset doesn't necessarily begin when you acquire it. For example, if you receive stock as a result of a stock split, the holding period of the new shares will be the same as for the old shares. Similarly, if you receive stock as a gift, your holding period is transferred from the person making the gift. If that person held the stock more than a year before you received the gift, you'll have long-term capital gain or loss on a sale even if you sell the same day you receive the gift.

Special holding periods go along with special basis rules, both of which are covered in Chapter 11. There's a general rule that makes it easier to remember when you have a special holding period. Generally, if you have a "tax-free" transaction such as a gift or a stock split, the holding period for the asset continues. Taxable transactions (most commonly sales) start a new holding period.

7

Taxation of Capital Gains and Losses

THE REASON WE MAKE SUCH A BIG DEAL about capital gains and losses, of course, is that they have some special tax rules. This chapter explains those rules, answering the following questions:

- How do tax rates and tax brackets work when you *don't* have capital gains and losses?
- What difference will you see when you add short-term capital gains and losses to your other income? How do capital loss carryovers work?
- How will long-term capital gains and losses affect your taxes?
- How do capital gains and losses interact when you have both short-term and long-term gains and losses?

Life without capital gains and losses

As explained in the previous chapter, *ordinary income* includes all forms of income other than capital gain. If you don't have capital gains and losses, your *taxable income* is simply your ordinary income reduced by your ordinary deductions. Taxable income is an important number: it's the one used to calculate your tax. It's less than your total income because you get to subtract either the standard deduction or the total of your itemized deductions. You may also qualify for other deductions that are allowed without itemizing, such as retirement plan contributions.

> **Example:** In 2023, the standard deduction for single filers is $13,850. Because of this "automatic" deduction, you could have $50,000 in earnings and still have less than $37,000 in taxable income even if you "don't claim any deductions."

Tax rates, tax brackets. Everyone knows tax rates start out low and get higher when your income grows, but things can get hazy after that. The confusion usually comes from talk about *tax brackets.* When people say they're "in the 22% bracket," it may sound like all their income is taxed at the 22% rate. That's not how it works.

Income tax rates start at 10%. No matter how large your income is, your first chunk of taxable income is taxed at the 10% rate. If your income is large enough, you'll have another chunk that's taxed at the 12% rate. That process continues through the other rates, up to a maximum of 37%. If you make millions, most of your taxable income will be taxed at the 37% rate, but you'll still have income that's taxed at the lower rates.

There's another way tax brackets sometimes cause confusion. Some people get the idea that the amount they earn at their regular job establishes their tax bracket, even if they have gobs of money from other sources. Sorry, that's not the case. Your tax bracket depends on your overall taxable income, which includes not just wages but also income like interest and dividends from sources other than your regular job.

When we say you're in the 22% tax bracket, we're really saying your taxable income is high enough so that some of it is taxed at the 22% rate, but not high enough for any of it to be taxed at 24%, the next higher rate. Knowing your tax bracket lets you know how much more tax you'll pay if you earn another $100, or how much you'll save if you come up with another $100 deduction. If you're in the 24% bracket, the answer in each case is $24. But consider the following:

Q: *Suppose your taxable income is just $100 below the borderline between the 24% bracket and the 32% bracket. Now you get an additional $200 of income. How much will your tax go up?*

A: The answer is $56. Although you're in the 24% bracket at the time you receive the added income, you have room for only $100 more in that bracket. So $100 will be taxed at the 24% rate and another $100 will be taxed at the 32% rate for a total tax of $56.

Q: *Suppose your taxable income is* exactly *on the line between the 24% bracket and the 32% bracket. If your income goes up by $100, how much more tax will you pay? If instead your deductions go up by $100, how much will you save?*

A: If your income goes up by $100 you'll pay $32 more in tax because there's no more room in the 24% bracket. Yet an additional $100 deduction will save only $24 because it eliminates income that was taxed in the 24% bracket. Of course, if you had *both* an added $100 of income and $100 of deduction, they would cancel each other out for no change in your tax.

These examples illustrate that knowing your tax bracket doesn't necessarily tell you exactly where you stand as to additional income or deductions. That's especially true when your taxable income falls near the levels where the sharpest changes in rates occur: between the 12% and 22% rates, and between the 24% and 32% rates. Knowing your tax bracket can be helpful, but sometimes you also need to know where you are within that tax bracket.

Short-term capital gains and losses

Now we're ready to see what happens when you throw capital gains and losses into the mix. We'll begin with short-term capital gains. Generally, you have a short-term capital gain if you sell stock for a profit after holding it *one year or less.* If you lose money on your sale—the amount realized was less than your basis—you have a capital loss.

Short-term capital gains alone. Suppose you have the good fortune to have no losses. Every time you sold stock, you had a short-term capital gain. The rule here is simple: your short-term gain is taxed at the same rates as ordinary income.

Consider the example above where you are in the 24% bracket but just $100 below the 32% bracket. We saw that adding $200 of ordinary income would increase the tax by $56, because half would be taxed in each bracket. The same would be true if we added $200 of short-term capital gain.

This isn't to say that short-term capital gain is *exactly* the same as ordinary income. We'll see in a few moments that short-term capital gain is *better* than ordinary income when you have capital losses. On the other hand, capital gain is potentially subject to the net investment income tax (Chapter 30), while many types of ordinary income escape this added tax.

Short-term capital gains and losses. Your luck won't always be that good! If you do enough trading, you're bound to have some losing trades. For now we're still excluding any long-term trades to get a clear picture of what happens with short-term gains and losses.

Start by finding a total for each category. Add up all your short-term gains to get the total amount of gain. Same thing with the losses. Then you subtract the total loss from the total gain.

- If the gain is greater than the loss, you end up with a positive number: a *net short-term capital gain.* That number gets added to your other income. It will be taxed at the same rate as if it were ordinary income.

- If the gain is exactly the same size as the loss, you end up with zero. The tax law isn't always sensible and fair, but in this case it is: you broke even in your stock trading, so the activity has no effect on the amount of income tax you pay.
- You may have losses that exceed your gains: a *net short-term capital loss*. In this unfortunate situation you may take some comfort in knowing that the Treasury will share your pain—but only up to a limit.

Capital loss limitation and carryover. A net capital loss is a deduction that reduces your other income, up to a maximum of $3,000 ($1,500 if married filing separately). If your capital loss is $3,000 or less, you get to claim the entire loss. If the loss is more than $3,000, you claim $3,000 and "carry" the rest to the next year.

> **Example:** Suppose your ordinary income and deductions leave you with taxable income of $40,000. In addition you have short-term capital gains that add up to $8,000 and short-term capital losses that add up to $10,000. Your net capital loss is $2,000. That's less than $3,000, so you can deduct the full amount, reducing your taxable income to $38,000.

Notice that you're getting the full benefit from $10,000 of capital losses. Some people get in a panic thinking they'll only get $3,000 of capital losses regardless of their gains. The $3,000 limitation doesn't come into play until after you net out the losses against the gains.

How carryovers work. A carryover sounds like something fancy and technical. Actually it's a pretty simple concept. Whatever capital loss you don't use this year because of the $3,000 capital loss limitation is treated like a brand-new loss in the same category (short-term or long-term) at the beginning of the following year.

> **Example:** Your capital gains add up to $2,000 and your capital losses add up to $10,000, leaving you with a net capital loss of $8,000. You get to deduct only $3,000 of the capital loss this year. The remaining $5,000 is carried over to the following

year. That means you're treated as if you had a new capital loss at the beginning of the following year.

Capital Loss Carryover	
Total short-term capital gain	$2,000
Total short-term capital loss	(10,000)
Net short-term capital loss	(8,000)
Used in current year	3,000
Carryover to next year	$ (5,000)

The $5,000 capital loss carryover works just like any other capital loss in the carryover year. If you have other capital gains and losses, it goes into the mix just like a "real" loss. If you don't have any other capital gains or losses, you can deduct $3,000 of this loss, and carry the remaining $2,000 to the *next* year. There's no time limit on this, because each year it's treated as a new loss. You can't take it with you, though, or even leave it behind: any unused capital loss carryover remaining at your death is worthless.

Forward, not back. Some kinds of losses (called *net operating losses*, or *NOLs*) carry back to previous years. Not capital losses! Unless you're a corporation, your capital losses carry forward only, never back.

I heard a sad story about someone who fell into a trap with these rules. She had a great winning streak in 1999 when the stock market was strong, piling up $400,000 in gains. When the air went out of some of the tech stocks early the next year she lost the whole bundle. She didn't even save enough to pay taxes on gains from the prior year! There's really nothing you can do in this situation. You can't carry the loss back to the previous year. In the current year the deduction is limited to $3,000. And unless you get another hot streak going, at

$3,000 per year it's going to take more than 100 years to use up a $397,000 capital loss carryover.

> **Note:** In Chapter 28 we'll see that individuals who qualify as traders can make the *mark-to-market election*, which converts trading gains and losses into ordinary income and loss. Traders who make this election can use trading losses against ordinary income, but the ability to carry net operating losses back as well as forward (which would have helped the taxpayer described above if she had made this election) was eliminated as of 2018.

Ordinary income less than $3,000. Some taxpayers don't have enough ordinary income to benefit from the capital loss deduction, even within the $3,000 limit. This situation is fairly common for minor children holding stock or mutual funds in a custodial account (see Chapter 21) but it can happen to adults as well. In this situation, the tax forms can make it look as if $3,000 of the capital loss disappears into thin air, without being used to reduce taxable income. That isn't the case, though.

For example, someone might have $4,500 of capital loss in a year when income tax would be zero even without the capital loss. When you follow the instructions for Form 1040, the return will show a $3,000 capital loss deduction, making it look as if the deduction is wasted and only $1,500 carries over. If you work through the capital loss carryover worksheet (found in the instructions for Schedule D or in IRS Publication 550), you should find that this $3,000 is restored as a carryover to the next year.

Long-term capital gains and losses

We've seen how ordinary income and deductions work without any capital gains or losses, and also what happens when you throw short-term capital gains and losses into the mix. Now let's eliminate the short-term gains and focus on what happens when you have long-term gains and losses: gains and losses from stocks and other assets held more than a year.

"Pass-through" gains. Depending on your investments, you may have a long-term capital gain that gets "passed through" from another source—for example, a capital gain dividend from a mutual fund. These are treated the same as long-term capital gains you have from selling stock or other assets.

Long-term capital gains alone. We'll start the same way we did for short-term gains and losses, looking at the situation where you have gains but no losses. The tax rate for long-term capital gain is lower than the rate for ordinary income. In fact, at the lowest income levels, the rate is zero. Once taxable income (including both ordinary income and net capital gain) reaches a level specified for your filing status, the rate becomes 15%. At much higher levels of income the rate is 20%. (As explained in Chapter 12, higher rates apply to some special categories of long-term capital gains.)

> **Example:** Suppose your taxable income, before taking long-term capital gain into account, is $2,000 below the level where the 15% capital gains rate begins. If your long-term capital gain is $2,000 or less, the entire gain will be taxed at 0%. If your long-term capital gain is greater than $2,000, then the 0% rate applies to the first $2,000 and the 15% rate applies to the rest, assuming the remainder fits below the income level where the 20% capital gains rate begins.

> **Example:** Suppose your taxable income, before taking any long-term capital gain into account, is $10,000 below the level where capital gains begin to be taxed at 20%, and you have a $30,000 long-term capital gain. In this case, the 15% rate will apply to the first $10,000 of long-term capital gain, and the 20% rate will apply to the rest.

> Prior to 2018, the income levels where capital gains rates changed matched up with tax brackets for ordinary income. Now, the zero rate for capital gains ends *approximately* where the 12% rate for ordinary income ends, and the change from 15% to 20% in capital gains rate falls within the income range for the 35% bracket.

The tax consequences of long-term capital gain are always tacked onto the end of your ordinary income, even if the gain came from a stock sale on January 1, before you earned any ordinary income. The rate that applies to the gain depends on how much ordinary income and short-term capital gain you had throughout the entire year. If that's enough to push the gain out of the lower brackets (where it would be taxed at 0%), the 15% (or 20%) rate will apply to the gain.

By the same token, long-term capital gain never pushes ordinary income into a higher bracket. Some people worry that they'll lose some of the benefit of the lower rates from long-term capital gain if it causes their ordinary income to be taxed at a higher rate. That doesn't happen: the tax rates apply first to ordinary income as if you didn't have any long-term capital gain, and then the special rates apply to your capital gain.

Indirect effects. Long-term capital gain can affect the rate you pay on ordinary income *indirectly*. That's because the gain is included in your *adjusted gross income*. That figure is used to determine whether various tax benefits should be reduced. A long-term capital gain, like any other additional income you might have, could reduce your itemized deductions, for example. Likewise, long-term capital gain can reduce the amount you're allowed to contribute to a Roth IRA, or reduce your deduction for a regular IRA contribution.

The special treatment of long-term capital gain is an important fact of life for people who buy and sell stocks or mutual funds. Knowledgeable investors seek to take advantage of this tax break whenever possible. An opportunity to receive long-term capital gain in place of ordinary income or short-term capital gain is a chance to preserve wealth by reducing your rate of tax on that income.

Long-term capital gains and losses. We've seen what happens if the only thing you have on your tax return, other than ordinary income such as wages, is long-term capital gain. If we throw long-term capital losses into the mix, we'll see a situation similar to the one we had when you had short-term capital gains and losses. You have to add up all your long-term gains, and also add up all your long-term losses. Then you subtract the total loss from the total gain.

If the result is a positive number, you have a net long-term capital gain. This is the amount that will be taxed at the special rates described above. If the gain and loss are exactly equal, they cancel each other out and have no effect on your taxes.

If the loss is greater than the gain, you have a net long-term capital loss. Just as in the case of a net short-term capital loss, you can claim up to $3,000 of the loss as a deduction. That means a net long-term loss of $3,000 or less has exactly the same effect as if the loss were short-term. If the loss is greater than $3,000, though, the category of the loss makes a difference, because the loss carryover will be long-term, not short-term. That could make a difference in your calculations for the following year.

Short-term and long-term gains and losses

Now we're ready to put it all together. Let's see what happens in a year when you have both short-term and long-term capital gains and losses.

The first step is to find a total for each of the four types of results: short-term gains, short-term losses, long-term gains and long-term losses. Then you subtract the losses in each category from the gains in the same category. In other words, subtract the short-term losses from the short-term gains, and subtract the long-term losses from the long-term gains. You end up with two numbers: one that represents a short-term gain or loss, and another that represents a long-term gain or loss. There are three possibilities: they are both positive (net gains), both negative (net losses), or one positive and the other negative.

Both positive. If you have a net short-term gain and a net long-term gain, the short-term gain is taxed at the rates that apply to ordinary income, just as it would be if you didn't have any long-term capital gain or loss. The long-term capital gain is taxed according to the overall level of taxable income, as discussed earlier. In this case, both ordinary income and short-term capital gain will be counted in determining which rate applies to long-term gain.

> **Example:** Before you take capital gains and losses into account, your taxable income is $2,000 below the level where long-term capital gain begins to be taxed at 15%. You have a short-term capital gain of $2,000 and a short-term capital loss of $500, giving you a net short-term capital gain of $1,500. In addition, you have a long-term capital gain of $3,800 and a long-term capital loss of $1,300, giving you a net long-term capital gain of $2,500.
>
> The short-term capital gain counts first, and is taxed at the same rate as ordinary income at that level. After that, you're only $500 away from the level where the 15% capital gains rate kicks in. That means $500 of your long-term gain will be taxed at 0% and the rest will be taxed at 15%.

Notice that you would come out better if you could apply the long-term loss against the short-term gain. That would give you a smaller short-term gain and a larger long-term gain, so that more of your gain would be taxed at the lower rates that apply to net long-term capital gain. Unfortunately, the tax rules don't permit you to do this. You always have to net long-term losses against long-term gains before you can apply them against any other kind of income.

> **Remember:** When it comes to capital gain, long-term is better than short-term. When it comes to capital loss, the opposite is true. Short-term loss is better because it reduces short-term gain.

Both negative. In a bad year you may have a net loss for both short-term and long-term transactions. When this happens, the $3,000 loss limitation applies to the total of *all* your capital losses. In other words, the largest amount of net capital loss you can claim in any year is $3,000, even if you have losses in both the short-term and long-term categories.

You're required to claim the short-term loss first. This rule doesn't matter if the total loss is less than $3,000. If the loss is greater than $3,000, this rule determines how much of your carryover is short-term and how much is long-term.

> **Example:** You have a net short-term loss of $2,500 and also a net long-term loss of $2,500. Your total capital loss is $5,000, but you can claim only $3,000 in a single year. You're required to use the short-term loss first, so the $3,000 you deduct this year will take up the entire short-term capital loss plus $500 of the long-term capital loss. That leaves you with a $2,000 long-term capital loss carryover.

You aren't allowed to use the long-term loss first, or use them both proportionately. The tax law requires you to use the short-term loss first.

Net loss and net gain. You may end up with a net loss in one category and a net gain in the other. When this happens, you apply the loss against the gain. The resulting number will belong to the category of the larger number.

- *Short-term loss greater than long-term gain.* The resulting number is treated as a net short-term loss, just like a short-term loss that arises purely from short-term transactions.
- *Long-term gain greater than short-term loss.* This situation gives you a net long-term gain, which will be taxed at the favorable long-term rates.
- *Long-term loss greater than short-term gain.* In this case you have a net long-term loss. You'll deduct up to $3,000 and carry any excess to the next year.
- *Short-term gain greater than long-term loss.* The result here is a net short-term gain, which will be taxed at the same rate as ordinary income.

That may seem like a complicated mess to try to remember, but in reality there's just one simple rule that applies: whichever item is larger determines the category for the net figure. It may not be pretty, but at least it's logical.

> **Example:** Suppose you net out all your short-term capital gains and losses and end up with a net loss of $2,000. At the same time, when you net your long-term gains and losses you come up with a gain of $8,000. Under these rules, you'll net the short-term loss against the long-term gain, leaving you with long-term capital gain of $6,000.

Tax terminology. You might think, quite reasonably, that you have a *net capital gain* whenever your total capital gain in all categories is greater than your total capital loss. Technically, though, the term *net capital gain* refers only to a net *long-term* capital gain that remains after subtracting any net short-term capital loss. If you have a net *short-term* capital gain, that gain isn't part of your *net capital gain.* It seems illogical, but that's the way the terms are defined in the tax law.

Why bother with this arcane factoid? The IRS sometimes uses this terminology in its instructions and publications. They may say that a particular rule applies only if you have a *net capital gain*. If you apply the rule to a net short-term capital gain you'll be wrong. Even the tax pros make this mistake once in a while, because it seems so logical to assume that a net capital gain includes a net short-term capital gain.

In a nutshell

Now we're ready to summarize the principal tax rules for the treatment of capital gains and losses. The best way to do this is to set forth the sequence of steps you go through to determine the correct treatment.

1. Begin by sorting all transactions into four categories: short-term gain, short-term loss, long-term gain and long-term loss. Find the total for each category.

2. Subtract the short-term loss from the short-term gain to arrive at a *net* short-term gain or loss. Do the same with the long-term gain and loss.

3. If you have a gain in one category and a loss in the other, subtract the loss from the gain. The resulting net figure is considered to be in the same category as the larger of the two numbers. For example, if you had a long-term loss and a smaller short-term gain, the resulting number would be a long-term loss.

4a. If you have an overall loss, use up to $3,000 of the loss as a deduction against your taxable income, applying short-term loss before long-term loss. Any loss that isn't used will carry over to the next year as if it were a new capital loss deduction.

4b. If you have an overall gain, the short-term gain (if any) will be taxed at the same rate as additional ordinary income. The long-term gain (if any) will be taxed at 0%, 15% or 20%, or a combination of these, depending on your level of taxable income and the size of the gain.

Chapter 34 lays out tax planning techniques that take maximum advantage of these rules.

8

Special Rules for Stock

So far we've been dealing with rules that apply to sales of all kinds of assets. In this chapter we'll look at some rules for capital gains and losses that apply specifically to shares of stock.

Date of a purchase or sale

The holding period for stock is determined the same way as for any other asset. You have to hold the stock at least a year and a day to have a long-term capital gain or loss. Yet there's some ambiguity as to when you buy or sell stock, because in a normal stock transaction two different dates are significant. One is called the trade date, and the other is called the settlement date.

The *trade date* is the date you entered into the transaction. That's often, but not always, the day you tell your broker to buy or sell. If you give instructions on Monday but the transaction doesn't take place until Tuesday (perhaps because you transmitted the instructions after the market closed, or you placed a limit order that couldn't be filled Monday), then your trade date is Tuesday. When in doubt, check the trade confirmation you get from the broker to learn your trade date.

The *settlement date* occurs a few days after the trade date. This is the day the shares and the cash will actually change hands. If you're the buyer, you need to have money in your account by the settlement date.

For tax purposes, the date that controls your holding period is the *trade date.* The settlement date is irrelevant in determining how long you held your stock. That's true for both purchases and sales. (There's an exception for short sales closed at a loss: see Chapter 15.) If you want to have a long-term gain, you have to make sure the trade date of your sale is on or after the first anniversary of the day after the trade date of the purchase. To get a short-term loss, you need to have the trade date of your sale before that date.

Year of sale. The trade date also determines *what year* you sold your stock. People sometimes ask what is the last day to sell stock for a gain or loss in the current year. The answer is December 31 (assuming the stock market is open that day). The fact that the transaction won't settle until January of the next year doesn't delay reporting of the sale, again with an exception for short sales described in Chapter 15.

Tax lots

The tax consequences when you sell stock or mutual fund shares depend on two things: your cost basis for the shares and your holding period. If you acquire shares of the same company or mutual fund at different times or different prices, your purchases are separated into *lots.* Each lot has its own cost basis and holding period. These are sometimes called *tax lots* because shares are identical in all respects except their tax characteristics. If you acquire multiple lots and subsequently make a sale in which you dispose of some but not all of the shares, you'll have different tax consequences depending on which lots were the source of the shares you sold.

> **Example:** You hold some XYZ stock you bought years ago, when the stock price was much lower than it is today. You also hold some XYZ you bought recently when the stock was trading above today's price. Now you want to sell some of this stock, but not all of it.

Plainly this is a case where it matters which shares you sell. A sale of the older shares will produce a gain, most likely increasing your tax for the year of the sale. Selling the newer shares will permit you to report a loss, potentially reducing your income tax.

Q: *Why not just use the average basis?*

A: In Chapter 9 we'll learn about optional rules for using average basis, but that method is available only for mutual fund shares and for stock held in a dividend reinvestment plan. Even when using average basis you have to maintain records for separate tax lots because the holding period affects the results of a sale.

All shares of a particular company are identical, so when you hold multiple tax lots of the same stock in the same investment account we need a way to determine which shares are being sold. The tax law handles this problem as follows:

- It provides a way for you to choose which shares you're selling, and
- It provides a rule for what happens if you don't choose.

We'll look first at what happens when you *don't* choose, and then see what you need to do if you want a different result.

If you don't choose

If you don't specify which shares you're selling, the law treats you as if you sold the *earliest* shares you bought. This is called the *first-in, first out* method, or *FIFO*.

Example: You bought 50 shares of XYZ at $40 three years ago and another 50 at $60 two years ago. Now you sell 50 shares at $80 without specifying which shares you're selling. The tax law says you sold the shares you bought three years ago.

Notice that you would report a smaller gain, and pay less tax, if you instead sold the shares you bought later. Sometimes it pays to choose which shares you're selling.

Adjusted holding period. The FIFO rule seems straightforward, but the regulations fail to resolve an important ambiguity. We're going to see that in various situations shares are treated as having a holding period that differs from the actual period of time you held the shares. For example, when you receive additional shares in a stock split, your holding period for the new shares is the same as for the ones you held before the split. This raises the question whether the FIFO rule should be applied to shares in the order in which they were actually acquired, or in the order implied by their adjusted holding period.

The tax regulations don't provide a clear answer to this question, but with a little thought we can see that using the actual acquisition date for this purpose wouldn't make sense. For one thing, such a rule would be unduly cumbersome, requiring taxpayers to maintain records with two sets of holding periods, one for determining whether gains and losses are long-term and another for determining the order of disposition.

Using the actual acquisition date would also produce surprising and undesirable results in some situations.

Example: Prior to a 2-for-1 stock split you hold 50 long-term shares and 50 short-term shares. After the split you hold 100 shares in each category, and you sell half your holdings.

The expected result, and the only one that makes sense, is to charge this sale against the 100 long-term shares. Yet if we apply the FIFO rule based on the actual acquisition date, you would be treated as having sold the 50 long-term shares and 50 short-term shares you held before the split. To avoid such problems, the FIFO rule should be interpreted as applying based on the date implied by the adjusted holding period of the shares, not the actual acquisition date.

Identification

As noted earlier, there are times when FIFO does not produce the optimal tax result. The law permits you to change the order in which you sell shares through a process called *identification* (or sometimes, redundantly, *specific identification* or *adequate identification*). In the normal situation where shares are held in a brokerage account, a valid identification has two requirements:

- *At the time of the sale*, you specify to the broker the shares you're selling, *and*
- *Within a reasonable time thereafter*, you receive written confirmation of that specification from your broker.

Before we turn to the details of these requirements, let's understand that they serve a dual purpose. First, by requiring you to make your choice at the time of the sale, the rules prevent you from using hindsight. You can't wait until later to determine which choice would produce the most favorable tax result. And second, the requirement for a timely confirmation from the broker creates a paper trail, so there is proof that you did in fact make your choice at the time of the sale.

> Over the years, many investors have been told incorrectly by tax advisors or brokers that they can wait until they file their tax returns to decide which tax lots they sold. Sometimes this erroneous advice was accompanied by the suggestion to match up the trade confirmation slips for purchases and sales, and staple them together as evidence of the choice. Frequent repetition gave these statements an aura of believability but they were supported by nothing more than wishful thinking.

Specifying the shares

Apart from the timing, there are no special rules about how to specify the shares. You can communicate your choice in any manner that's acceptable to the broker, including electronically. If your broker accepts sell orders over the phone, including share identification, oral communication will satisfy the requirement. It is the broker's confirmation, not your original choice, that has to be in writing. Be aware, however, that not all brokers will be flexible enough to accept an oral share identification.

Likewise, there are no magic words you have to use. You simply need to identify the shares in a way that makes it clear which shares you sold. Any of the following might do the trick:

- The shares I bought on March 12, 2006.
- The shares I bought for 40.85.
- The shares I bought most recently.

In theory, it shouldn't matter if the instruction is meaningless to the broker—at least for shares you acquired in the days before brokers were required to maintain records of tax basis. For example, you may have had a different broker when you bought the shares, so your present broker has no idea what shares you bought on March 12, 2006. That's okay: the only thing the broker has to do in this situation is provide written confirmation that you chose to sell those shares.

When to choose. Generally, unless the choice is handled by a standing order as described below, investors specify which shares they're selling when placing the order to sell. Strictly speaking, however, the regulations say you have until the settlement date (or, if sooner, the date settlement would normally occur according to SEC rules) to make this choice. Assuming your broker will cooperate, this rule offers some leeway (generally two business days) to correct an error or change your mind.

Standing orders

These rules don't require you to make a separate identification every time you sell some of your shares. If you always identify shares according to a particular rule, you can establish a standing order with your broker. One possibility is to automatically sell the shares with the highest basis (and therefore report the smallest amount of gain or largest amount of loss). This approach has been used often enough to obtain the informal name *HIFO*, a play on FIFO meaning "highest in, first out."

HIFO does not produce optimal results in all cases, however. Depending on circumstances, it might be better to have a smaller short-term loss instead of a larger long-term loss, for example. For maximum tax efficiency you may wish to adopt a more sophisticated rule, or use HIFO as a default method that you'll override with other instructions when necessary.

Because brokers are now required to maintain basis records, it is impractical for them to accept methods other than those that have been programmed into their computers. Many offer HIFO, and some offer a menu of other choices. If your broker doesn't offer the method you want to use, you'll need to identify shares at the time of individual sales—or use a different broker.

Broker's confirmation

Identifying shares is a two-step process: you have to communicate your choice to the broker, and you also have to receive written confirmation of the identification from the broker within a reasonable time after the transaction. The tax regulations have been modernized to specify that this requirement can be satisfied by electronic communication. It can be a separate communication related to the individual transaction or it can be included in an account statement.

The broker does not have to physically transfer a specific lot of shares. The broker merely has to confirm that you communicated your choice at the time of the sale.

Switching methods

Some of the writing about these rules seems to suggest that you can get locked into one or another method for determining the order in which you sell shares. That's incorrect: you can use any method you want for any sale. Relying on FIFO for some of your sales does not preclude you from identifying shares in subsequent sales. Likewise you can drop back into using FIFO after identifying shares on some sales. FIFO is simply a default that applies whenever you fail to identify shares.

Similarly, adopting a method such as HIFO as a standing order does not limit your flexibility. You can terminate that standing order at any time and do something different for future sales. If your broker's systems are flexible enough, you can also override a standing order on a particular sale while leaving it in place for other sales. The tax rules offer complete freedom of choice—provided that you choose at the time of the sale.

If you hold certificates

It used to be commonplace for shareholders to hold *certificates* for their shares of stock. Nowadays that's unusual. If you hold certificates, the way you choose which shares you're selling is to deliver the certificate that represents those shares. It's your responsibility to determine which certificate represents the shares you want to sell and deliver that certificate. It won't help to tell the broker (or the IRS) you meant to sell some other shares if you deliver the wrong certificate.

It's possible you'll end up holding a single certificate that represents shares bought at different times or different prices. In that case, assuming you're using a broker to sell the shares, you need to identify the shares you're selling (as explained above) when you deliver the certificate to the broker. If you sell some of the stock represented by a certificate *without* using a broker or other agent, you simply have to maintain a written record of which shares you sold.

Threat to the identification rules

A proposal to do away with the identification rules, and require the use of average basis, has been floated repeatedly since the 1990s. This unfortunate idea is based on the mistaken notion that taxpayers gain an unfair advantage when they identify shares for sale. In reality, the opportunity to identify shares merely preserves *neutrality*, putting the investor who adds to existing holdings of a particular stock in the same position as one who instead chooses to invest in a different stock. The investor who buys a different stock is free to choose to sell the newer or older investment first, and the investor who buys more of the same stock should have the same choice.

Repeal of the identification rules would be a policy blunder, vastly complicating the lives of investors and in many cases producing grossly unfair tax results. Proponents have repeatedly failed to enact this mistaken change, but the possibility that it will eventually become law cannot be discounted.

9

Special Rules for Mutual Funds

MUTUAL FUNDS OFFER THE INVESTOR an opportunity to obtain in a single purchase indirect ownership of a diversified portfolio. Part of the deal is a modified form of *flow-through* taxation under which, for example, if the mutual fund has a long-term capital gain, a portion of the dividend paid on your shares will appear as long-term capital gain on your income tax return. We address mutual fund dividends in Chapter 13. This chapter covers special rules that apply to sales of mutual fund shares:

- You are permitted, but not required, to use the average basis of shares in an account, rather than the separate basis of different tax lots, to determine gain or loss on a sale.
- A loss on a sale of mutual fund shares you've held less than six months will receive special treatment if you received a capital gain dividend or an exempt interest distribution during the period you owned the shares.

- Another special rule applies to any gain or loss incurred on shares held 90 days or less if you paid a reduced load on shares subsequently purchased by reason of having owned the shares sold at a loss.

We turn to these rules after a brief survey of the different types of mutual funds.

Types of mutual funds

There are thousands of mutual funds to choose from, and various ways of classifying them. We won't try to give a full picture of what's available, but a few remarks on various types of mutual funds are appropriate.

Open-end mutual funds. This is the type of mutual fund familiar to most people. The name comes from the fact that these funds grow in an open-ended way by selling shares directly to investors. At the close of each day, the fund determines the total market value of its assets. This number is used to arrive at the *net asset value* of shares in the fund. The net asset value, or *NAV*, is the price you'll see for fund shares on websites or in the financial section of your newspaper. Most open-end mutual funds will automatically reinvest your dividends unless you request otherwise.

Closed-end mutual funds. This type of mutual fund has been around for a long time, but has not been nearly as popular as open-end mutual funds. When you want to buy shares in a closed-end mutual fund, you make a purchase in the stock market, just as you would if you were buying regular shares of stock. The price of the mutual fund shares isn't necessarily the same as the value of the assets held by the fund. It can be higher, but more often it's somewhat lower.

Exchange-traded funds. This is a relatively recent innovation that has quickly become very popular. Like closed-end funds, ETFs offer shares you can buy and sell throughout the day on the stock exchanges. These funds are specially designed to have a market value that closely reflects the value of the underlying assets, however, so you are less likely to see much deviation between the trading price and the net asset value of the ETF's holdings.

ETFs vary greatly in their legal structure and the types of assets they hold. As a result, they're subject to varying tax rules, not all of which are covered in this book. Before buying ETFs that hold non-traditional investment assets such as commodities or currencies, investors should review tax considerations published by the firm offering the fund. We note, however, that ETFs holding more traditional assets—stocks and bonds—are generally structured in a way that makes them subject to the rules that apply to mutual funds. In particular, the rules for losses on shares held less than six months, described later in this chapter, would apply to ETF shares just as they do to shares in traditional mutual funds.

Money market funds. Some mutual funds are set up to make very short-term investments that are unlikely to change significantly in value. While it's possible to have a loss in one of these *money market funds*, that's extremely rare. When one of these funds had a loss in the 2008 financial crisis, it was only the second time in nearly 40 years that this had happened. You also won't have a gain in one of these funds, because they declare dividends *daily* to keep the price of shares at exactly $1.00. Your profit comes in the form of interest income received by the fund and paid out to you as nonqualifying dividends (that is, dividends that don't qualify for special low tax rates).

In response to problems that became evident in the 2008 financial crisis, money market funds that have institutional investors are now required to let their share price float, so that it won't always equal $1.00. The traditional fixed price of $1.00 will continue to apply to *retail* funds that cater only to individual investors. Anticipating that individual investors will generally be directed to use these retail funds, we omit discussion of special rules that will apply to floating price money market funds.

Exempt bond funds. Some mutual funds are set up to invest in tax-exempt bonds. Investors sometimes assume that they won't have to worry about taxes on this investment because the bonds are tax-free. Although you won't pay federal income tax on the dividends from exempt interest, you can have taxable gain (or deductible loss) when you sell shares in these funds, or a taxable dividend if the fund itself has gains from selling bonds. Note also that there's a special rule for losses from these funds, explained later in this chapter.

Buying and selling mutual fund shares

When you buy regular stocks, you determine the number of shares you want to buy, and the price of the stock determines the amount of money you invest. Mutual funds generally work the opposite way: you determine the amount of money you want to invest, and the price determines the number of shares you'll acquire with that much money. For example, an investment of $500 might translate into 19.273 shares, based on the net asset value of the shares at the end of the day the mutual fund received your money.

Because the transactions are in dollar amounts, they may seem like deposits in a bank account. The essence of the transaction, though, is a purchase of shares. More importantly, any time you pull money out of a mutual fund, you're *selling* shares. That's true even if you merely move money from one fund to another in the same family of mutual funds. Perhaps you never saw the money, but for tax purposes you're treated the same as if you sold shares in the first fund—with a gain or loss—and used the money from that sale to buy shares in the second one.

This point sometimes comes as a surprise to people who are new to mutual fund investing. Perhaps they've grown accustomed to moving money from one fund to another within their 401k account or IRA. There's no gain or loss to report in retirement accounts, so it never hits home that they're buying and selling shares when they make these fund switches. They take the same approach with their non-retirement investments and learn the truth when Form 1099-B arrives at tax time, telling them a sale has been reported to the IRS.

Basis and holding period

To determine how much gain or loss you have on a sale of mutual fund shares, you need to know your *basis* in those shares. Chapter 8 explains the general rule for determining the basis of shares of stock, and that rule applies to mutual fund shares as well: your basis is equal to the amount paid for the shares, including any costs directly related to the purchase. If you paid a brokerage commission or similar charge when you made your investment, that amount is included in your basis. Some mutual funds impose a charge on the initial purchase, called a *load*. This would be included in your basis, too.

> **Example:** You invested $20,000 in a mutual fund that charges a 5% front-end load. Only $19,000 was actually used to buy shares, because $1,000 was used to pay the sales charge. Yet your basis for these shares is $20,000, because basis includes expenses incurred in purchasing the shares.

Dividends. Most mutual funds are set up to reinvest your dividends in additional shares of the same fund. The tax law treats you as if you received the dividend in cash, and then used the cash to buy additional shares. That means you have to report the dividend as income. It also means you have additional shares with cost basis equal to the amount of the dividend.

> **Example:** You invested $20,000 in a mutual fund, acquiring 828.844 shares at $24.13 per share. Later, when the net asset value of the fund was $24.93, the fund paid a dividend of $1.04 per share. This payout reduces the mutual fund's net asset value by an equal amount, changing it to $23.89 ($24.93 minus the $1.04 per share dividend). Your dividend is $862.00, and you receive an additional 36.082 shares at $23.89 per share. You now have a total of 864.926 shares. Unless you use the average basis method described later, they don't all have the same cost basis. The original shares have a basis of $24.13 per share, and the ones acquired later have a basis of $23.89 per share.

> Note that immediately after the dividend is paid, the NAV quoted for the fund will show a decrease, because cash in the amount of $1.04 per share flowed out, reducing NAV. This event didn't change the value of your holdings following the dividend reinvestment, though, because you acquired additional shares with a value that exactly offsets the reduction in NAV.

It's also worth noting that your shares don't all have the same holding period. Your holding period for some shares goes back to the date of your original investment, while the other shares have a holding period that begins on the date the mutual fund paid the dividend. This is important when you have to determine whether your gain or loss is short-term or long-term.

> **Example:** You sell your mutual fund shares more than a year after the date of the original investment but less than a year after the date of the dividend. Your gain or loss on the original shares is long-term, but your gain or loss on the shares you acquired from dividend reinvestment is short-term.

Later in this chapter we'll look at the average basis method, which makes it easier to determine the basis of the shares you sell. Yet even when you use that method, you have to know the holding period of your shares. This information tells you whether some or all of your gain is short-term, and is used for other purposes as well:

- The wash sale rule may apply if you sell some shares at a loss within 30 days before or after a dividend, because the dividend reinvestment is a purchase. Chapter 10 explains the wash sale rule.
- The special rule for sales of mutual fund shares at a loss within six months of purchase (explained later in this chapter) can apply to shares you bought automatically as a result of dividend reinvestment.

Basis of particular shares

For those who don't use the average basis method, determining the basis of particular shares in a mutual fund can be a tedious process. This is particularly true if you've made a large number of purchases over a period of years. Fortunately the number-crunching challenge has been largely shifted to financial firms for shares purchased after 2011.

Consider the following example. You've invested $100 per month over a period of four months with the following results:

Month	Amount	Price	Shares
March	$100.00	25.43	3.932
April	$100.00	25.80	3.876
May	$100.00	25.65	3.899
June	$100.00	26.03	3.842

The price per share of the mutual fund varies from time to time. As a result, the number of shares you receive for each $100 is different.

If you sell all the shares at one time, it's easy enough to see that your basis is $400. But suppose you withdraw only a portion of your account. You take $250, resulting in a sale of 8.477 shares. How do you determine the basis of those shares? As it turns out, there are three different possibilities.

- First-in, first-out (FIFO)
- Identification
- The average basis method

First-in, first-out

One approach for determining the basis of mutual fund shares you've sold is the first-in, first-out method, or FIFO as described in Chapter 8 for regular shares of stock. The only difference is that it's often a great deal more difficult to apply this method in the case of mutual funds because of multiple purchases and fractional shares.

We asked earlier what the result would be if you sold 8.477 of the shares represented in the table. Applying the FIFO method, we would treat the first shares purchased as the first shares sold. Spending a few moments with a calculator, you can determine that you sold all the shares bought in March, all the shares bought in April, and 0.669 of the shares bought in May. You're left with 3.230 of the shares bought in May and all the shares bought in June. The basis for the shares you sold is as follows:

Month	Shares	Per Share	Basis
March	3.932	25.43	$100.00
April	3.876	25.80	$100.00
May	0.669	25.65	$17.16
Total	8.477		$217.16

You'll report a sale of 8.477 shares for $250.00, with a basis of $217.16, resulting in gain of $32.84.

This certainly isn't rocket science, but you can see where you could run into a major headache if you continued to buy shares on a monthly basis over a period of years, and in addition had dividend reinvestments to deal with. That's where the average basis method comes in handy. But first a few words about identification.

Identifying shares

Chapter 8 explains the rules for identifying shares of stock. It's somewhat unusual to see investors use those rules for mutual fund shares, yet the same rules apply here if you aren't using the average basis method. The mutual fund company may allow you to set up a standing order, such as one that sells the shares with the highest basis first, or you might specify the order of sale some other way. As in the case of regular stock sales, identifying shares may reduce your tax bill.

In the example above, you might specify that you're selling the newest shares, rather than the oldest ones. The newer shares have a higher basis than the older ones, and that means you report a smaller gain (or a larger loss) when you sell them. The tax regulations say you have to tell the broker or mutual fund which shares you're selling at the time of sale. In addition, you have to receive written confirmation of the identification within a reasonable period of time after the sale. See Chapter 8 for more on identification.

Introduction to average basis method

Now we come to a choice that isn't generally available when selling regular stocks. People sometimes ask whether they can use average basis, instead of the basis of each individual lot of shares, to determine gain or loss on a sale of shares. For mutual funds, and for shares of regular stock held in a dividend reinvestment plan, the answer is yes.

Changes in the rules. The averaging rules were extensively revised in connection with the adoption of rules requiring brokers and other financial institutions (including mutual fund companies) to report basis and holding period, in addition to proceeds, when customers make sales. Here are the key differences:

- Average basis was previously used only at the election of the taxpayer but may now apply automatically unless the taxpayer chooses *not* to use average basis.
- Average basis previously applied across all accounts in which the taxpayer held shares of the same mutual fund but now applies separately to each account. Even within a single account, it applies separately to covered shares (those acquired after 2011) and noncovered shares (those acquired earlier).
- Taxpayers previously elected averaging by indicating this choice on their tax returns, but now for covered shares they must notify the broker or other financial institution.
- Taxpayers previously could not terminate or undo an election to use averaging except through a cumbersome and expensive ruling process, but are now permitted to terminate, and in some cases undo retroactively, an averaging election.
- We previously had two methods of averaging but now have only one. The double-category method no longer exists, and the single-category method is now simply known as the average basis method.
- Averaging previously applied only to mutual fund shares but now can apply also to shares of ordinary stocks if held in a dividend reinvestment plan.

Calculating average basis

Mutual fund companies are required to perform average basis calculations for covered shares (acquired after 2011), and many of them provide calculations for older, noncovered shares as well. There are situations where you may need to perform your own calculations, however. Figures provided for noncovered shares may not be accurate because the mutual fund company incorrectly assumes you used the average basis method for sales in prior years. Figures for covered shares can be incorrect as well in some situations, such as when you make a wash sale by selling shares in one account and buying replacement shares in a different account.

In broad outline the average basis method is simple enough. We maintain a running tally of the total basis of all shares that are being averaged. If you buy more shares, the purchase price goes into this total. If you've chosen to have dividends reinvested, the same thing happens each time the mutual fund pays a dividend, because reinvestment involves a purchase of additional shares with a basis equal to the amount of the dividend. We don't have to know the basis of individual tax lots because all shares have a basis equal to the average, determined by dividing the total basis by the total number of shares. We still need records of individual tax lots, but generally only for the purpose of determining your holding period for those shares.

When you sell shares, we multiply the average basis per share by the number of shares sold to determine the basis of those shares. Then we subtract that figure from the total basis of shares remaining in the account. Immediately after the sale, the basis per share of the remaining shares is the same as for the shares you sold, but that basis could change as a result of a subsequent purchase of additional shares.

Example: You contributed $100.00 per month to your mutual fund account for a period of 27 months. During that period, $147.00 of dividends were reinvested. Your total basis is $2,847.00. According to your mutual fund statement, at this point you own 112.342 shares, so your average basis is $25.34 per share.

Then you take $500.00 from the fund. Your statement says you sold 18.277 shares. To determine your basis in those shares, multiply the average basis by the number of shares.

That gives you a basis of $463.14 ($25.34 times 18.277). You'll report a gain of $36.86 ($500.00 minus $463.14).

Before the sale, the total basis of your shares was $2,847.00. Now you've sold shares with a basis of $463.14, so your remaining shares have a basis of $2,383.86. The next time you sell shares, you'll start from this number and increase it for any amounts added to the account, including reinvested dividends.

This may not seem like the easiest calculation in the world, but in a lot of cases it's a far sight easier than determining exactly what shares you sold when you withdrew $500 and figuring the basis of those particular shares. The main requirement is to keep a running tally of the total basis: your purchases, plus reinvested dividends, minus the basis of shares you sold. Divide that total by the number of shares you held at the time of the sale (a number you can get from your mutual fund statement) to get the average basis.

The following table lays out the calculations in the preceding example.

Averaging Calculation

1	Previous basis	$ 0.00
2	Additions	2,700.00
3	Reinvested dividends	147.00
4	Basis adjustments	0.00
5	Total basis	2,847.00
6	Number of shares owned	112.342
7	Average basis per share	25.34
8	Number of shares sold	18.277
9	Basis of shares sold	463.14
10	Total basis before sale	2,847.00
11	Basis of shares sold	(463.14)
12	Basis remaining after sale	$2,383.86

In this calculation, the "previous basis" is zero because this is the first time using averaging. The next time you sell shares, your "previous basis" will be $2,383.86, the ending number from the calculation above. Lines 2 and 3 will show only the additions and dividends that occurred after the sale reflected in this calculation. Line 4 allows for basis adjustments that may result from return of capital distributions (a negative number) or capital gain allocations (a positive number) described in Chapter 13.

> Remember, the key to this calculation is a running tally of your basis, adjusted to reflect added investments, reinvested dividends and sales, as indicated above. If you know the total basis of your shares, the averaging calculation is easy.

Holding period

Calculating basis is only part of the task. In addition to basis, you also have to know your *holding period* for the shares you sold. In other words, you need to know if the shares you sold were all long-term, all short-term, or some of each. You can average your basis, but you can't average your holding period!

When you use the average basis method, you're required to treat the shares you sold as the *earliest* shares you bought. All shares have the same basis, so this rule doesn't affect the amount of gain or loss, but it does affect the *category* of gain or loss. If you have long-term shares, they are treated as the first ones sold, even if you would prefer to sell the short-term shares.

> **Example:** You're selling mutual fund shares at a loss using the average basis method. Because you have a loss, you would prefer to sell your short-term shares. That way you would have a short-term loss, which reduces short-term gain. You aren't allowed to make this choice, though. You have to treat this as a sale of the oldest shares.

In most cases the easiest way to determine whether you sold any shares with a short-term holding period is to look at the shares you *didn't* sell. If the number of shares remaining in your mutual fund account after the sale is greater than the number of shares you acquired (including dividend reinvestments) during the 12 months preceding the sale, then all of your gain or loss on the sale is long-term. If not, you'll have to determine how many of the shares you sold were short-term.

Separate accounts

Under the old rules, if you held shares of the same mutual fund in two separate accounts, and you chose to use averaging for that mutual fund, you were required to use a global average. It seems unlikely that many investors held shares of the same fund in more than one account, and unlikelier still that they were aware of the rule and followed it. Nevertheless, this is what the regulations required.

This ill-considered rule was eliminated when the new averaging rules came into effect in 2012. Investors are now permitted—strike that, *required*—to maintain separate averages for each account in which they use averaging. What's more, they're allowed to make different elections for different accounts. You can use averaging for shares held in one account, and maintain distinct basis records for each tax lot of the same mutual fund held in a different account.

Covered and noncovered shares

Two thousand twelve was a watershed year in tax reporting for mutual fund shares. Before 2012, financial institutions were not required to report basis when customers sold mutual fund shares. In fact, the tax law didn't even require them to maintain records from which basis could be determined, although many did so, with varying degrees of detail, as a service to their customers. If mutual fund companies did not have full and accurate information concerning the basis of shares acquired before 2012, any *average* basis that included those shares would also be suspect. To assure that the IRS receives accurate basis information for shares acquired in 2012 and later years, the rules say that any account holding both older and newer shares must be treated as two separate accounts.

As in any other case where you have shares in separate accounts, you can choose to use averaging for both accounts, or for either one, or for neither. You might, for example, use averaging for the older shares, but preserve the separate basis of each tax lot for newer shares as a way of increasing your tax planning flexibility. If you choose averaging for both, you will have two separate averages for the two groups of shares.

The regulations refer to the two groups of shares as *covered* and *noncovered* shares. Newer shares are covered—that is, covered by the rules that required financial institutions to report basis when shares are sold. Many mutual fund companies provide basis information to customers who sell noncovered shares, but generally they do not report this information to the IRS. The distinction between covered and noncovered shares is important for other reasons, including the manner in which you choose whether or not to use averaging, as discussed later in this chapter, and the manner in which you report sales on your tax return, as discussed later in this book.

> The rules include a provision called the *single account election* which permits noncovered shares to be treated as covered shares if requirements are met. This election is available to the financial institution, not to the individual investor, and for technical reasons we believe it is unlikely to see much use.

Electing the average basis method

We now arrive at a topic that is far more complicated than we'd like. The old (pre-2012) rules limited our choices as to the use of an averaging method. We could make different choices for different mutual funds, but there was only one way to elect averaging, and once you made the election, it applied to all shares of that mutual fund, across all accounts in which you owned shares of that fund, for as long as your remained an investor in that fund. The new rules are more flexible but potentially bewildering. You might find that you're using averaging even though you never chose to do so. You may or may not have an opportunity to undo that averaging and restore separate basis for the tax lots you've purchased. You can use averaging for shares you hold in one account but not use averaging for shares of the same fund that you own in a different account. You can choose to stop the use of averaging for future purchases, or resume the use of averaging after having stopped.

Averaging by default. Financial firms are now permitted to establish a default treatment for mutual fund shares acquired after 2011. Many mutual fund companies have responded by setting the average basis method as the default, on the theory that this is what most of their customers would prefer. If you buy mutual fund shares at one of these companies, *you will be bound by their default method unless you act to preserve your ability to use the cost basis of separate lots.*

You have two ways to avoid averaging for new shares in an account with a company where averaging is the default. One is to specify at the time of the first investment that you intend to use separate basis. The other way is to *revoke* the averaging election (in this case, the "election" made for you by the company's choice of a default). See below for rules on revoking an averaging election.

Note that you have a separate choice between average basis and cost basis for each mutual fund in which you invest, even within the same overall investment account. Telling the company you don't want to use average basis for your shares in a balanced fund won't necessarily prevent the company from defaulting you into averaging for your shares in a small cap fund. If you want to avoid using the average basis method while investing at a company that has this method as the default, be sure to understand the procedures for overriding their default on all your investments.

Electing averaging. The procedures for electing averaging differ depending on whether you hold covered shares (generally, shares bought in 2012 or later years) or noncovered shares (acquired in 2011 or earlier).

For covered shares, if you want to use averaging and this is not the default method of the company where you maintain the investment account, you elect averaging by notifying the company. The notification must be in writing, but electronic communication is permitted, so clicking on a checkbox in an online form would suffice if the company offers that opportunity. You're allowed to make the election separately for each mutual fund and for each account, or you can specify that it applies to all accounts you now have or will later establish with that company. The election will apply only to covered shares, however. In addition, it will apply only to sales occurring after you make the election. You can't apply this election retroactively to earlier sales, even if they occurred in the same year. Also, you can't apply the election to some of the covered shares but not to other covered shares of the same fund in the same account.

The procedure to elect averaging for older, noncovered shares is different. You make this election on your tax return for the first year you use averaging for shares of this mutual fund. This means the election is effectively retroactive to the beginning of the preceding year (that is, the year for which you're filing the tax return). The regulations require you to "indicate on the tax return that [you] used the average basis method in reporting gain or loss," so you should include a statement to that effect when you elect averaging. (My sense is that this rule has been largely ignored by both taxpayers and the IRS, so there is no need to be concerned if you failed to include this statement for previously filed returns.) The statement is required only for the first year you use averaging for that mutual fund.

> See below for additional procedure required if your account includes shares received as a gift.

Averaging information provided by the fund

Many mutual funds provide averaging calculations for noncovered shares, based on the assumption this is the method the customer is most likely to want to use. They send a schedule that tells you the basis per share, the number of shares sold, and the total basis of the shares you sold. This information is not reported to the IRS. In fact, the mutual fund is not required to provide this information at all. It's simply a service that some funds provide.

Just because they send this information doesn't mean you have to use it. You may find that you're better off if you use the first-in, first-out method to determine your gain or loss. If you used averaging for noncovered shares of this fund in prior years, you have to stick with that averaging method, but otherwise you're free to use the method of your choice.

Bear in mind that the mutual fund company doesn't know what method you used for noncovered shares in prior years. If you made previous sales that didn't use the average basis method, the company's basis calculation may not be correct. If you've used the FIFO method or specific identification for noncovered shares in the past and then switch to averaging, you'll have to do your own averaging calculation.

Revoking the average basis method

We'll see later that you can stop using the average basis method whenever you choose. The decision to do so would affect only subsequent purchases, however. To *undo* averaging, so that all the affected shares revert to their original cost basis, you need to *revoke* the averaging method.

You can use this revocation procedure in either of two situations. One is where the average basis method was applied to your account as a result of the financial firm having chosen that method as the default. The other is where you affirmatively elected to use the average basis method but afterward change your mind.

> The procedure for revoking an averaging election does not apply when you elect averaging for noncovered shares. As described above, this election is made on your tax return, and can be changed only by amending that return on or before its extended due date (generally October 15 of the year you filed the return).

You lose the ability to revoke the averaging method when you sell any of the shares to which it applies. There is a possible trap here in that you could have been defaulted into the averaging method without your knowledge and found out about it only after you saw the results of your first sale. For this reason, if you want to avoid averaging, you need to be alert to the possible need to revoke an averaging method that may be in place by reason of the financial firm's default.

Assuming you haven't made any sales, the financial firm is required to permit you to revoke the averaging method for a period of one year after it began to apply (one year after you made the election or one year after you made the first purchase to which the averaging method applied by default). The regulations say financial firms can provide a longer period of time to revoke the average basis method, and some have chosen to do so. It's safest not to assume you'll have more than a year to act.

The effect of revoking the averaging method is to treat your shares as if that method never applied in the first place. Each tax lot, whether acquired in a regular purchase or by dividend reinvestment, will have a basis equal to its cost when acquired, subject only to any adjustments that might have applied without regard to use of the averaging method.

> Revoking the average basis method is retroactive in the sense that it undoes averaging that took effect in the past. It is not retroactive to previous sales, however. Making a sale with averaging in effect terminates your ability to revoke averaging.

Changing from the averaging method

For covered shares, you can also *change from* the averaging method without revoking it. There are no restrictions on your ability to take this action. You can do it whenever you want, regardless of whether you've already sold some of the shares to which the averaging method applies. When you change from the averaging method (instead of revoking it), the shares already in the account do not revert to their original cost basis. Their basis continues to be whatever the average basis was at the time you switched to using cost basis. Any shares you acquire in the future, however, would have a separate cost basis and would not affect the basis of shares already in the account.

When might you use this rule? Perhaps you simply want more flexibility for tax planning in connection with sales of shares you purchase in the future. There are other situations where it may be particularly advantageous to change from the average basis method.

One possibility would be a situation where the basis of newly acquired shares is quite a bit different from the average basis of shares you already own. For example, if the value of the shares has gone down, you might want to buy additional shares without diluting the basis of older shares. In this way you would preserve your ability to harvest tax losses in subsequent sales of those older, high basis shares.

Another possibility would be a desire to work around the rule that requires you to sell the oldest shares first when using the average basis method. You might hold both short-term and long-term shares with high average basis that can be sold at a loss. In a situation where a short-term loss would be more valuable, you could change from using the average basis rule before making a sale. It appears that you would then be permitted to use identification to make a sale of your short-term shares while continuing to hold the long-term shares.

Should you use averaging?

Averaging originated in the idea that its methods provide a measure of simplification in performing the basis calculations for investments that are often purchased in installments and include fractional shares. For some investors, particularly those who are not motivated to engage in detailed tax management of their accounts, this advantage will suffice to justify using the average basis method.

Yet the advantage is greatly diminished now that mutual fund companies are required to maintain basis records. In the course of upgrading their systems for compliance with these rules, many companies raised their game in terms of tax management opportunities for their investors. It may be much easier now than it was in the past to identify shares when making a sale. What's more, you may be able to select a tax-efficient method of selling as a standing order, automatically selling the shares with the highest basis, for example. You may find that you can achieve greater tax efficiency while suffering little or no inconvenience.

Although averaging deprives you of flexibility, there are times when it can produce a tax result superior to any that can be achieved through identification. Consider the situation where the value of your mutual fund has gone up quite a bit in the last 18 months or so. Throughout that period you were adding to your investment, but now you want to take some money out. If you use the first-in, first-out method, you'll be selling shares you held more than a year (good) but those shares have the lowest basis, meaning you'll report a large gain (bad). If you identify the shares you're selling as ones you bought more recently, you'll have a smaller gain (good) but your gain will be short-term (bad).

The average basis method provides a solution. You can sell the long-term shares, but report a smaller gain than you would under the FIFO method. That's because the more costly shares you bought recently give you an average basis that's higher than the per-share basis of the older shares. You get the lower rate that applies to long-term capital gain, but your gain is smaller than it would be if you didn't elect to use the average basis method.

Averaging can help in the reverse situation, too. Suppose shares have declined in value while you acquired them, and you now plan to sell all the shares for a capital loss. If the oldest shares have the highest basis, averaging will shift some of that basis to newer shares. The effect may be to convert some of your long-term loss to short-term loss, which is sometimes more valuable because it is used first to offset short-term capital gain.

Double-category averaging

Taxpayers were previously permitted to choose an averaging method called double-category averaging, which averaged the basis of shares held a year or less (short-term shares) separately from the basis of shares held more than a year (long-term shares). This averaging method offered tax planning flexibility but required meticulous recordkeeping because both averages would change every time a tax lot passed the first anniversary of its purchase, graduating from short-term to long-term. Because it was so cumbersome the method was rarely used, and the Treasury did away with it when the averaging rules changed in 2012.

Averaging when you have gift shares

There's a special rule that applies to certain shares received by gift if you elect to use the average basis method. The rule applies only if the shares have a basis greater than their value at the time of the gift. In other words, the rule applies if the person who gave you the shares could have sold them at a loss. The purpose of this special rule is to prevent you from getting the benefit of this loss when you use the average basis method.

If you have gift shares and you want to use the average basis method, you have to do one of the following:

- You can include in your election a statement that you'll use the *date-of-gift* value as the basis of the shares for all purposes. That means you won't get the benefit of the higher basis the shares had in the hands of the person who made the gift. You might do this if the date-of-gift value is only a little bit lower than the donor's basis. Bear in mind, though, this choice will apply to any gift shares you receive in the future, too.
- Your other alternative is to hold the gift shares in a separate account that's excluded from your averaging calculations. This choice involves some added paperwork, but preserves the possibility that you'll benefit from the higher basis if the value of the shares rises. For more about gifts and basis, see Chapter 11.

Losses within six months

We're through talking about averaging but not quite finished dealing with special rules for mutual funds. Here's a rule even your tax pro may not know. If you have a loss from selling mutual fund shares you've held less than six months, you have to treat some or all of that loss as a long-term loss if you received a capital gain dividend (or had to report undistributed capital gain) on those shares. What's more, if you received an exempt interest dividend on those shares, part or all of your loss will be nondeductible.

Background. When a mutual fund pays a dividend, the value of the fund goes down by the amount of the dividend. For example, if your mutual fund shares are valued at $29.75 immediately before a dividend of $1.50 per share, the value will be $28.25 per share immediately after the dividend. No problem there—that's just the way stocks work in general. But that means a special rule is needed for certain capital losses on mutual fund shares.

Capital gain dividends. Consider what would happen if you bought shares in a mutual fund at $29.75 per share just before the fund paid a *capital gain* dividend of $1.50. You'll treat that dividend as long-term capital gain even if you held the mutual fund shares only a day before the dividend. Then you *sell* the mutual fund at $28.25—the value right after the dividend. Under the normal rules, you would get a short-term capital loss. That could provide you with a significant tax advantage if you also have short-term capital gains.

> **Example:** Overall for a particular year you had $15,000 of long-term capital gain and $5,000 of short-term capital gain. Your short-term capital gain would be taxed at your marginal rate of 32%, while the long-term gain is taxed at 15%. Being a crafty investor, but unaware of the special rule we're discussing, you find a mutual fund that's about to pay a capital gain dividend. You buy enough shares so you'll receive a $5,000 capital gain dividend. Right after receiving the dividend, you sell the shares for a $5,000 capital loss.
>
> Now your totals for the year are $20,000 of long-term capital gain and $0 of short-term capital gain. The $15,000 long-term gain you had before is increased by the $5,000 capital gain dividend from the mutual fund, and the $5,000 short-term gain you had before is eliminated by the $5,000 loss on sale of the mutual fund shares. Your total amount of gain is still $20,000, but now it's all long-term, meaning a lower rate of tax—if this special rule didn't apply!

The rule applies only if you sell your mutual fund shares at a loss *six months or less after you bought them.* (It's OK to sell less than six months after the *dividend,* if you held the shares more than six months.) Note that this doesn't match up with the amount of time you need to hold the shares to have a long-term capital gain or loss upon selling the shares. The idea is that if you've held the shares six months, that's long enough so that your loss (if you have one) probably relates to genuine changes in the value of the mutual fund rather than the effect of a single dividend.

When the rule applies, you have to treat some or all of your short-term loss as a long-term loss. The amount that's treated as a long-term loss is limited to the amount of the capital gain distribution or allocation you received. So if your loss is greater than the amount of that distribution or allocation, the remaining portion of the loss is treated as a short-term capital loss.

> The same rule applies if, instead of a capital gain dividend, you had to report undistributed capital gain. Chapter 13 explains capital gain distributions and allocations.

It appears that the six-month rule does not apply to qualifying dividends, even though they are taxed at the same rate as long-term capital gains. However, you don't get the benefit of the lower tax rate unless you hold your mutual fund shares at least 61 days. See Chapter 13.

Exempt interest dividends. The same principle applies if you receive an exempt interest dividend and then sell shares at a loss. But in this case, your short-term loss becomes nondeductible.

> **Example:** You buy shares in a municipal bond fund just before it pays an exempt interest dividend of $1,200. Then you sell the shares at a loss of $1,300. If you held the shares six months or less, you're permitted to deduct only $100. The remaining $1,200 represents the exempt interest dividend you received.

This rule does *not* apply to nontaxable return of capital distributions. Those distributions reduce your basis in the mutual fund shares, so your loss calculation automatically takes this item into account.

Load rollover rule

There's one other rule that can change the tax consequences when you sell mutual fund shares. It has to do with reinvestment rights offered by some mutual fund companies. When you pay a sales charge, often called a *load*, the company may permit you to sell those shares and buy into another fund, or buy back into the same fund, without paying a load charge, or with payment of a reduced load charge. The *load rollover rule* applies when all three of the following are true:

- You acquired a reinvestment right when you paid a load charge in connection with a purchase of mutual fund shares;
- You sold those shares within 90 days after purchasing them; and
- On or before January 31 of the year following the year in which the sale occurred, you used the reinvestment right to buy mutual fund shares (in the same or a different fund) with a reduction in the load charge you would otherwise have paid.

When all these conditions exist, you have to figure your gain or loss from selling the original shares without taking the load charge into account, except to the extent the load charge exceeds the reduction in load charge on the new investment. This rule prevents taxpayers from using a load rollover to create artificial losses.

> **Example:** You want to invest $20,000 in the XYZ Growth Fund, which charges a 5% front-end sales load. That means $1,000 of your investment will be used to pay the sales charge, leaving you with a $19,000 investment. You're allowed to switch your money between funds maintained by XYZ without paying an additional load.
>
> If the load rollover rule didn't apply, you might be tempted to try the following maneuver. Instead of buying the fund you're really interested in, you would buy the XYZ Balanced Fund, paying the $1,000 load. Then you would

immediately switch the $19,000 investment to the XYZ Growth Fund (where you wanted to be all along), claiming a $1,000 capital loss on sale of your shares in the Balanced Fund.

The load rollover rule prevents you from getting a tax advantage if you use this technique.

The disallowed sales charge is added to your basis in the newly purchased shares, so your tax benefit isn't lost entirely, just delayed until you sell the shares you bought with the reduced sales load.

10

The Wash Sale Rule

WHEN THE VALUE OF YOUR STOCK GOES DOWN you get that sinking feeling—you've lost money. But the tax law doesn't allow that loss until you sell the stock. In a way that's good, because it means you can control the timing of your deduction, taking it when the benefit is the greatest.

The problem is, you may have a conflict. You want to deduct the loss, but you also want to keep the stock because you think it's going to bounce back. It's tempting to think you can sell the stock and claim the loss, then buy it back right away. And that's where the wash sale rule comes in. If you buy replacement stock shortly after the sale—or shortly before the sale—you can't deduct your loss. At least, you can't deduct it until you sell the replacement stock.

This chapter provides a complete explanation of wash sales under the following headings:

- The basic rule
- Consequences of a wash sale
- Substantially identical securities

- Replacement stock
- Matching Rules
- IRAs and other related "persons"
- Wash sales and traders
- Planning for wash sales

The basic rule

People in business sometimes say a combination of two things that offset each other, eliminating any advantage, is a *wash*. *"The profit from increased sales was just enough to cover the cost of the advertising, so it turned out to be a wash."* This may not be a common use of the word—I checked two good-sized dictionaries without finding a definition corresponding to this meaning—but this use gives us the name of a tax rule that has been with us for many years: the *wash sale rule.*

In general you have a wash sale if you sell stock at a loss, and buy substantially identical stock within 30 days before or after the sale. The two transactions leave you in the same position as before you started: it was a wash.

> **Example:** On March 31 you sell 100 shares of XYZ at a loss. On April 10 you buy 100 shares of XYZ. The sale on March 31 is a wash sale. You can't deduct the loss on this sale.

Wash sale period. The *wash sale period* for any sale at a loss consists of 61 days: the day of the sale, the 30 days before the sale and the 30 days after the sale. (These are calendar days, not trading days. Count carefully!) If you want to claim your loss as a deduction, you need to avoid purchasing the same stock during the wash sale period. For a sale on March 31, the wash sale period includes all of March and April.

Losses only. The wash sale rule only applies to *losses*. You can't wipe out a *gain* from a sale by buying the same stock back within 30 days.

Example: On June 10 you sell 100 shares of XYZ for a $2,000 profit. On June 15 you buy 100 shares of XYZ, replacing the shares you sold. The wash sale rule doesn't apply because you had a gain, not a loss. You have to report the gain.

Consequences of a wash sale

The wash sale rule actually has *three* consequences:

- You aren't allowed to claim a deduction for the loss on your sale.
- Your disallowed loss is added to the basis of the replacement stock.
- Your holding period for the replacement stock includes the holding period of the stock you sold.

The first one is clear enough, but the other two may require some explanation.

Basis adjustment. The basis adjustment is important: it preserves the benefit of the disallowed loss. You'll receive that benefit on a future sale of the replacement stock.

Example: Some time ago you bought 80 shares of XYZ at $50. The stock has declined to $30, and you sell it to take the loss deduction. But then you see some good news on XYZ and you buy it back for $32, less than 31 days after the sale.

You can't deduct your loss of $20 per share. But you add $20 per share to the basis of your replacement shares. Those shares have a basis of $52 per share: the $32 you paid, plus the $20 wash sale adjustment. In other words, you're treated as if you bought the replacement shares for $52. If you end up selling them for $55, you'll only report $3 per share of gain. If you sell them for $32 (the same price you paid to buy them), you'll report a loss of $20 per share—unless you buy replacement stock again, creating a second wash sale.

Because of this basis adjustment, a wash sale usually isn't a disaster. In most cases, it simply means you'll get the same tax benefit at a later time. If you receive the benefit later in the same year, the wash sale may have no effect at all on your taxes. There are times, though, when the wash sale rule can have truly painful consequences:

- If you don't sell the replacement stock in the same year as the wash sale, your loss will be postponed, possibly to a year when the deduction is of less value.
- If you die before selling the replacement stock, neither you nor your heirs will benefit from the basis adjustment.
- You can also lose the benefit of the deduction permanently if you sell stock and arrange to have a related person—or your IRA—buy replacement stock. We'll discuss this point later in this chapter.

Holding period. When the wash sale rule applies, your holding period for the replacement stock includes the period you held the stock you sold. This rule prevents you from converting a long-term loss into a short-term loss.

> **Example:** You've held shares of XYZ for years and it's been a dog. You sell it at a loss but then buy it back within the wash sale period. When you sell the replacement stock, your gain or loss will be long-term—no matter how soon you sell it.

In some situations you get more tax savings from a short-term loss than a long-term loss, so this rule generally works against you. If the price of the stock recovers and you sell for a gain, you may benefit from this rule.

Gaps and overlaps. You can have a wash sale because of a purchase that's up to 30 days before or after your sale. The law says your holding period for the replacement shares "includes" the holding period of the shares that were sold. That raises the question of how to handle gaps and overlaps. For example, suppose you bought the original stock on May 5. Somewhere along the way you had a wash sale, and there was a gap of several days before you bought the replacement shares. If you sold the replacement stock on May 6 of the following year, is your gain or loss long-term, even though several days elapsed between the sale of the original stock and purchase of the new shares? Or do you subtract the days you didn't own the stock?

There are no regulations or rulings that would resolve this issue. For years, the IRS said in Publication 550 that your holding period for the replacement shares begins on the same day as the holding period for the shares you sold. In my view, this is the more reasonable interpretation. Unfortunately, someone at the IRS had a different idea, changing the language of the publication to use the ambiguous language of the statute, saying the holding period "includes" the holding period of the stock you sold, without explaining how to include it.

Brokers and other financial firms were forced to decide how to interpret this rule when the programmed their computers for basis reporting that began in 2011 for regular stocks and 2012 for mutual fund shares. It appears that many of them viewed the change in Publication 550 as an indication that the IRS now rejects the "same day" interpretation previously appearing in that document. As a result they may use an interpretation that counts the number of days you held the stock that was sold, and adds that number of days to the holding period of the newly acquired stock. This interpretation can produce strange results, especially when holding periods overlap, but it is now baked into so many computer systems that it is unlikely the IRS will ever again issue guidance in favor of the more sensible alternative.

Substantially identical securities

You don't have a wash sale unless you buy *substantially identical securities* within the 61-day wash sale period. As a general rule, stock of one company isn't substantially identical to stock of a different one, even if they're both in the same industry. For example, Dell isn't substantially identical to HP. If you have a loss on one of these companies, you can buy the other one without having a wash sale.

This rule presents one of the most effective ways of dealing with the wash sale rule. If you want to report a loss but you're afraid the market will get away from you while you wait out the wash sale period, you can sell your losing shares and buy another stock that's likely to move in the same direction as the one you're holding. Of course, things don't always work that way: one company can have good news while another in the same industry has bad news. What you're doing is *reducing* the chance of missing an upswing in your stock's value, not *eliminating* that possibility.

Related stocks. There are times when a change in the value of one stock will be reflected directly in the value of another stock. This often happens in situations where a merger or other acquisition is pending. Investors know that company A is going to be acquired, with each share of its stock exchanged for 2.7 shares of company B, so the market value of company A's stock is simply 2.7 times the value of company B's stock. In this situation, the tax regulations treat the two stocks as substantially identical for purposes of the wash sale rule. You can't claim a loss on selling one of these stocks if you purchase shares of the other within the wash sale period.

Mutual funds. There's some debate, but no direct authority, on the question of whether two mutual funds keying off the same index are substantially identical for purposes of the wash sale rule. Can you sell one S&P 500 index fund at a loss and buy a different S&P 500 fund the same day without having a wash sale?

Because there is no direct authority dealing with this question, reasonable minds may differ. It's always possible to identify differences between funds managed by different companies, such as expense ratios and "tax load." Some people conclude on this basis that funds maintained by two different companies should never be considered the same for purposes of the wash sale rule.

My feeling is that those differences aren't enough to prevent the two funds from being *substantially* identical, which is all the wash sale rule requires. The point of the wash sale rule is to determine whether you've changed your position relative to the market. If you can lay the price graph for your new investment on top of the price graph for the old one and never see a significant disparity (as would be the case for two high quality S&P 500 funds), the investments should be considered substantially identical for purposes of the wash sale rule.

If I were sitting with a loss in an index fund and wanted to get around the wash sale rule, I would invest for 31 days in a fund that doesn't precisely track the same index, but emphasizes stocks of the type that are in that index. A fund that has similar stocks but doesn't track the same index shouldn't be considered substantially identical to the index fund. Yet a diversified holding of stocks that are mainly in the same index should have a relatively small likelihood of diverging significantly from the index within 31 days. That's not to say there's zero likelihood of that happening. The managed fund may have some heavy bets go sour during that time. Bear in mind, though, that the reverse is equally likely: the managed fund may outperform the index for this period.

The bottom line is that risk and the wash sale rule are tied together. If you have a strategy that completely eliminates market risk, you bear the *tax risk* that the IRS will say you have a wash sale. The idea is that you can't report a loss for tax purposes without changing your investment position.

Replacement stock

There are situations where your purchases and sales may fit within the literal language of the wash sale rule, but where the rule shouldn't apply because the stock you bought didn't replace the stock you sold. Unfortunately, you won't find exceptions to cover these situations in the Internal Revenue Code or the tax regulations. Some of the possibilities are covered by common sense, and there's an IRS ruling that covers another one. Still others leave some doubt as to the correct interpretation.

The easiest way to understand what I call the *replacement stock* issue is through a series of examples.

> **Selling all.** On June 1 you buy 200 shares of XYZ for $10,000. On June 12 you sell all 200 shares for $8,000 (a loss of $2,000).

Most people wouldn't even think about applying the wash sale rule here. You know instinctively it shouldn't apply, even though there's a sale at a loss, and a purchase within 30 days before the sale. Your instincts are correct: the wash sale rule doesn't apply because the stock you bought isn't *replacement stock* for the stock you sold. That's because you sold the same stock you bought.

> **Selling half.** On June 1 you buy 200 shares of XYZ for $10,000. On June 12 you sell 100 shares for $4,000 (a loss of $1,000). You continue to hold the other 100 shares.

The answer here is a little less obvious. After the sale, you hold shares identical to the shares you sold, and you bought those shares less than 31 days before the sale. But you probably still feel that the wash sale rule shouldn't apply here. Fortunately, the IRS agrees, at least in situations where you bought the 200 shares in a single lot. They issued a ruling saying this sequence doesn't produce a wash sale.

The result shouldn't change if you gave a single order to buy 200 shares and your broker happened to execute it by buying two lots of 100 shares each. It's clear in this situation that the shares you have left after the sale weren't bought to replace the shares you sold. Yet the IRS ruling telling us you're okay if you buy the shares in a single lot doesn't tell us what happens if a single buy order is split into two lots, so the result here is a little less certain.

> **Separate purchases.** You buy 100 shares of XYZ in the morning, and decide to buy another 100 shares in the afternoon of the same day. Within 30 days you sell the morning shares at a loss.

This is a situation where the wash sale rule probably *does* apply. The shares you bought in the afternoon are likely to be considered replacement shares for the ones you bought in the morning and later sold.

> **Old shares.** You've held 100 shares of XYZ for more than 30 days. You buy an additional 100 shares for $5,000. Less than 31 days later, you sell these shares (the new ones) for $4,000 (a $1,000 loss). You continue to hold the old shares.

There are no rulings that mention this situation. Yet I believe the implicit requirement for replacement stock should prevent the wash sale rule from applying here. After your sale, you don't hold any shares that were purchased in the preceding 30 days.

Note that you have to use *identification* to sell the newer shares. Unless you follow this procedure (explained in Chapter 8), the tax law assumes you sold the older shares. If you have a loss on a sale of the older shares, the wash sale rule applies because you bought replacement shares within 30 days before the sale.

> **Not so old shares.** This example is the same as the previous one, except the "old" shares aren't as old. You bought the old shares on June 1, the new shares on June 10, and sold the new shares at a loss on June 20.

Once again, you had to use specific identification to sell the new shares. The question is, do you have a wash sale here because you bought the old shares less than 31 days before you sold the new ones?

As a matter of logic, it's clear that the answer should be no. The old shares can't possibly be replacement shares for the newer ones. You bought them before you bought the shares you sold, so it seems they should be ignored in applying the wash sale rule.

Unfortunately, in a ruling dealing with an unrelated issue, the IRS gave an example like the one above, and said the wash sale rule applied. The ruling was designed to cover an entirely different point, and it's probably just an unfortunate coincidence that the example came out the way it did. The person who drafted the ruling may not have thought about the fact that the shares in the example weren't replacement shares. Perhaps if the IRS were to focus on this issue, they would agree with my interpretation. I can't promise that result, though.

> My feeling is that the wash sale rule should never apply if the replacement shares were bought at the same time as, or earlier than, the shares that were sold. There isn't any opportunity for abusive tax planning in this situation. The issue is in doubt, though, because the IRS has issued a ruling containing an example that seems erroneous.

Matching rules

There are times when you know the wash sale rule applies, but it isn't obvious exactly *how* it applies because of multiple purchases and sales of the same stock. The tax law provides *matching rules* for telling which shares are affected by a wash sale.

The general rule is to resolve ambiguities by analyzing transactions in chronological order. If there are multiple sales that can match a particular purchase, you match the earliest sale first. Similarly, if there are multiple purchases that can match a particular sale, you match the earliest purchase first. *You're required to follow these rules even if a different way of matching would produce a better tax result.*

Example: You sold 100 shares of XYZ at a loss on March 12. On March 14 you bought 60 shares, and on March 20 you bought another 90 shares. You bought a total of 150 shares during the wash sale period, but only 100 are *replacement* shares under the wash sale rule. You need to know *which* shares are replacement shares because that affects the basis and holding period of those shares. *The replacement shares are the ones acquired earliest:* the 60 shares you bought on March 14 and 40 of the 90 shares you bought on March 20. The other 50 shares you bought on March 20 are not affected by the wash sale rule.

Example: You sold 100 shares of XYZ at a loss on March 12, and another 100 shares, also at a loss, on March 14. On March 20 you bought 150 shares. In this case, *all* of your new shares are replacement shares, but now you need to determine which loss is disallowed. *The wash sale rule applies to the earliest sale first,* so all the loss from the March 12 sale is disallowed. In addition, the wash sale rule disallows the loss from 50 of the 100 shares sold on March 14.

There's one other rule that acts as a tiebreaker. You may have a situation where you can't tell which shares were sold first. In that case, the wash sale rule applies first to the shares you *acquired* first.

Example: On January 5 you bought 100 shares of XYZ at $55, and on January 10 you bought another 100 shares of XYZ at $65. On March 12 you sold 200 shares of XYZ at $40. Then you bought 100 shares of XYZ on March 18, creating a wash sale as to 100 shares of the 200 shares you sold.

First you look at which shares were sold first. You may not be able to tell which were sold first because you sold all 200 shares at the same time. If that's the case, you apply the wash sale rule to the shares you *bought* first: the shares you bought on January 5. Your loss on the shares you bought on January 10 is allowed.

IRAs and other related "persons"

One of the most frequently asked questions about the wash sale rule goes like this:

Suppose I sell my stock at a loss and buy the same stock in my IRA. Does the wash sale rule apply?

Early editions of this book pointed out that the IRS was likely to apply the wash sale rule in this situation, but noted that the issue had not been addressed in any official guidance. In December 2007 the IRS issued a ruling that confirmed their position: you can't avoid the wash sale rule by buying replacement stock in an IRA.

The ruling adds that the disallowed loss is not added to the taxpayer's basis in the IRA. This means the wash sale rule can have a more painful consequence in this situation. In a normal wash sale, your basis in the replacement shares is increased by the amount of the disallowed loss. That means you can recover the tax advantage associated with that loss by selling the replacement shares. When the replacement shares are in an IRA, there's no way to claim a loss on a subsequent sale. Without a basis adjustment in the IRA itself, you can't reduce the amount of income you report on your IRA distributions. In short, you get no future tax benefit at all.

Other related "persons." The IRS ruling was strictly limited to situations where the replacement purchase is in a traditional or Roth IRA. What if you have a spouse or other member of your family purchase replacement shares? Or a trust or business entity you control?

The IRS says the answer depends on whether the purchase of replacement shares was part of a prearranged plan. You can claim the loss if it's "purely coincidental" that another member of your family bought the same stock you sold, but not if the purchase was part of a prearranged plan. This statement is often overlooked because it appears in the part of IRS Publication 550 dealing with related party transactions rather than the wash sale rule. The IRS position is consistent with the outcome of some cases where the courts ruled against taxpayers who used a purchase by a related person in an effort to avoid the wash sale rule., although the IRS is treating the transactions as an indirect related party sale rather than a wash sale.

Wash sales and traders

At one time the wash sale rule didn't apply to *traders* (other than corporations), but Congress changed the law. (The income tax regulations have not been updated to reflect this change in the law, but taxpayers cannot rely on regulations that contradict the statute.) If you're a trader under the rules described in Part VI of this book, you have to deal with the wash sale rule until and unless you make the mark-to-market election (Chapter 28). That's unfortunate, because by the very nature of what they do, traders normally have a large number of wash sales.

Working through all the basis adjustments for scores of wash sales is a major headache. You need to analyze every trade on which you have a loss to determine if it's a wash sale. If it is, you have to make a basis adjustment to the replacement stock. What's more, the basis adjustment can turn a cash profit into a tax loss, so even profitable trades can result in losses that are subject to the wash sale rule.

> **Example:** You lost $300 on a sale of XYZ and bought the same stock again the next day. That's a wash sale, so you have to eliminate the loss and add $300 to the basis of the replacement stock. Then you sell the replacement stock for a profit of $100 (relative to the purchase price). Because of the extra $300 of basis, this is a loss of $200 for tax purposes. If you have another purchase of the same stock, the wash sale rule can apply again.

Prior to 2011, for active traders with thousands of transactions per year it was all but impossible to perform all the wash sale analysis required by these rules without specialized software. Brokers are now required to perform wash sale analysis and report the results. Unless you have reason to believe the analysis provided by your broker is incorrect, it will generally make sense to rely on the wash sale analysis provided in the broker's annual tax report.

Planning for wash sales

Before you spend too much brainpower figuring out how you can plan for wash sales, ask yourself *why* you need to do this planning. In many cases the reason boils down to the fact that you're kicking yourself for buying the stock in the first place, and you'll kick yourself even more if it recovers after you sell it. Try to convince yourself that you should kick yourself just as much if some *other* stock goes up when you don't own it. Sell the loser, and buy something else.

If you're one of those people who can't move on after a loss, you may want to know what you can safely do to plan around the wash sale rule. No technique is completely safe. Here are some ideas to consider:

- Most obviously, you can sell the stock and wait 31 days before buying it again. (Check your calendar carefully!) The risk here is that the price of the stock may rise before you can repurchase it.
- If you're truly convinced the stock is at rock bottom, you might consider buying the replacement stock 31 days *before* the sale. If the stock happens to go up during that period, your gain is doubled. If it stays even you can sell the older stock and claim your loss deduction. But if you're wrong about the stock, a further decline in value will be doubly painful.
- If your stock has a strong tendency to move in tandem with some other stock, you may be able to reduce your risk of missing a big gain by purchasing stock in a different company as "replacement" stock. This is not a wash sale because the stock you're buying is not "substantially identical" to the stock you're selling. Thirty-one days later you can switch back to your original stock if that's your wish. But there's no way to be certain that any two stocks will move in the same direction, or in the same magnitude.

There's no risk-free way to get around the wash sale rule. But then again, continuing to hold a stock that has lost value isn't risk-free, either. In the end it's up to you to evaluate all the risks, and balance them against the benefit you'll receive if you can claim a deduction for your loss.

More on wash sales

Further complexities of the wash sale rule apply to people who engage in short selling, and people who trade stock options. Those specialized applications of the wash sale rule are explained in Chapters 15 and 16.

11

Special Transactions

THERE ARE A VARIETY OF SPECIAL TRANSACTIONS that can affect the way you figure your gain or loss on shares of stock. Some of them apply to all kinds of property, and others relate only to stock. This chapter covers the situations you're most likely to encounter:

- Stock received as a gift
- Stock acquired from your spouse
- Stock received from a decedent
- Stock dividends and splits
- Mergers and spin-offs
- Dividend reinvestment plans (DRIPs)
- Stock acquired by exercising employee options
- Stock that becomes worthless
- Cash in lieu of fractional shares

Stock received as a gift

If you're lucky enough to receive stock as a gift, you need to know the special rules for determining gain or loss on sale of that stock. These rules don't apply to stock you receive from your spouse or from a decedent. We'll get to those rules a little later.

Good news. To begin with, you'll be happy to learn that the value of the gift isn't *income.* The gift may seem as good as a paycheck (or better!) but you don't have to report it or pay income tax. You don't have to pay gift tax, either. If there's a gift tax, the *donor* pays it, not the person who received the gift.

Stock has gone down. The rules for gifts depend on whether the stock is *appreciated* or *depreciated*—in other words, did it go up or down while the donor held it. We'll start with the rule for depreciated stock: stock that has gone down. In other words, we're talking about a situation where the donor's basis (usually the amount paid to acquire the stock) is greater than the current value.

> **Example:** Your uncle bought 100 shares of XYZ when it was at $72. His basis for the 100 shares, including a $50 commission, was $7,250. He gave the stock to you when it was at $60 and had a fair market value of $6,000. If he sold it instead, he would have had a loss of $1,250.

In this case you have *dual basis* for the stock. You use one number for basis if you have a *gain* when you sell the stock, and a different one if you have a *loss.* This may seem confusing, but the rule isn't hard to apply:

- If you sell the stock for more than the donor's basis ($7,250 in the example) you'll use that basis to measure your gain. For example, if you sell for $7,600, you report a gain of $350 ($7,600 minus $7,250).
- If you sell the stock for less than the value at the time of the gift ($6,000 in the example), you use that value to measure

your loss. For example, if you sell for $5,250, you report a loss of $750 ($6,000 minus $5,250).

- Another possibility is that you sell the stock for a price somewhere between the value on the date of the gift and the donor's basis. For instance, you might sell for $6,375 in the example. In this case your gain or loss is zero.

The idea behind this rule is to prevent your uncle from transferring a tax loss to you when he makes the gift. At the time of the gift he could have sold the stock for a loss of $1,250. Instead, he gave the stock to you. You get the full benefit of his basis when you sell the stock for a gain, but you aren't permitted to claim a loss unless the stock declines in value after you receive it.

Tax planning. In this situation, it's sometimes better for the donor to sell the stock and claim a loss, then make a gift of the sale proceeds. Otherwise, it's possible that no one will get the benefit of the donor's basis in the stock.

Example: You bought XYZ for $30,000 but it now has a value of $12,000. You want to make a gift to your daughter. If you give the stock and your daughter subsequently sells it for $12,000, no one will get a deduction for the $18,000 loss in value. If you sell the stock for $12,000 and give the cash to your daughter, you can claim the $18,000 loss (subject to the capital loss limitation). If the idea is for your daughter to own XYZ stock, she can use the $12,000 to buy this stock—preferably at least 31 days after your sale, to avoid any risk that the IRS will apply the wash sale rule as explained in Chapter 10. The tax savings from being able to claim the loss may be greater than the costs of this sale and purchase.

See Chapter 9 for a special rule that applies when you use the average basis method for a mutual fund account that includes depreciated gift shares.

Stock has gone up. Now let's look at what happens when the value of the stock has gone up. In other words, the value of the stock is greater than the donor's basis. In that case, your basis for the stock is the same as the donor's basis—with a possible increase if the donor paid gift tax on this gift.

> **Example:** Your grandmother gives you 100 shares of XYZ she bought many years ago. The current value of the stock is $8,500, but her basis is only $1,200.

Unless the gift tax adjustment described below applies, your basis for the stock is the same as your grandmother's: $1,200. If you sell it for $8,000, you must report a gain of $6,800—even though the stock went down while you were holding it.

Gift tax adjustment. Gift tax doesn't apply to most gifts because of the *annual exclusion* and the *unified credit*, both of which are explained in Chapter 20. If the gift tax applies in spite of these exclusions, you may be able to increase your basis in the stock you receive. The increase applies only if the stock was appreciated—that is, it had a value greater than the donor's basis at the time of the gift. In this case, your basis includes the portion of the gift tax that relates to the stock's appreciation. Here's how you figure the basis increase:

- **Step 1.** Determine the amount of appreciation for the gift. This is the fair market value of the property minus the donor's basis. For example, suppose your mother gave you stock with a value of $50,000, and she had a basis of $20,000. The appreciation is $30,000.
- **Step 2.** Determine the *appreciation ratio.* This is the amount of appreciation (determined in step 1) divided by the amount of the gift. In our example, the appreciation ratio is 60% ($30,000 divided by $50,000).
- **Step 3.** Determine the amount of the gift tax paid on the gift. Let's say your mother paid $9,000 gift tax on this gift.

- **Step 4.** Multiply the gift tax by the appreciation ratio. In our example, you would get $5,400 (60% times $9,000).

In this example, you end up with a basis of $25,400, which includes your mother's basis of $20,000, plus $5,400 gift tax adjustment.

Holding period. As always, it isn't enough to know how much gain or loss you have when you sell something. You also need to know whether the gain or loss is long-term or short-term. In other words, you need to know your holding period.

The rule for stock or other property received by gift is unique. If you end up using the donor's basis to figure your gain or loss on the stock, you take the donor's holding period. In other words, if the donor acquired the stock on June 5, 2003, you're treated as if *you* acquired it on that date.

On the other hand, the rules described above may require you to use the fair market value of the stock on the date of the gift to determine your basis. If your basis is determined under this rule, your holding period begins on the date of the gift, and you'll have a short-term gain or loss if you sell less than a year and a day after receiving the gift.

- **Tax planning.** When you make a gift of stock, you can transfer the *gain* in that stock to the recipient of the gift. That can mean a smaller tax bill on sale of that stock if the donee is in a lower tax bracket than you are. Just make sure it's a legitimate gift: the IRS is likely to object if you give stock to your son or daughter just before a sale, and he or she gives you the cash afterwards.

  The flip side doesn't work. You can't transfer a loss to someone else by making a gift. If you're thinking of giving away stock that's gone down while you held it, you should consider selling the stock and making a gift of the proceeds.

Stock acquired from your spouse

The usual rules for determining basis don't apply when you acquire stock from your spouse. This is true if you receive stock in any of the following ways:

- You receive a gift from your spouse.
- You buy stock from your spouse.
- You receive stock as part of a settlement or decree in a divorce or separation.

In any of these situations, the rule is very simple, and it is hard and fast: your basis is the same as the basis your spouse had immediately before you acquired the stock. Your spouse's holding period also transfers to you.

> **Note:** This rule doesn't apply if your spouse dies and you inherit stock from his or her estate. The rules for that situation are described later.

Although this rule is quite simple, it's worth taking a moment to think about what it means.

Gifts. As explained above, there's a tricky little rule that means you can have dual basis for stock you received as a gift. This rule doesn't apply to gifts between spouses. You simply take the same basis and holding period your spouse had.

Purchases. Here's the really strange part of this rule. (So strange, in fact, that even some tax professionals have a hard time believing it.) If you buy stock from your spouse, you get the same basis your spouse had—no matter what you pay for the stock.

> **Example:** Your spouse bought 200 shares of XYZ at $80 per share (a total of $16,000). Later, when XYZ is at $125, you buy the stock from your spouse for $25,000. Your basis is only

$16,000. If you sell it the next day for $25,000, you'll have to report a "gain" of $9,000.

This may seem unfair, but there's another side to the coin. Your spouse didn't have to report any gain when you bought the stock. There's no reporting of gain or loss on sales of stock (or anything else) between spouses, and that's why the basis doesn't change.

Divorce and separation. The same rule applies to divorce and separation. Let's suppose you and your spouse are splitting up, and part of what you're splitting includes 100 shares each of two different stocks. One has been Wall Street's darling, rising from $20 to $60; the other has been a dog, falling from $90 to $55. At a tender moment during the divorce proceedings, your spouse says you can take either stock, and your spouse will keep the other one. You can't believe what a dope your spouse is as you grab for Darling, Inc.

But when you sell your Darling stock for $60, you have only $20 of basis and have to report a gain of $40. By the time you're finished with federal and state taxes, you may get to keep only $50 per share. Meanwhile your dopey spouse is selling Dog Corp. for $55 and paying no taxes at all. In fact, your spouse reports a loss that results in lower taxes. The end result is that your spouse pockets something like $63 per share: $55 in sale proceeds and $8 in tax savings. That's $13 per share more than you got out of your Darling stock. All's fair in love and war.

Stock received from a decedent

Now we turn to rules that apply when stock held by an individual passes to another individual at the death of the first one. These rules don't necessarily apply to stock held by a trust or a family limited partnership rather than directly held by the decedent. You may need to consult a tax professional to learn the basis of stock you receive in special circumstances.

Background. Cash or other property you inherit from a decedent isn't considered income. You don't have to report it on your income tax return. Of course, if you later receive income from that property (such as dividends on stock) you have to report that income.

Basis and holding period. The basis and holding period rules for property received from a decedent don't follow the pattern for other rules. Normally, the basis of an asset changes only in a *taxable transaction*: an event that requires someone to report income, gain or loss. Also, your holding period for an asset is usually either the actual amount of time you held the asset or a holding period transferred from another asset or another person. There's a certain logic to all these rules, but that logic doesn't apply when it comes to estate property.

Your basis in stock you inherit is the fair market value of the stock on the valuation date. In most cases (see exception below) the valuation date is the date of death. In tax lingo we say the stock's basis is *stepped up* (or stepped down) to the date-of-death value. The basis is adjusted even though no one reported gain or loss at the time the owner died. Furthermore, the holding period for the stock is automatically long-term. That's true even if the decedent bought the stock less than a year before death.

> **Example:** Your grandfather bought 800 shares of XYZ many years ago for a total of $1,600. You inherited the stock when he died. On his date of death, the value of the stock was $32,000. Your basis in the stock is $32,000. If you sell it for $28,000, you have a loss of $4,000; if you sell it for $40,000 you have a gain of $8,000. Your gain or loss is long-term, even if you sell the stock right away after receiving it.

This tax rule provides a significant benefit on these facts. No one had to pay income tax on all that increase in value that occurred while your grandfather owned the stock. Yet you get the same basis as if you bought the stock for $32,000.

This rule can work the other way, though. Suppose your grandfather bought the stock for $32,000, but it was worth only $1,600 when he died. Now the basis will be stepped *down*. No one will receive an income tax deduction for the loss of value while your grandfather owned this stock.

Exception for alternate valuation date. There's a special rule under the estate tax that allows the executor or administrator to elect a different valuation date in certain cases. If the estate qualifies for this election, and the executor makes the election, the valuation date is six months after the date of death. The principal reason for making this election is to reduce the amount of estate tax that must be paid. Yet the election also has an effect on income tax, because it means you will now use the later date to determine your basis in the stock.

> **Example:** In the example above, the stock had a value of $32,000 on the date of death. Six months later, the stock had a value of $27,000. If the estate qualifies for the alternate valuation date, and the executor makes the election, you'll take the stock with a basis of $27,000.

In this example, you end up with a lower basis, which means you may have to pay more income tax when you sell the stock. Overall, though, the beneficiaries of the estate received a benefit because the alternate valuation date is used in circumstances where it reduces estate tax.

Stock dividends and splits

Companies sometimes increase the number of shares outstanding (and at the same time reduce the value of each share) by issuing stock dividends or stock splits. These events are usually nontaxable, but change the number of shares you own and the basis of those shares. (In the unusual case where you receive a *taxable* stock dividend, the company should notify you of this fact and explain how to report it.)

A stock dividend is generally declared in terms of a percentage. For example, in a 5% stock dividend, you'll receive one additional share for every 20 shares you already own. A stock split is usually declared as a fraction. In a 2-for-1 split, you receive one additional share for every share you own (so that you end up owning two shares for every one you owned before the split). Stock splits can occur at odd fractions. For example, if you stock splits 3-for-2, you receive one additional share for every two you owned before the split (and end up owning three for every two you had before). A 3-for-2 stock split has the same effect as a 50% stock dividend.

> If your stock pays a cash dividend and the dividend is reinvested, you end up with more stock as a result of the dividend reinvestment, but this is *not* a stock dividend. You have a stock dividend only if the dividend itself is paid in stock.

Determining your basis. When you receive additional shares as a result of a nontaxable stock dividend or split, your total basis in your stock remains the same. The basis is divided among the shares you already owned and the new shares in proportion to the value of the shares. In the usual case, where the new shares are exactly the same as the old ones, the value per share is the same, and basis is allocated equally to each share.

Example: You own 400 shares of XYZ with a basis of $33 per share (total basis of $13,200). XYZ declares a 10% stock dividend. You receive 40 additional shares and now own a total of 440 shares. Your total basis is unchanged, so your basis per share is now $13,200 divided by 440, or $30.

Example: You own 150 shares of XYZ with a basis of $24 per share, and another 100 shares of XYZ with a basis of $28 per share. The stock splits 2-for-1. After the split, you own 300 shares with a basis of $12 per share, and 200 shares with a basis of $14 per share. This is true even if you receive a single certificate representing your 250 new shares.

Holding period. You're treated as if you held the new shares as long as you held the old shares. For example, if you bought 400 XYZ two years ago and received 40 new shares in a nontaxable stock dividend this year, any gain or loss on a sale of the 40 new shares will be long-term even if you sell these shares immediately after you acquire them.

Mergers and spin-offs

Sometimes one company merges with another, going out of existence and leaving its shareholders with stock in the acquiring company. Other times a company that owns another company (a *subsidiary*) will distribute or *spin off* stock in the subsidiary to its shareholders, who find that they own stock in two companies where they formerly held just one.

Brokers are now required to make the necessary basis adjustments in connection with these corporate transactions, but only for covered shares—that is, shares bought in 2011 or later (2012 for mutual fund shares). You (or your tax professional) will have to do basis calculations for noncovered shares.

Companies engaged in these transactions generally provide their shareholders with detailed information about the tax consequences. If you mislaid this information, guidance should be available on the company's website or upon request from the investor relations department of the company. I urge you to obtain information from the company because it will be more detailed than the guidance offered here. Because of the complexity of these rules, what follows is merely a broad outline of the main points.

Cash merger. In some mergers, the owners of the acquired company receive cash. The owners are treated as if they sold their stock for an amount equal to the cash proceeds. If you have a gain, the fact that the "sale" was involuntary doesn't excuse you from reporting it.

Stock merger. You may receive stock instead of cash in the merger. When this happens, the merger is nearly always tax-free. You don't report gain or loss on the exchange of your old shares for shares of the new company. The new shares have the same basis and holding period as the old shares.

> **Example:** Six years ago you bought 100 shares of XYZ at $36 (total of $3,600). Then Bigco acquired XYZ in a tax-free merger and you received 60 shares of Bigco. Your basis for the Bigco shares is $3,600 ($60 per share), and you're treated as if you bought the Bigco shares six years ago.

Merger for stock and cash. This type of merger can be taxable or tax-free. If it's taxable, you're treated as if you sold your shares for an amount equal to the sum of (a) the amount of cash you received, plus (b) the value of the shares you received. The new shares have a basis equal to their value when you received them, and your holding period for those shares begins when you receive them.

If the merger is tax-free, it may be really only *partly* tax-free because part of your consideration was cash. If you have gain on the exchange, you report that gain, but only up to the amount of cash you received. If you received cash in excess of any gain, you'll reduce your basis in the stock by the amount of excess cash.

> **Example:** Some time ago, you bought 100 shares of XYZ at $36 (total of $3,600). Now XYZ merges into Bigco, and you receive 40 shares of Bigco plus $800 in cash. There are three possibilities:
>
> *Gain is larger than cash.* Suppose the Bigco shares are worth a total of $4,000. You also received $800 in cash, for total consideration of $4,800. Your gain is $1,200 ($4,800 minus original cost of $3,600). You report gain of $800 because that's the amount of cash you received. Your stock has a basis of $3,600.
>
> *Cash is larger than gain.* Suppose the Bigco shares are worth only $3,000. Now your total consideration is $3,800, giving you a gain of $200. You report $200 of gain. You received

another $600 in cash, and that reduces your basis in the new shares from $3,600 to $3,000.

No gain. Suppose the Bigco shares are worth only $2,000. Your total consideration was $2,800, which is less than you paid for the XYZ shares. You can't report a loss on the transaction, but you get to receive the $800 cash without reporting any gain or income. You have to reduce your basis in the new shares by this $800, from $3,600 to $2,800.

In each case, your holding period for the new Bigco shares includes the time you held the old XYZ shares.

Spin-offs. If you receive stock in a tax-free spin-off, you don't report gain or loss (or dividend). Your basis from the shares you held before the spin-off is allocated among all your shares in proportion to their fair market value at the time of the spin-off. The new shares have the same holding period as the original shares.

Example: You bought 100 shares of Bigco at $72 (total of $7,200). Bigco decides to spin off XYZ, distributing one share of XYZ for every two shares of Bigco. After the spin-off, you hold 100 shares of Bigco and 50 shares of XYZ.

Some people think they should allocate two-thirds of the basis to the Bigco shares, because two-thirds of the shares are Bigco shares. *Don't make that mistake!* The basis allocation is based on relative *value*, not the number of shares. The company should inform you of the proper allocation ratio. The amount of basis allocated to the XYZ shares may be greater than or less than one-third of the total.

If you receive shares in a *taxable* spin-off, you should rely on information from the company to determine the tax consequences.

Dividend reinvestment plans

Many publicly traded companies maintain *dividend reinvestment plans* (sometimes called *DRIPs*). If you hold stock in XYZ and participate in a DRIP maintained by that company, cash dividends on your stock are automatically reinvested in XYZ stock. The tax consequences are *not* the same as receiving a stock dividend (a dividend paid in the form of stock).

Different companies design their DRIPs with different features. As a result, the tax consequences of DRIPs may differ. Here are some of the ways plans may vary:

- Some DRIPs charge a periodic service charge, which may be deducted from the dividends paid on your stock. For example, you may be required to pay a service charge of $30 per year to participate in the DRIP.
- Some DRIPs acquire stock directly from the company, while others may use your dividends to buy stock on the open market. If the plan buys stock on the open market, it may incur brokerage commission costs, and the date of purchase will not necessarily be the same as the date of the dividend.
- Some companies that maintain DRIPs will pay brokerage commission costs on purchases made through the plan. In other cases, the commission is paid out of the dividend and reduces the number of shares you receive.
- Some DRIPs permit participants to buy additional shares by sending a cash payment to the trustee of the plan. These are called *optional purchases.*
- Some DRIPs provide a discount on purchases of dividend reinvestment shares, or on optional purchases, or both.

When you're considering whether to participate in a DRIP, you should receive a prospectus that describes the features of the plan. The prospectus will point out advantages of participation, which may include avoiding brokerage commissions or buying stock at a discount. It will also point out possible disadvantages of participation. For example, if you decide to sell the stock you hold in the plan, you may not be able to do so as quickly as if you held the shares in a regular brokerage account.

The prospectus will also include a section describing the tax consequences of participation. If possible, you should rely on that discussion, and on information supplied by the company, to determine how to report. If the tax information in the prospectus isn't available, or isn't clear, the following explanation may be helpful.

You're the owner. The tax law treats you as the owner of shares you hold in a DRIP. The prospectus may refer to a *trustee* that holds your shares and administers the plan, but for tax purposes your stock is *not* held in trust. The administrator of the DRIP is merely acting as your agent, the same way your stockbroker does if you maintain a brokerage account. You don't have to report income when you take your shares out of a DRIP because you owned those shares even before you took them out. If you take cash out of a DRIP, you'll report capital gain or loss on the sale of shares to provide the cash.

Service charges. If your DRIP imposes a service charge, this charge is *not* included in the basis of shares you buy through the plan. Instead, it's an investment expense. Beginning in 2018, no deduction is allowed for these costs.

Amount of dividend. When you participate in a dividend reinvestment plan, the amount of your dividend may not be the same as if you held your shares outside a plan:

- If the plan incurs brokerage commissions to reinvest dividends and the company pays the commissions rather than deducting them from the dividend, your share of the commission is treated as an additional dividend. When this happens, the additional dividend is usually very small.
- If the company provides a discount on dividend reinvestment purchases, the amount of the discount is treated as an additional dividend. The same is generally (but not always) true for a discount on optional purchases.

In general, you can rely on your annual Form 1099 to tell you the amount you must report as a dividend.

Basis in your shares. Your basis in shares you purchase through a DRIP includes:

1. The amount (if any) you paid for the shares, plus
2. The amount taxed to you as a dividend, minus
3. The amount (if any) deducted from your dividend as a service charge.

This basic rule can spin out in different ways:

- Suppose the stock you already own in a DRIP pays a dividend of $300. The DRIP buys shares directly from the company at a 5% discount, so your account is credited with $315 worth of stock. The IRS treats the additional $15 worth of shares as a further dividend, so you're taxed on a dividend of $315, and that's your basis in the shares.
- Suppose the DRIP buys shares in the open market instead of buying them from the company. The company doesn't provide a discount, but it does cover the brokerage commission. The IRS treats your share of the brokerage commission as an additional dividend. If your share of the commission is $8, you're taxed on a total dividend of $308, and that's your basis for the shares.
- Suppose you send in $1,000 to make an optional purchase through the DRIP. The DRIP buys shares directly from the company at a 5% discount. Your account is credited with $1,050 worth of stock. Generally, the IRS will treat the discount as a dividend. When this is so, you report a dividend of $50 (in addition to any other dividend you received) and take a basis of $1,050 in your stock.

Holding period for your shares. For shares that are received in lieu of cash dividends, you're treated as if you bought the stock on the date of the dividend. If you make an optional purchase through a DRIP, you're treated as if you bought the stock on the date the plan makes the purchase (*not* the day you send in your money).

Keeping records. Maintaining accurate records of basis and holding period for shares in a DRIP is a difficult chore for the reasons mentioned in Chapter 9 for mutual funds: investors tend to accumulate many tax lots, each with a different cost and date of purchase, and most including fractional shares. These difficulties are greatly reduced now that brokers are required to maintain records of basis and holding period and provide that information for each sale. Furthermore, beginning in 2012 the average basis method, previously available only for mutual fund shares, is also optionally available for shares in a DRIP. The rules described in Chapter 9 for using the average basis method for mutual fund shares apply to DRIPs as well.

Brokers are not required to provide basis and holding period records for shares purchased before 2012, so you may have to rely on your own records to determine the basis of older shares.

> If you sell some but not all of your DRIP shares, and have a loss on the sale, be alert to the possibility of a wash sale if you had a purchase from dividend reinvestment within 30 days before or after your sale.

Employee stock options

Employee stock options come in different varieties with different tax consequences. The subject is too large to cover here; in fact, I've written an entire book on the subject with the catchy title *Consider Your Options*. Here are some of the main points having to do with reporting gain or loss on a sale:

- If you exercise a nonqualified stock option, you'll report compensation income either at the time of exercise or when the stock vests. This income increases your basis in the shares, so you don't get taxed twice on the same income. For example, if you pay $800 to exercise an option and report $400 of compensation income, you're treated as if you bought the stock for $1,200.

- You don't report compensation income at the time you exercise an incentive stock option, but you may have to pay alternative minimum tax (AMT). When you sell the shares, you'll have a higher basis (and a smaller gain) under the AMT than under the regular tax.
- If you sell shares from an incentive stock option too soon (typically within a year after exercising the option), you'll have a *disqualifying disposition.* In that case you have to report compensation income equal to the *spread* at the time you exercised the option (the difference between the value of the stock and the amount you paid under the option) or the amount of gain you have on the sale, whichever is *smaller.* This income increases your basis. If your profit is larger than the amount of the spread, any excess is capital gain (which may be long-term or short-term, depending on how long you held the stock before selling).
- You may have to report compensation income on a sale of shares from an employee stock purchase plan. If you do, the income increases your basis in the shares, so you don't pay double tax on that income.

Worthless shares

Companies sometimes fail, leaving shareholders with worthless stock. The general rule is that if your stock becomes worthless, you claim a capital loss as if you sold the stock on the last day of the year in which the stock became worthless.

> **Example:** You bought XYZ stock in November. In June of the following year, a disaster of some kind struck the company and the stock became worthless. Although you held the stock less than a year when it became worthless, you'll have a long-term capital loss because you're treated as having a loss on the last day of the year, and that's more than a year after you bought the stock.

The chief difficulty with this rule is determining which year a stock became worthless. Some companies crash and burn fairly rapidly leaving little doubt as to the year they became worthless, but others die a lingering death. It isn't necessarily enough that trading in the stock has terminated, making it difficult or impossible to sell your shares. Even if the company is in bankruptcy, the stock may not be worthless because some companies emerge from bankruptcy and continue operations. If the stock has any present *or future* value, it isn't worthless. You can't claim your loss in a year before the year the stock becomes worthless.

To make matters worse, you also aren't allowed to claim a loss in a year *after* the stock became worthless. That means you're entitled to the deduction in a particular year only if you can show (1) some identifiable event or events caused the stock to become worthless in the year you claimed the loss, *and* (2) the stock had at least some value at the end of the preceding year. If you postpone your deduction to a later year because you're uncertain whether the stock truly is worthless, the IRS may disallow your deduction on the basis that you should have claimed it in an earlier year. To soften this rule a bit, the law permits you to go back and amend the return in the year the stock actually became worthless, as many as seven years after you filed the return for that year.

Dealing with uncertainty. What should you do if you think your stock is worthless, but you aren't sure? One approach is to try to arrange a sale of the stock. Some brokers will accommodate their customers by purchasing shares that may be worthless for a nominal amount. Then you can claim a loss on the sale, without worrying about whether the stock is worthless. If the stock actually became worthless in an earlier year, though, the IRS may challenge the deduction and say you should have claimed it in the earlier year.

> If you have the idea of selling the shares to a relative, or to a business you own, remember that you can't claim a deduction on a sale at a loss to a related person.

A regulation adopted in 2008 allows you to establish that a security is worthless by abandoning it. Presumably you could do this by telling your broker you no longer want the stock, and it should be removed from your account. Here again, you'll be treated as if you sold the shares on the last day of the year, not the date you abandon them. Bear in mind that abandonment is not the same as a gift, so you can't deduct your loss if you give the shares to a relative.

If you continue to hold shares that may or may not continue to have value, the safest approach is to claim your deduction in the earliest year the stock may have become worthless. It's possible the IRS will challenge the deduction, but there shouldn't be a penalty if you believed in good faith that the stock may have been worthless that year. In fact, the judicial opinion in one case dealing with worthless securities suggested exactly this approach in situations where it's unclear when stock has become worthless.

Cash in lieu of fractional shares

In some of the transactions described above you may receive cash representing the value of a fractional share. Generally this cash should be reported as proceeds from the sale of that fractional share. You allocate basis to that fractional share just as you would if it were a full share.

> **Example:** You paid $8,000 for 100 shares of XYZ. Later, Bigco acquired XYZ in a tax-free merger. Under the formula used in the merger, you're entitled to receive 92.5 shares of Bigco stock. You receive 92 shares plus $75.00 representing the value of the fractional share.
>
> To find your basis per share, divide your total basis of

$8,000 by 92.5 (*not* by 92!). Your basis per share is $86.49. Your basis for the fractional share is $43.24, so you'll report a gain of $31.76 ($75.00 received in cash minus basis of $43.24).

12

Special Categories of Gains and Losses

SO FAR WE'VE TALKED ABOUT "PLAIN VANILLA" capital gains and losses. This chapter discusses special categories of gains and losses that receive different treatment under the tax law:

- Unrecaptured section 1250 gain
- Collectibles gain or loss
- Qualified small business stock
- Opportunity zones
- Specialized small business investment companies (repealed)

The rules for unrecaptured section 1250 gain, and for collectibles gain or loss, usually don't apply to stock. We cover them briefly because it's possible these gains and losses will interact with your gains or losses from buying and selling stock.

Cryptocurrency and other digital assets

The huge volume of transactions involving digital assets has captured the attention of the IRS. They now require all individuals who file Form 1040 to declare at the top of the form whether they had any reportable transactions in digital assets. This is their blanket term covering cryptocurrency, stablecoins and nonfungible tokens (NFTs). It also covers any other digital representations of value that are recorded on a blockchain or similar technology.

Reportable transactions include pretty much any in which you receive digital assets other than by purchase using "real" currency such as U.S. dollars. For example, if you accept payment in bitcoin or other digital currency for goods or services you provide, you have a reportable transaction. Likewise if you received a reward or award of digital assets. It's also possible to receive digital currency through activities known as mining or staking, or as a result of an event known as a hard fork. These would also require you to check "yes" on the Form 1040 question about transactions in digital assets.

Similarly, you have to check "yes" if you disposed of digital assets. For example, you need to report if you sold digital assets, exchanged them for goods or services, or exchanged them for other digital assets. Check "yes" if you disposed of digital assets in any other way, including a gift.

The IRS points out a few transactions you do not need to report. You don't have to report holding digital assets in a wallet or account, or moving them from one wallet or account you own or control to another wallet or account you own or control. As mentioned earlier, a purchase of digital assets using real currency is not reportable.

The tax treatment of all these transactions is based on a simple principle: digital assets are "property" as that term is used in the tax law. For example, if you accept digital currency for services you perform, you have compensation income in the amount of the value of the digital currency at the time you receive it. Probably few individuals in this situation would be surprised that this is the proper tax treatment. Those among them who are hoping to avoid making the required tax payment by accepting cryptocurrency for services may be surprised at how aggressive the IRS has become in seeking out noncompliance in this area. Reports indicate that IRS "John Doe" summonses, previously used to ferret out information about foreign bank accounts, are now being used to investigate illegal nonreporting of transactions in digital assets.

Perhaps the issue most likely to cause genuine confusion is the use of cryptocurrencies to make purchases or make other payments. We're used to the notion that merely buying something isn't a taxable event. If we think of cryptocurrencies as money, it may seem that the same should be true when we use them the same way. Yet cryptocurrencies are "property" in the eyes of the IRS. When you "spend" cryptocurrency, you're disposing of property, and you have to report gain or loss on the transaction.

Unrecaptured section 1250 gain

I can't blame you if your eyes glaze over at the thought of something called *unrecaptured section 1250 gain.* It's possible some of this gain will show up on a year-end statement you receive from a real estate investment trust (REIT), or possibly from a mutual fund that holds stock in one or more REITs. You can also run into this category of gain if you personally sell real property after claiming depreciation deductions, or you're a member of a partnership that does so.

Briefly, this item represents past depreciation deductions that were converted into long-term capital gain. Depreciation deductions reduce ordinary income, which is taxed at higher rates than long-term capital gain. In effect, when you sell property for which you previously claimed depreciation, you're converting ordinary income into long-term capital gain. To reduce the benefit of this conversion, the tax law imposes a maximum rate of 25%, rather than 20%, on capital gain from this source. (Gain that falls into a tax bracket where ordinary income is taxed at a rate lower than 25% is taxed at that lower rate.)

> **Example:** You bought rental property for $80,000. Over the years you held it, you claimed $20,000 of depreciation deductions, reducing your basis to $60,000. Then you sold it for $90,000, securing a $30,000 gain. A portion of this gain ($20,000) is unrecaptured section 1250 gain, taxable at a maximum rate of 25%. The remaining $10,000 is taxed as "regular" long-term capital gain, at a maximum rate of 20%.

If you have gain in this category and prepare your tax return by hand, you'll have to figure the amount of the gain on an "Unrecaptured Section 1250 Gain Worksheet" (18 lines) and then figure their tax on a "Schedule D Tax Worksheet" (47 lines), both found in the Schedule D instructions. At that point you may decide it's time to use software or see a tax pro.

Collectibles gain or loss

You probably won't run into this item in connection with your stock investing. If you have gains from investing in certain items classified as *collectibles*, though, your maximum tax rate on this gain is 28%. Collectibles include works of art, rugs, antiques, metals, gems, stamps, coins, alcoholic beverages, and any other items the Treasury designates as belonging to this category. If you hold any of these items more than a year and sell for a gain, your tax will be higher than on a normal long-term capital gain.

Contrary to popular belief, collectibles do not include many other items people collect and sometimes value highly, at least until the Treasury designates them as such. For example, it appears that baseball cards or comic books are not collectibles as defined in the tax law, although I suppose the IRS could argue that they are works of art.

> If you're considering a charitable donation of property, appreciated collectibles held more than a year make a good choice. You get to claim the full value of the property and avoid the 28% tax.

Qualified small business stock

The first two items above are taxed under rules that are less favorable than for regular capital gains. Now we come to a special category that's taxed under *more* favorable terms. To take advantage, though, you have to acquire *qualified small business stock.*

To give a complete explanation of these rules would require an entire chapter—more space than we can afford for a benefit most people can't claim. What follows is an overview that will enable you to get an idea what these benefits are, and find out whether they might apply to you. If it looks as if you might qualify, you'll have to follow up with a tax professional who can look into the details.

Qualified small business stock. Stock you buy in the stock market isn't *qualified small business stock.* To qualify for these tax benefits, you have to buy stock directly from the company, perhaps as a founder, venture capital provider, or employee who exercised an option, or else own an interest in a partnership, REIT or mutual fund that has acquired qualified small business stock.

The company has to meet various requirements. It must be a "C corporation" (in other words, a corporation that hasn't made the "S corporation" election). It has to be in an active business (not just an investment company)—but various types of active businesses aren't allowed. Furthermore, the company may not have more than $50 million in assets at the time you buy the stock (or during certain other specified periods).

Benefits. Two different benefits are potentially available to people who hold qualified small business stock. The first one allows you to "roll over" gain from qualified small business stock you held more than six months. That means you don't pay tax when you sell the stock, provided that you invest the money in *new* qualified small business stock within the 60-day period beginning on the date of the sale. Your basis for the new stock is reduced by the amount of gain postponed from the sale of the old stock. That means you'll still pay tax on that gain if you sell the new stock. You may be able to avoid that tax altogether, though, if you hold the stock until death or donate it to a charity. Your holding period for the new stock includes the holding period for the old stock.

The other benefit allows you to exclude some of your gain when you sell the stock, subject to certain limits. The portion you exclude can be any of several percentages from 50% to 100% depending on when you bought the stock and other factors (Congress likes to tinker here). The part you don't exclude is taxed at 28%, so you get an effective rate of 14% if you qualify for the 50% exclusion. The exclusion is partially disallowed for purposes of the alternative minimum tax (AMT).

The amount of gain you can exclude from any one company is limited, but the limit is pretty generous. It's the greater of two figures. One is $10 million ($5 million if you're married filing separately). The other is—well, if your gain is more than that you should be relying on a high-priced accountant or tax lawyer rather than the information in this book. (The other limit is ten times the basis of the shares in that company you sold that year.)

Qualified opportunity funds

An extraordinary provision added by the Tax Cuts and Jobs Act makes it possible for taxpayers to defer almost any kind of capital gain and potentially secure additional tax benefits if they invest in a *qualified opportunity fund.* (Proposed regulations make exceptions for gain from section 1256 contracts or offsetting positions.) You need to make this election during the 180-day period beginning on the day you have the gain, and then show on your tax return that you elect to invoke this provision. Your gain, up to the amount you invest, will not be taxable that year, but instead will become taxable when you sell this investment, or on December 31, 2026, if the investment remains unsold on that date.

Depending on how long you hold this investment, some of that gain may disappear. After five years your basis is increased by 10% of the amount that was deferred, eliminating 10% of the gain from the original sale. Another 5% of that gain disappears if your holding period stretches to seven years. As a final kicker, reaching the ten-year milestone lets you avoid paying tax on any gain from an increase in the value of this investment during your holding period. Depending on their structure, however, some of these funds can be expected to liquidate in 2026 when the deferred gain becomes taxable, which would preclude a ten-year holding period.

What's the catch? For one thing, a qualified opportunity fund has to be at least 90% invested in properties and businesses in certain low-income areas, which may not be prime areas for profitable investing. That's the underlying idea: to revitalize these areas by attracting investment dollars that wouldn't otherwise give them a second look. These funds will say they intend to achieve lofty investment returns, and perhaps some of them will succeed, but if they were such great investment opportunities, we wouldn't have needed these generous tax benefits to bring them into existence. Keep in mind that the tax benefits will be awfully expensive if the investment fails.

Most of these investments are available only to *accredited investors*—those who make over $200,000 per year (or $300,000 with their spouse), or have net worth, excluding their home, above $1,000,000. What's more, you may face a hefty minimum investment, and you may have less flexibility than you'd like when it comes to pulling your money out.

Be aware there are a number of traditional mutual funds that happen to use the words "opportunity fund" as part of their name but provide no special tax benefits because they are not *qualified opportunity funds.*

Specialized small business investment companies

For a number of years we had a rule under which taxpayers could defer gain from selling publicly traded securities if they were willing and able to invest sale proceeds in a type of business known as a *specialized small business investment company* (SSBIC). The Tax Cuts and Jobs Act repealed this little-used provision for sales after 2017.

Part III
Other Investment Income and Expense

13

Dividends from Stocks and Mutual Funds

We seem to have emerged from a period of several decades in which dividends dwindled in importance as companies changed their emphasis from cash payouts to stock buybacks. Capital gains became the primary goal for most investors in stocks and mutual funds, partly because of favorable tax treatment and partly because that was where they found the bulk of their investment profits. Recent years have changed the outlook for dividends. Spurred by investor demand and lower tax rates for qualified dividends, many companies have increased their dividend payouts, or announced new dividends when they did not pay any in the past.

We'll begin by looking at the rules for dividends from companies. These are somewhat more complicated than in the past because of the special tax rates for dividends. Later, we'll turn to dividends from mutual fund companies—which are even more complicated.

Dividends from companies

In the first edition of this book we were able to say dividend income was "simple city." Now we have lower tax rates for qualified dividends, but these come with some added complexity.

Rates. The rates for qualified dividends are the same as for long-term capital gain. In fact, the tax calculation for qualified dividends is combined with the capital gains tax calculation on your tax return. At the lowest income levels you pay 0%. Most taxpayers pay 15%, and those with the highest income, 20%.

> **Q:** *Does that mean I can use dividends to soak up capital losses?*
>
> **A:** No. Even though qualified dividends are now taxed at the same rates as long-term capital gains, these dividends are treated as ordinary income for other purposes, including the $3,000 capital loss limitation.

Sixty-one day holding period. There's a special holding period for qualified dividends. Generally you have to hold the stock at least 61 days, not counting the date of purchase but counting the date of sale. You don't have to hold the stock 61 days *before* the dividend, and you don't have to hold it 61 days *after* the dividend—but you have to hold it at least 61 days during the 121-day period beginning 60 days before the ex-dividend date.

The main idea here is that you can't buy stock just before a dividend, use the long-term rate on that dividend, and then sell the stock, possibly taking a short-term capital loss that will reduce income that would be taxed at a higher rate.

> **Example:** You buy 1,000 shares of XYZ at $40 just before the ex-dividend date and capture a $2 per share dividend. Right after that you sell the stock at $38. You have a $2,000 dividend and a $2,000 short-term capital loss, but overall no economic profit or loss. In this situation your dividend is ordinary income that does not qualify for the favorable tax rate.

This rule can produce unfavorable tax results even if you aren't trying to do anything fancy.

> **Example:** In the previous example, suppose you already have more than $3,000 of net capital loss for the year. The additional short-term capital loss will not do you any good except as a carryover to a later year. Yet you still have to report the dividend as ordinary income.

> **Example:** Going back to the previous example again, suppose you have an overall capital gain for the year, but all your gain is long-term. Now you'll be able to use the capital loss from selling the XYZ shares, but the loss will count against income that would have been taxed at the favorable rate for long-term capital gains. Meanwhile, your dividend income doesn't qualify for that rate because you didn't hold the stock long enough.

These problems existed before the change in the law, but they are likely to crop up more often now that companies are paying more dividends and many investors are seeking out dividend-paying stocks. The moral of the story: be wary of dividends if you do short-term trading.

Preferred stock. You have to meet a longer holding period requirement—91 days instead of 61 days—if you hold preferred stock that pays a dividend attributable to a period of more than 366 days. Otherwise the normal 61-day period applies to preferred stocks.

Mutual fund dividends. Mutual fund dividends can include income from various sources: long-term capital gains, short-term capital gains, interest and dividends. The part of a mutual fund dividend that comes from qualified dividend income *received by* the mutual fund gets treated as qualified dividend income on *your* return—just as you get the benefit when the mutual fund distributes long-term capital gains. Other portions of the mutual fund dividend have to be treated as ordinary income, taxed at the regular tax rates. For example, if part of the mutual fund distribution represents interest income or short-term capital gains received by the mutual fund, you'll report that part of the mutual fund distribution as a nonqualified dividend.

> The tax information you get from the mutual fund in January or February will tell you how much of the dividend qualifies for the lower rates.

REITs. The idea behind the lower dividend rate is to make up for the fact that corporate income is taxed twice: the corporation pays tax on this income, and then the shareholder pays tax on the same income when it is paid out as a dividend. Real estate investment trusts (REITs) that follow certain rules don't pay tax on their income, so the lower rates don't apply to most REIT income. REIT dividends that come from income that was subject to corporate income tax will qualify for the lower rates, but this is normally a small fraction of REIT income, if any.

> The tax information you get from the REIT in January or February will tell you how much of the dividend qualifies for the lower rates.

Dividends from foreign companies. Foreign companies can pay qualified dividends if their stock trades on an exchange in the United States. This includes stock that trades through ADRs (basically a substitute for actual shares of stock, used to overcome certain difficulties in trading stock of a foreign company). It's also possible to receive qualified dividends from a foreign company that does not trade on a U.S. exchange, so check the tax information you receive from the company.

Investment interest deduction. As explained in Chapter 14, qualified dividends don't count as investment income for purposes of applying the limitation on investment interest expense deduction unless you choose to give up the benefit of the lower tax rates.

Don't get fancy. Advanced trading techniques or special transactions can disqualify you from claiming the lower rate on dividends. There's a rule that says you don't have a qualified dividend if you're obligated to make a payment to someone else with respect to the dividend. That rule would apply if you sell stock *short against the box* as explained in Chapter 15. And there's another rule that says you aren't treated as the owner of the stock, for purposes of the 61-day holding period, during any period when you've used stock options or similar arrangements to protect yourself against loss from a decline in the value of the stock.

> **Example:** You hold 1,000 shares of XYZ and decide to sell short 1,000 shares of this stock while continuing to hold these shares. XYZ pays a dividend of $1.25 per share while the short position is open.

In this situation, you have to pay $1,250 to the person from whom you borrowed the shares to make a short sale. You also receive $1,250 as a dividend on the shares you continue to hold. This is not a qualified dividend, however, because you were obligated to make a payment related to this dividend.

More on dividends

People sometimes get tripped up if they have cash dividends reinvested. It's important to keep a record of dividend reinvestments, because they count as additional purchases of stock. These purchases create *basis* in your shares, and that means you'll report a smaller gain (or larger loss) when you sell the shares. Brokers are now required to maintain basis records for new purchases, including purchases that result from dividend reinvestment, but these requirements don't apply to purchases before 2011 for regular stocks or 2012 for mutual funds.

In theory, a regular company can pay a tax-free return of capital dividend, although this rarely happens. A company can pay this type of dividend only after it has paid out all its "earnings and profits," not just for the current year, but over its entire life as a corporation. If you receive a notice telling you part of your dividend is a tax-free return of capital, read about this type of dividend in the discussion of mutual fund dividends below.

Mutual fund dividends

Mutual fund dividends can be much more complicated. In fact, mutual funds can pay four different types of dividends, and in addition make two different types of *allocations* that affect your tax return. Some of these items are further broken down into subcategories. That may seem like a lot to learn, but chances are that any one mutual fund you invest in will generate only two or three of these items.

We'll start by looking at the reports you'll receive from your broker or mutual fund company. Then we'll identify each type of dividend and explain how to handle it.

> **Note:** Your mutual fund dividends are taxable even if you choose to reinvest them. Generally, when you choose to reinvest your dividends you're treated the same as if you received the dividend in cash and then used it to buy additional shares.

Reports you'll receive. From time to time during the year you may receive statements concerning activity in your mutual fund account. Those statements will provide information concerning dividends, but these are not your official tax reports. The tax reports normally arrive in January or February, and consist of one or more of the following items:

- Form 1099-DIV, Dividends and Distributions
- Form 2439, Notice to Shareholder of Undistributed Long-Term Capital Gains
- A tax report from the mutual fund company or your broker

Form 1099-DIV. This form was expanded in 2012 and now reports nearly all the information you're likely to need regarding mutual fund distributions. Companies are permitted to use the official IRS form, or provide you with a *substitute* Form 1099-DIV that gives the same information. The substitute form doesn't have to be on a separate sheet of paper. It can be printed on the same page as other information. This form tells you:

- The total *ordinary dividends* you received for the year and the portion that may be qualified dividends.
- The total *capital gain distributions* you received for the year, and the portion, if any, that is in any of the special subcategories of capital gain.
- The total *nondividend distributions* you received for the year.
- Your share of the fund's *foreign tax paid* for the year.
- The amount of exempt interest dividend you received for the year, and the portion that may be subject to alternative minimum tax.
- In the unlikely event that tax was withheld from your distribution, the amount of federal and state withholding.

Form 2439. This form reports information about undistributed long-term capital gains that are *allocated* to you, even though they were not paid out to you. If you didn't get one of these forms, don't worry. Most mutual funds don't make this type of allocation, so most mutual fund investors don't receive this form. If you *do* get one, read the discussion of mutual fund capital gain allocations below.

Mutual fund tax report. The mutual fund may send you a report providing additional tax information you may need in preparing your state income tax return:

- How much of your exempt-interest dividend is from various states. (This information doesn't affect your federal income tax return, but may affect your state income tax return.)

- How much of the ordinary dividend represents interest on federal obligations that's exempt from state income tax.

There's no special format for this report, but it's usually easy enough to identify. Just make sure you don't throw out anything you receive from your mutual fund or broker in January or February!

January dividends. There's a special rule you should be aware of if you receive dividends in January. Mutual funds are permitted to treat certain January dividends as if they were paid in the previous year. It may seem like a mistake when the mutual fund reports this income as if you received it in December of the previous year. It's not a mistake though, just a special feature of the way the tax law treats mutual funds.

Ordinary dividends

Most mutual funds pay at least some ordinary dividends. Even if the mutual fund is designed to generate other types of income, such as tax-exempt interest, it may have a small amount of income it must pay out as an ordinary dividend.

Almost any type of income other than long-term capital gain or tax-exempt interest will be treated as an ordinary dividend when paid out by a mutual fund. In particular:

- *Taxable interest* that's received by a mutual fund will be treated as an ordinary dividend when the mutual fund pays this income to its shareholders. That's why you'll get a dividend report, not an interest report, if you invest in a money market mutual fund. If the taxable interest includes interest on federal obligations, you may be able to exclude that portion on your state income tax return.
- *Short-term capital gain* that's received by a mutual fund is also treated as an ordinary dividend when paid to the shareholders.

That last statement may seem surprising if you're familiar with the way capital gains work. Short-term capital gains often end up being taxed at the same rate as ordinary income, but they're not *treated* the same as ordinary income. In particular, if you have a large capital loss—long-term or short-term—you may be better off if you have short-term capital gain than if you have ordinary income. That's because you can deduct only $3,000 of the loss against ordinary income.

Nevertheless, you aren't allowed to treat any part of your mutual fund dividend as short-term capital gain. That's true even if the mutual fund includes information in its report telling you how much of the dividend came from short-term gains. You have to treat that amount as part of your ordinary dividend.

Capital gain distributions

If a mutual fund has long-term capital gains, it can designate part of its dividend as a capital gain distribution. The shareholders report this part of the dividend as if it were their own long-term capital gain. These amounts are called *capital gain distributions* or *capital gain dividends*. As noted above, this treatment does *not* apply to short-term capital gains.

A capital gain distribution is taxed as long-term capital gain. That's true even for shareholders who have held the mutual fund shares less than a year. Generally this means favorable rates apply: you're likely to pay less tax on this type of dividend than on an ordinary dividend. Be alert to special categories of capital gain that may appear in boxes 2b, 2c or 2d of Form 1099-DIV. If you see amounts reported in these boxes, follow the instructions on the form carefully.

Important: A special tax computation is needed to get the benefit of lower tax rates for long-term capital gains. There's a long calculation on page 2 of Schedule D, and a shorter one in the tax return instructions for people in simpler situations. Tax software will of course perform these calculations automatically if you enter a capital gain distribution, but you need to be alert to this additional calculation if you're one of the hardy individuals who still don't use software to prepare their returns.

Note: If you receive a capital gain distribution and subsequently incur a short-term capital loss on mutual fund shares held six months or less, read about the special rule for losses within six months in Chapter 9.

Capital gain allocations

Mutual funds that have long-term capital gains have a choice. They can pay the capital gains out to their shareholders: a capital gain distribution. If they don't want to do that, they can retain the capital gain, pay a tax, and make a *capital gain allocation.*

It's easy to tell which one you received. Capital gain dividends are reported in box 2a of Form 1099-DIV, as described earlier. If the mutual fund decides instead to make a capital gain allocation, this item won't appear on Form 1099-DIV. Instead, you'll receive a special form: Form 2439, *Notice to Shareholder of Undistributed Long-Term Capital Gains.*

Where is it? This form may arrive at a different time than other tax forms. Mutual funds and other companies are supposed to mail Form 1099-DIV by February 15. They have 60 days after the end of their tax year (which isn't necessarily December 31) to provide Form 2439. If your shares are held by a nominee, this form may arrive even later.

What to do. When you receive Form 2439, you need to do four things:

- Report the capital gain on your income tax return for the year.
- Claim a credit for the tax paid by the mutual fund.
- Attach copy B of Form 2439 to your completed tax return.
- Adjust the basis of your shares in the mutual fund.

Reporting the capital gain. You'll report the capital gain from this form in the same way as a capital gain dividend, discussed earlier. If preparing the return by hand, be sure to do the tax rate calculation for capital gains, or you lose the benefit of the lower rates. The rule for losses on shares held less than six months applies to capital gain allocations as well as capital gain distributions.

Claiming the credit. Now for the good part. You get to claim credit for the tax paid by the mutual fund. That tax is paid at the rate of 21%, the tax rate corporations pay on capital gains (since 2018). If this additional credit means you have an overpayment, you can use it to claim a refund.

Add the amount from box 2 in every Form 2439 you receive and report the total on Form 1040 Schedule 5. You'll get credit for this figure just as if it were an additional amount of tax you paid to the IRS.

Attach Copy B. You should receive two copies of Form 2439, called Copy B and Copy C. (The mutual fund sends Copy A to the IRS.) When your income tax return is completed, attach Copy B to your return. Retain Copy C for your records.

Basis adjustment. There's one more piece of business that's easy to overlook, and it's an important one. When you receive a capital gain allocation on Form 2439, you get to increase the basis in your mutual fund shares by 79% of the amount of the allocation. If you overlook this adjustment, you'll pay too much tax when you sell your shares.

Why 79%? That's the amount that's left after you get credit for the 21% tax mentioned above. Be sure to record this basis adjustment in your records for this mutual fund. It'll save you money when the time comes to sell your shares.

If all your shares are covered shares (acquired after 2011), your broker or mutual fund company should make this basis adjustment for you. You may need to make your own calculations if you have any older shares. Multiply the amount of the capital gain allocation by 79% to find the amount of the basis adjustment, then divide by the total number of shares you hold (covered and noncovered) to determine the amount of basis adjustment per share. Then apply this adjustment to your noncovered shares.

Be sure to retain Copy C of Form 2439 in your tax records as proof that you're entitled to this basis adjustment.

Comment. Overall, this tax treatment is neither good nor bad. It puts you in about the same place you'd be if you received a capital gain dividend in cash, paid tax with part of that cash, and then bought additional shares with the cash that was left over.

Exempt interest dividends

Some mutual funds are established to provide a way to invest in municipal bonds and other securities that produce tax-exempt interest. Dividends from these mutual funds are usually composed mainly of tax-exempt interest. Under the special tax rules for mutual funds, you should treat the tax-exempt interest portion of your dividend the same as if you received the tax-exempt interest directly.

Although these dividends are generally tax-free, you can't simply ignore them:

- Your dividend from this type of mutual fund isn't necessarily entirely tax-exempt. You may have to report part of your dividend as ordinary income or capital gain.
- Exempt interest dividends must be reported on your income tax return, even if they don't affect the amount of tax you pay.

- These dividends may affect the amount of tax you pay on your social security income.
- Exempt interest dividends may affect your deduction for investment interest expense.
- Exempt interest dividends may be partly or entirely subject to the alternative minimum tax (AMT). See Box 12 on Form 1099-DIV.
- Some or all of your exempt interest dividend may be subject to state income tax. Look for supplemental information from the mutual fund providing details.

Reporting exempt interest dividends. Exempt interest dividends appear on Form 1099-DIV. Find the total of your exempt interest dividends for the year. Add this amount to any exempt interest income you have from other sources and report that amount on the appropriate line of Form 1040.

Federal interest dividends

In general, states are not permitted to impose an income tax on interest from federal obligations, even though this interest is subject to federal income tax. For purposes of state income tax, interest on United States savings bonds, United States treasury bills, and various other bonds or obligations of the Unites States and territories are exempt. (The exemption doesn't extend to Ginnie Mae Bonds, Fannie Mae Bonds, or FHLMC securities.) If your state has an income tax and you receive this type of income, look for a line on your state income tax return where you can exclude the interest.

This rule applies to certain mutual funds on a "flow-through" basis. To qualify, the laws of most states say the mutual fund must meet a requirement that at least half its assets consist of obligations that are exempt from state income tax. If this is the case, the portion of the mutual fund dividend that represents exempt interest is excluded from income on the state form.

Reporting federal interest dividends. Information about the amount of federal interest included in your mutual fund dividend won't appear on Form 1099-DIV. Your mutual fund should provide this information in an annual statement or report, which may accompany Form 1099-DIV or may arrive somewhat later. If you believe your mutual fund has this type of income but can't find this information, contact the mutual fund or your broker.

There's nothing special to do on your *federal* income tax return for this type of interest. It's included in the ordinary dividend reported on Form 1099-DIV, and you should report it just like any other ordinary dividend. To determine the proper reporting on your state income tax return, review the form and instructions carefully. Look for information about interest on savings bonds and other federal obligations.

Nondividend distributions: return of capital

Mutual funds sometimes make cash distributions that don't represent earnings. When you receive this type of distribution, you're considered to be getting back some of the money you invested in the fund. That's why these payments are sometimes called *return of capital distributions.* On Form 1099-DIV they're shown as *nondividend distributions.* The IRS used to call them *nontaxable* distributions, but changed the terminology, probably because they can be taxable in limited circumstances.

Don't confuse these payments with exempt interest dividends. Those dividends represent interest received by the mutual fund from municipal bonds and similar investments. Return of capital distributions don't come from exempt interest or from any other type of earnings. These two categories of distributions appear in two separate, clearly labeled boxes on Form 1099-DIV.

Adjusting your basis. Before you can determine how to report your distribution, you have to take care of an important piece of business:

adjusting the basis of your shares. Remember, your *basis* is a measure of your investment in the shares. When you receive a return of capital, you're getting part of your investment back, so your basis in the shares goes down.

Your broker or mutual fund company should perform the basis adjustment calculation for you on any covered shares (shares bought after 2011). You may have to do your own arithmetic for older, noncovered shares. If you use the average basis method for those shares, the basis adjustment is simple. All you have to do is subtract the amount of the nontaxable distribution received on those shares from the total basis of those shares.

If you use any other method, you have a little more work to do. Determine the amount of the distribution per share. Then reduce your basis for each share by this amount. Note that if you have the distribution reinvested, the new shares are covered shares, so your broker or mutual fund company will track the basis of those shares.

In nearly all cases, the amount of the return of capital distribution is smaller than your basis in the shares. That lets you know the distribution is truly nontaxable. If you receive a return of capital distribution that exceeds the basis in your shares, you have to report capital gain as explained below.

Tax reporting. You don't have to report a nontaxable distribution. That means you have nothing at all to report if the distribution is less than or equal to your basis, which is nearly always the case. But what if the distribution is greater than your basis? You aren't allowed to have negative basis. If your return of capital distribution is larger than your basis, you reduce the basis to zero—and you report the additional amount of the distribution as capital gain on Schedule D.

> **Example:** At a time when your basis in your mutual fund shares is $170, you receive a nondividend distribution of $250. You'll reduce your basis in the shares to zero. In addition, you'll report a capital gain of $80.

Report the gain as short-term or long-term depending on how long you held the shares to which the distribution relates.

14

Investment Expenses

EFFECTIVE IN 2018, THE TAX CUTS AND JOBS ACT eliminated the entire category of itemized deductions known as *miscellaneous deductions subject to the 2% floor.* One of the casualties was the deduction for investment expenses. Previously allowed to itemizers (but only to the extent deductions in this category exceeded 2% of adjusted gross income), these expenses are now entirely disallowed.

This change does not apply to costs of buying and selling shares of stock or other investments. These costs have never been allowed as itemized deductions, but instead are used to adjust gain or loss when you sell. The Tax Cuts and Jobs Act did not alter those rules.

Also unaffected are expenses connected with a trade or business. Under the tax law, investing is not considered a trade or business. However, *traders* (discussed in Part VI) are by definition conducting a trade or business, so they can claim expenses that might otherwise be disallowed by this rule.

Another exception, important to many investors, is the investment interest expense deduction, which will consume the remainder of this chapter. If you borrow money and pay interest in connection with your investing activity, you need to understand these special rules. You can't deduct investment interest unless you itemize. Even if you itemize, your deduction is limited by the amount of investment income you report. This chapter answers the following questions:

- What interest expense counts as *investment* interest expense?
- How does the investment income limit work?
- What is the special rule if you have long-term capital gains or qualified dividends?

Investment interest

The tax law divides interest expense into various categories, each with its own tax treatment. It's important to determine how much interest expense you have in each category because different limitations apply in each case. In addition to investment interest, the other main categories are business interest, home mortgage interest, personal interest, student loan interest and passive activity interest.

If you borrow money in connection with a business, the interest you incur is *business interest.* You'll deduct that interest in determining the amount of income or loss you have from that business.

> **Traders.** Investing is *not* considered a business. However, if you're a *trader* as defined in Part VI of this book, interest expense you incur in connection with your trading activity is business interest, not investment interest. The limit discussed in this chapter doesn't apply to such interest.

Interest expense that isn't connected with a business or investment is generally considered *personal interest* for which no deduction is allowed. Interest on credit cards typically falls into this category, as does most interest on auto loans and amounts borrowed for consumer items like home appliances. Yet you're allowed to deduct *home mortgage interest* if you itemize, and a limited deduction for *student loan interest* is available even if you don't itemize.

Some people confuse *passive activity interest* with investment interest. Don't make this mistake, because the rules for passive activity interest are very different. (Those rules are beyond the scope of this book. See IRS Publication 925, *Passive Activity and At-Risk Rules*, for more information.) Buying and selling stocks is *not* a passive activity. A passive activity is generally a *business* activity (not an *investing* activity) in which you have some ownership without having enough direct involvement to be "materially participating" under the tax regulations.

General rule. *Investment interest* generally includes any interest you pay on money borrowed to buy stock or other investment property.

> As a general rule, home equity loans that are not used for specified purposes no longer offer a mortgage interest deduction. If your home equity loan is used to buy investment property, the interest paid on that loan can be treated as investment interest.

Investment property generally includes anything that produces interest, dividends or annuities, and anything that produces capital gain or loss, provided that you don't hold the property as part of a business. Stocks, mutual fund shares and stock options are all considered investment property. You may also hold other types of investment property, such as land or precious metals.

Margin interest. Many people who buy and sell stocks arrange with their broker to borrow against the investments held in their accounts. This type of loan is called a *margin loan*. Interest on a margin loan is investment interest only if you use the loan to buy stock or other investment property. For example, if you take out a margin loan to buy a home entertainment system, interest on the loan is non-deductible personal interest. You don't get to treat this interest as investment interest merely because the money came from a margin loan.

Straddles. If you buy and sell options, your investment activity may produce *straddles* as explained in Chapter 19. When you pay interest on loans incurred in connection with straddles you have to add the interest to the cost of your investment instead of claiming a deduction for investment interest.

Short sales. If you make short sales of stock, you may be required to make a payment in lieu of dividend to the person from whom you borrowed stock for the short sale. If the payment is treated as investment interest, it's subject to the rules described in this chapter. Chapter 15 explains when these payments are treated as investment interest.

Interest allocation. You may take out a single loan for more than one purpose. When this happens, you have to allocate the interest according to the way you used the money.

> **Example:** You borrowed $12,000, using $9,000 of that amount to buy stock and the remaining $3,000 to buy furniture for your home. You used 75% of the loan to buy investment property, so you'll treat 75% of the interest on this loan as investment interest.

Actually, you'll probably end up treating *more* than 75% of the interest on this loan as investment interest. The reason is that as you repay the loan, you're treated as if you paid the *personal* (non-investment) part of the loan first. When you've paid the loan down to $10,000, for example, the remaining debt is 90% investment debt, and at that point you'll treat 90% of the interest payments as investment interest.

Investment interest limit

To claim a deduction for investment interest, you must *itemize.* This means you claim specific deductions for items like state taxes, home mortgage interest and charitable contributions instead of the standard deduction. Changes made by the Tax Cuts and Jobs Act are likely to reduce the number of itemizers to only about 10% of all taxpayers, so this deduction will be unavailable to many.

Even if you itemize, your deduction for investment interest expense is limited to your net investment income. If your net investment income is zero, you can't deduct any investment interest expense. If your net investment income is smaller than the amount of your investment interest expense, you'll be able to deduct some but not all of that expense. If you aren't able to deduct the full amount of your investment interest expense, the part you didn't deduct *carries over* to the next year, when you'll be able to claim the deduction if you itemize and have net investment income.

> **Example:** Last year you had investment interest expense of $3,000 and net investment income of $2,000. You deduct $2,000 of investment interest expense and carry $1,000 to the next year. This year you have investment interest expense of $500 and again have $2,000 of net investment income. Your total investment interest expense is $1,500: $500 from the current year plus $1,000 carried over from the previous year. You can claim the entire $1,500 as a deduction because it doesn't exceed your net investment income.

Net investment income. *Net investment income* is your gross income from property held for investment reduced by any deductible investment expenses other than investment interest expense. Investment expenses subject to the 2% floor are no longer deductible, so those types of expenses will not affect the calculation. Certain types of investments can still produce deductible expenses, such as depreciation on investment real estate.

Investment income includes interest, nonqualified dividends, annuities and certain royalties, but doesn't include Alaska Permanent Fund dividends. It also includes short-term capital gain, but doesn't include long-term capital gain or qualified dividends unless you make the election described below.

Net capital gain. Here's a point that confuses many people, including some tax professionals. IRS instructions say net investment income doesn't include *net capital gain.* That makes it sound like you don't include any kind of capital gain, short-term or long-term. But they're using the term *net capital gain* with a special meaning: the excess of long-term capital gain over short-term capital loss. In other words, it's the amount that's eligible to be taxed at the lower tax rate for long-term capital gain. If you have a net *short-term* capital gain, you include that in your net investment income, because that's not part of your *net capital gain* under this special definition.

Election to include long-term capital gain or qualified dividends. If your investment interest expense is greater than your net investment income, you might consider electing to treat some or all of your long-term capital gain or qualified dividends as investment income. The benefit of doing this is that you can claim your investment interest deduction in the current year, instead of carrying it forward to the next year. There's a downside, though: you lose the benefit of long-term capital gain tax rates for the portion of your gain covered by this election.

It's a good idea to make this election if the amount of investment interest is so large you might not be able to deduct all of it in the foreseeable future. On the other hand, if you think you can deduct the investment interest within the next year or two, you might be better off not making the election so you can preserve the benefit of the lower capital gains tax rate.

Example: Normally you have only a very small amount of investment income. This year, you played the market more than usual and ended up paying $10,000 of margin interest, all of which was used to buy stocks. Your only investment income was $500 of interest and $18,000 of long-term capital gain from selling stock you bought a few years ago.

If you don't make this election, your entire $18,000 capital gain will be taxed at a favorable rate, but you'll deduct only $500 of the margin interest. You may not get the full benefit of the investment interest deduction for many years, if ever. In this situation, you elect to treat $9,500 of the long-term capital gain as ordinary income so you can deduct all your margin interest. The remaining $8,500 of long-term capital gain still qualifies for the favorable tax rate.

Example: Change the facts so that your margin interest is $2,000 and you expect to have at least $1,500 of net investment income next year. In this case you don't make the election, even though that means waiting a year before you can get the full benefit of your investment interest deduction. The benefit of the deduction is greater in the later year because it will reduce your ordinary income, not your long-term capital gain.

The way I think about this is that you deduct the investment interest "against" some other investment income. The greatest benefit comes from deducting it against investment income that's taxed at regular tax rates, not long-term capital gain. Yet deducting it against long-term capital gain is still better than waiting an eternity before claiming the deduction—or failing to deduct it at all.

Part IV
Capital Gains: Advanced Topics

15

Short Sales

THIS CHAPTER DESCRIBES SHORT SALES of stocks and other securities, and explains the general tax rules relating to short sales. It also explains how the wash sale rule applies to short sales. Chapter 18 explains *constructive sales*, which can occur if you sell *short against the box* (see below).

> The sale of a home at a price below the mortgage debt owed on that home is sometimes called a short sale. The transactions described here are not in any way related to those home sales.

How Short Sales Work

If you've never done a short sale, the concept is likely to seem strange. When you sell stock short, you're selling stock you don't own. You borrow the stock from someone else, promising to "repay" those shares of stock later. You sell the shares you borrowed, receiving cash.

When you're ready to close the short sale, you deliver shares back to the person from whom you borrowed them.

As a practical matter, the borrowing takes place automatically. Your broker takes care of that. The fact remains that you owe a debt that has to be repaid in stock. That means there are two ways to close a short sale: you can *buy* shares to repay the loan, or you can deliver stock you owned at the time of the short sale.

If you buy shares to close the short position, you're in exactly the opposite position of someone who owned shares during that period of time: you make a profit if the stock went *down* between the time you sold and the time you bought, and lose money if the stock went *up*. For this reason, short sales can be used as a way of betting that the price of a particular stock will decline.

> **Example:** You sell short 100 shares of XYZ at $60 per share. You receive $6,000 in the sale, and have an obligation to replace the 100 shares at some future time. If the stock price declines to $47, you can satisfy your obligation by purchasing 100 shares for $4,700, retaining $1,300 as your profit. On the other hand, if the stock goes up, you may end up having to pay more than $6,000 to satisfy your obligation to repay the stock. In that case you would have a loss on your short sale.

Short against the box. The other way to close a short sale is to deliver shares you held at the time of the short sale. If you hold shares of a particular stock and decide to sell short—instead of selling the shares you own—you are selling *short against the box*. This is a way of neutralizing a stock position without selling the shares you own.

> **Example:** You hold 100 shares of XYZ. You want to eliminate your risk from a decline in value of the stock, but you aren't ready to sell the stock. You sell short 100 shares while continuing to hold the original shares. In other words, you sell short against the box. Now, if the value of the stock goes down, you'll have a gain on the short sale that exactly matches your loss on the shares you hold.

When you're ready to close the short sale, you can buy shares in the market, but you don't have to do so. You can simply deliver the shares you started out with.

> Selling short against the box can bring the constructive sale rule (Chapter 18) or the straddle rules (Chapter 19) into play. Also, as noted in Chapter 13, any dividends you receive on stock you've sold short against the box do not get the lower tax rate for qualified dividends.

Simple short sales

Special rules apply if you make a short sale and at the same time own substantially identical stock. Before we turn to those rules, let's look at the simpler situation where you don't own the stock at the time you make the short sale, or at any time before you close the short sale.

At the time you make the short sale, you borrow shares and sell them, receiving cash. Although you've received cash, you have nothing to report on your tax return at this point. You won't know whether you have a profit or a loss until you close the short sale.

To close the short sale, you'll have to buy shares at the current price. Your broker will return these shares to the account from which you borrowed at the time you made the short sale. If you're able to buy the shares for a smaller amount than you received at the time of the short sale, you have a profit. You'll report that profit as a short-term capital gain. Note that the gain is short-term even if your short position was open more than a year. That's because the thing you sold was stock you held less than a year. If you have to pay more for the stock than the amount you received at the time of the short sale, you'll report a short-term capital loss.

Closing date. The date of sale for a regular sale of stock is the trade date. Yet a short sale isn't closed by the purchase of shares. It's only closed when the shares are *delivered.* As a result, if you close a short sale by purchasing shares in the market, the tax law looks at the settlement date, not the trade date—except when you have a profit on the short sale. So the only time you have to look at the settlement date instead of the trade date is when you're closing a short position at a loss.

> **Example:** You made short sales of the stock of two different companies, A and B. Stock A went down, giving you a profit of $10,000. (Remember, when you sell short, you make money when the stock goes down.) Stock B went up, giving you a loss of $10,000. On December 31 you close both positions by purchasing shares in the market.

You have to report your profit on stock A in the current year, because profits on short sales are recorded on the trade date. Yet the loss on stock B does not get recorded until the following year, when the trade settles. Although you have two transactions that offset each other economically, from a tax standpoint they occur in different years. What's more, you can't carry the loss back to the previous year when you had the profit.

Owning Identical Stock

At some point, you may make a short sale of stock you already own (selling *short against the box*), or you may buy stock to hold (rather than to close a short position) at a time when you have a short position in the same stock. Three sets of rules potentially come into play in this situation. First, we have for many years had rules that apply specifically to short sales against the box. These rules, described below, were mainly designed to prevent you from using short sales against the box to convert short-term capital gain into long-term capital gain. In 1997 Congress enacted the constructive sale rule, described in Chapter 18, which can cause you to be treated as if you sold shares even if you continue to hold them while selling short against the box. Then in 2004 Congress changed the straddle rules so they apply to most short sales against the box. The rules described in this section apply to offsetting positions established before October 22, 2004; offsets established later are subject to the straddle rules described in Chapter 19.

Short-term gain. If you hold substantially identical stock (defined the same as for the wash sale rule) for one year or less at the time of the short sale, or if you acquire substantially identical stock after the short sale but before you close the short sale, then two rules apply:

- If you have a gain on the short sale, the gain will be short-term, regardless of how long you held the stock that was used to close the short sale.
- Your holding period for the substantially identical stock begins when you close the short sale, or when you sell the stock, whichever occurs first.

Example: You bought 100 shares of XYZ six months ago. You sell short 100 shares of XYZ while continuing to hold these shares. Nine months later you use the original shares to close the short sale. If you have a gain on the sale, it's a short-term gain, even though you held the shares a total of 15 months before using them to close the short sale.

Example: Start with the same situation as the previous example, but this time you close the short sale by buying shares in the market. You continue to hold your original shares for another nine months, and then sell them for a gain. The gain is short-term even though you held the shares a total of two years. Your holding period for those shares started over again when you closed the short sale.

Example: You sold short 100 shares of XYZ at a time when you didn't own any shares of that stock. Then, while your short position was still open, you bought 100 shares of XYZ. You hold the shares more than a year, and then sell them for a gain. The gain is short-term unless you held the shares *more than a year after closing the short sale.*

Note that these rules apply to gains, not losses. Any loss from sale of the stock is long-term if you held the stock more than a year before selling it or using it to close the short sale.

If you work through this rule, you'll see that all of the following must be true for you to get a long-term gain on a short sale:

- At the time of the short sale, you hold long-term shares but no short-term shares in the stock you're selling short.
- You don't acquire any shares of that stock while the short sale is open.
- You use your long-term shares to close the short sale.

Long-term loss. On the flip side, there's a special rule for losses. If you held substantially identical stock for more than a year as of the date of a short sale, any loss from closing the short sale is a long-term loss, even if you use stock you held less than a year to close the short sale.

> **Example:** You held 100 shares of XYZ more than a year when you decided to sell short 100 shares of that stock. The price of the stock went up, and you closed the short sale at a loss, using newly purchased shares. Your loss is long-term, even though you used newly purchased shares to close the short sale.

This rule applies to losses, not gains. If you used newly purchased shares to close your short sale at a gain, you would have a short-term gain even though you owned long-term shares at the time you made the short sale.

Larger amount sold short. If you sell short more than the number of shares you hold, the special rules described above don't apply to the excess shares. For example, if you hold 100 shares of XYZ and sell short 150 shares of that stock, the special rules would apply to 100 shares but the rule for simple short sales would apply to the other 50.

> For situations not covered by the rules described above or the straddle rules (Chapter 19), the category of gain or loss (short-term or long-term) is determined by your holding period for the stock used to close the short sale.

Stock becomes worthless

Sometimes stock becomes worthless. A company may fail and leave nothing but scraps for the creditors to fight over. That's a sad event if you're unlucky enough to own the stock when it happens. If you've made a short sale of that company's stock, however, the company's failure is your success. You'll never be called upon to pay anything to close your short sale because the stock is worthless.

It might be tempting, in this situation, to simply leave the short sale in place indefinitely. After all, you've already received your profit. You received cash at the time you made the wash sale. The longer you delay closing the short sale, the longer you can avoid reporting the gain.

That *used* to be the rule. Because of a 1997 change in the law, you have to report gain from a short sale on the date the stock becomes substantially worthless. It may be difficult to determine exactly when that day occurs, but the point is that you can't avoid reporting your gain by simply leaving a short position open indefinitely. If events in a particular year indicate that the stock has become substantially worthless, that's the year when you have to report gain from your short position, even if the position remains open at the end of the year.

Short sales and the wash sale rule

As explained in Chapter 10, the wash sale rule prevents you from claiming a deduction from selling stock at a loss if you buy replacement stock within 30 days before or after the sale. The idea is that you shouldn't get a deduction because you're maintaining an investment in the stock with at most a small interruption in ownership. The wash sale rule also applies to losses from short sales.

Applying the wash sale rule to short sales is tricky because there are two different ways it can apply. You can have a wash sale as a result of another *purchase*, or you can have a wash sale as a result of another *sale*. Even the IRS gets confused here: their explanation in Publication 550 combines elements of the rule for purchases with the rule for sales, making it difficult to tell what rule actually applies to either situation.

Replacement purchases. The rule applying the wash sale rule to replacement purchases in a short sale situation has been in place for many years. Here's an example (it used to appear in IRS Publication 550, but for some reason has been deleted) showing why the wash sale rule applies to replacement purchases:

> **Example:** On June 2, you buy 100 shares of stock for $1,000. You sell short 100 shares of the stock for $750 on October 6. On October 7, you buy 100 shares of the stock for $750. You close the short sale on November 17 by delivering the shares bought on June 2.

You have a loss on the short sale because the sale was at $750 and you closed it by delivering stock you bought for $1,000. Yet at the end, after you closed the short sale on November 17, you're in the same position you were in before the short sale: you still own 100 shares. What's more, from October 7 to November 17, you were in an *equivalent* position: you held 200 shares but you were short 100, and that's economically the same as simply holding 100 shares. There was only one day (October 6) when your position was different. The idea behind the wash sale rule is that you have to change your position for at least 31 days if you want to claim a loss, so the wash sale rule applies in this situation.

Notice, though, that you closed the short sale more than 30 days after you bought the replacement shares. We've already learned that your loss from a short sale occurs when you close it, not when you enter into the short position. How can the wash sale rule stretch back from November 17 to October 7?

The answer is a special rule that says *solely for purposes of applying the wash sale rule* a short sale is considered to occur on the date you make the short sale (*not* the date you close it) if both of the following are true:

- On the date of the short sale, you own identical stock, or an option or contract to acquire identical stock, and
- You later deliver the stock you owned (or stock acquired using the option or contract you owned) to close the short sale.

That's exactly what happened in the example above. That means we determine whether you have a wash sale by looking at October 6, not at November 17. You made a replacement purchase within 30 days before or after October 6, so the wash sale rule applies. You can't deduct the loss from closing the short sale on November 17. Instead, you have to add that loss to your basis for the replacement shares you bought on October 7.

A questionable case. The regulation laying out how the wash sale rule applies to replacement purchases seems to imply that if the two conditions described above are *not* both true, you apply the wash sale rule by looking at purchases made within 30 days before or after the date you close the short sale. The result could be to apply the wash sale rule in situations where it doesn't make sense.

> **Example:** You sell short 100 shares without owning any of the same stock. Contrary to your expectations, the stock rises (which means you're losing money on your short sale). You buy stock in the market to close the short sale and, because you're so impressed with the way the stock's price is rising,

you buy 100 more shares (a "long" position) to hold as an investment.

Clearly the wash sale rule shouldn't apply here. The loss arose from a short position, and the 100 shares you bought did not replace that short position. I think there's a good chance the IRS would agree that the wash sale rule doesn't apply here, but there's no official pronouncement to that effect, and if you read the regulation literally, it seems as if the wash sale rule might apply.

Replacement sales. Prior to 1984, the wash sale rule applied to replacement *purchases* but did not apply to replacement *sales.* Congress amended the law that year to bring replacement sales within the scope of the wash sale rule. The Treasury has never issued regulations providing details on how this rule works. That's unfortunate, because the language in the law is somewhat vague. It says simply that "rules similar to" the regular wash sale rule apply to losses from closing short sales.

The rule applies if, within 30 days before or after closing a short sale at a loss, you sell substantially identical stock, or enter into another short sale of substantially identical stock. Here are examples of the two different situations.

Example 1: You sell short 100 shares of XYZ at a time when you don't own any XYZ. You're betting that the stock price will fall, but instead it rises, leaving you in a losing position. At this point you're more certain than ever that the stock is overpriced and you want to hang on to your short position to profit from the inevitable fall. Yet you want to deduct your loss on this year's tax return. So you close your short position at a loss, and then open another short position the next day. This is a wash sale because you replaced your losing short position with an identical short position within the wash sale period.

Example 2: You buy 100 shares of XYZ and at the same time make a short sale of 100 shares (short against the box). Just before the end of the year, the price of the stock is up, so you have a profit in your long position and a loss in your short position. You close the short position at a loss on December 29. On January 2, you sell the stock for a profit equal to your loss from the short position. Overall you have no profit or loss, but you want to claim a deduction for your loss in the year you closed the short position. The wash sale rule prevents this deduction, because you made an additional sale of stock within 30 days after closing the short sale at a loss.

Another questionable case. Consider the following sequence of transactions. On February 1, you buy 100 shares at $45. On March 10, you make a short sale of 100 shares at $38 (a short sale against the box). On April 15, you close the short sale by delivering the stock you bought on February 1 (a loss of $7 per share). On April 20, you make another short sale without owning any shares.

You have a short sale at a loss, followed within 30 days by another short sale. Under the literal language of the Internal Revenue Code, it appears this would be a wash sale. Yet this shouldn't be a wash sale because the loss was from the *long* position, not the short position, and you didn't replace the long position. Possibly you avoid having a wash sale by referring to the rule in the regulations that says you look to the date you made the wash sale, not the date you closed it, if you close it using stock you owned at the time you made the wash sale. The result isn't clear, however, because the regulation was written for the replacement purchase rule, not the rule for subsequent sales (which didn't exist when the regulation was written).

Short sale expenses

Consider what happens when a company pays a dividend while you have a short position in that stock. The dividend will go to the person who bought the shares from you. Meanwhile, the person who loaned the shares to you expects to be reimbursed for the dividend. After all, that person merely loaned you the shares, she didn't sell them.

That's why you're required to reimburse the lender for the dividend she would have received if you hadn't borrowed shares for your short sale. That's part of the promise you make when you borrow the shares: you'll not only replace the shares, but also make up for any dividends lost prior to closing of the short sale. This is sometimes called a *payment in lieu of dividend.* If you make such a payment, you need to know how to treat it on your tax return.

General rule. In general, you treat these payments the same way you treat interest on money you borrowed to make an investment. You claim a deduction, but only if you itemize, and only to the extent of your net investment income, with any excess carried over to the following year. See Chapter 14 for an explanation of the investment interest expense deduction.

"Short short" exception. If you close the short position by the forty-fifth day after the date of the short sale, you can't deduct your payment in lieu of dividend. Instead, you have to add that amount to the basis of the stock you used to close the short sale. That way, it either decreases your gain or increases your loss from the short sale. The reason for this exception is to prevent you from using short sales to convert capital losses into ordinary deductions.

Extraordinary dividends. A period of forty-five days is long enough to prevent tax planning for normal dividends, but not long enough if you make a short sale of stock in a company that pays a very large dividend. In that situation, the tax benefit from claiming an ordinary deduction from making a payment in lieu of dividend might be large enough to justify the risk of holding the short position open more than forty-five days. If a company pays an *extraordinary dividend,* you aren't allowed to deduct the payment in lieu of dividend unless you keep the short sale open more than a year. You've received an extraordinary dividend if the total amount of dividends received during the time the short sale was open is greater than 10% of the amount you received in the short sale (5% if you sold short preferred stock).

> **Example:** You sold short XYZ at $45 per share. While the short sale was open, XYZ paid a dividend of $5 per share. You're required to pay $5 per share to the lender of the shares. If you hold your short position open more than a year you can deduct this amount as investment interest. Otherwise, you have to treat it as a reduction in the amount you received in the sale.

16

Stock Options

OPTIONS GIVE YOU THE RIGHT TO BUY OR SELL stock or other property at a specified price during a specified period of time. In this book we're concerned primarily with options to buy or sell stock. (A brief discussion of index options appears in Chapter 17.) If you trade options on other kinds of property, such as commodities or foreign currencies, you should be aware that additional rules may apply.

You should also be aware that the rules described here don't apply to options received as compensation for services. For an explanation of nonqualified stock options, incentive stock options and other forms of equity compensation, refer to my book on that subject: *Consider Your Options.*

> Option trading can involve hidden cost and a high degree of risk. Before trading options, be sure to study the principles of option trading—and don't rely solely on materials from a firm that promotes option trading.

Option Terminology

A *call option* is an agreement or contract that permits the holder to buy stock at a specified price for a specified period of time. For example, if you hold a call option on XYZ stock at $45, you can use that option to buy XYZ at that price even if the stock is trading in the market at a much higher price. In other words, you can force someone to sell you the stock at a bargain price.

A *put option* permits the holder to *sell* stock at a specified price for a specified period of time. If you hold a put option on XYZ stock at $45, you can use that option to sell XYZ at that price even if the stock is trading in the market at a much *lower* price. In other words, you can force someone to "overpay" for the stock.

> The standard size for a stock option trading in the market is 100 shares. If you buy three call options, you're acquiring the right to buy 300 shares.

The price specified in the option agreement is the *strike price* (also called the *striking price* or the *exercise price*). The last day to exercise the option is called the *expiration date* (in some countries, the *date of expiry*).

There are two sides to each option agreement. The person who has the right to exercise the option is the *holder* of the option. The person who must buy or sell the stock if the holder exercises the option is the *writer* (also called the *grantor*) of the option.

> **Example:** You hold XYZ stock and decide to sell a call option on this stock. You don't own an option on the stock, so you're creating a new option, which makes you the *writer* of the option.

A call option is *in the money* if the stock is trading at a price higher than the strike price. It's *at the money* when the trading price of the stock is the same as the strike price of the option. When the trading price of the stock is below the strike price of the option, the option is *out of the money* (or *under water*).

The opposite relationships hold for a put option. These options are in the money when the stock trades at a price below the strike price of the option, and out of the money when the stock trades above the strike price. In each case, saying that an option is *in the money* means the option has value built into it, given the price at which the stock is trading.

An option is *deep in the money* when it's in the money to a large extent. Most of the time the term is used loosely, so there's no precise measure of how much difference you need between the market price of the stock and the strike price of the option before the option is deep in the money. The usual notion is that the option is so far in the money that it is almost certain to be exercised. A more technical definition of this term is used in connection with straddles (see Chapter 19).

Straddles, constructive sales

Option traders and investors may run into special rules that are covered in other chapters. The discussion in this chapter assumes your options are not part of a *straddle* (Chapter 19) and that your options don't create a *constructive sale* (Chapter 18). Generally, these special situations arise when you hold different positions that are related (such as holding XYZ stock and, at the same time, holding a put option on XYZ stock or selling a call option on XYZ stock).

Holders of call options

If you buy a call option, you acquire the right to buy stock. You can't claim a deduction at the time you purchase the option. Instead, your call option has a basis equal to the amount you paid for it (including brokerage commissions and other costs, if any). There are three different ways your option may terminate:

You exercise the call option. In this case, you're using the option to buy stock. Your basis for the option is added to the amount paid for the stock. Your holding period for the stock begins when you exercise the option: it does *not* include the time you held the option.

> **Example:** You buy a call option on XYZ with a strike price of $45, paying $500 for the option to buy 100 shares at this price. Later, when the stock is trading at $60, you exercise the option, paying $4,500 to buy 100 shares. Although you have a built-in profit (you paid a total of $5,000 to buy stock worth $6,000), you don't report gain or loss at this time. Instead, you hold XYZ stock with a total basis of $5,000 ($4,500 paid for the stock plus $500 paid for the option).

Your call option expires. You may hold the call option until it expires unused. In this case you're treated as if you sold the option for $0 on the expiration date. You'll report a capital loss, which may be short-term or long-term, depending on whether you held the option more than a year.

> **Example:** You pay $500 to buy a call option on 100 shares of XYZ at $45 per share. Two months later, the stock is trading at $42 and you allow the option to expire unused. You'll report a capital loss of $500 on the expiration date.

You sell the call option. The third possibility is that you sell the option you purchased earlier. Treat this situation the same as if you sold any other capital asset. You report a gain or loss based on the difference between the amount you received in the sale and the amount you paid for the option. The gain or loss is long-term if you held the option more than a year.

Holders of Put Options

If you buy a put option, you acquire the right to sell stock. As in the case of a call option, you can't claim a deduction at the time you purchase the option. Instead, your put option has a basis equal to the amount you paid for it (including brokerage commissions and other costs, if any). Here again, there are three different ways your option may terminate:

You exercise the put option. If you exercise the put option, you're using it to sell stock. You don't report gain or loss on your option, but you reduce the amount you received in the sale by the cost of the option.

> **Example:** You paid $500 for a put option to sell 100 shares of XYZ at $45. Later, you exercise the put option, selling 100 shares at the strike price of $45. You received $4,500 in the sale, but the option cost $500, so the net amount you received is only $4,000. You'll report that you sold the stock for $4,000.

Your put option expires. You may hold the put option until it expires unused. The tax treatment here is the same as if you hold a call option until it expires: You'll claim a capital loss as if you sold the option for $0 on the date of expiration. The loss is long-term if you held the option more than a year before it expired.

You sell the put option. If you purchase a put option and subsequently sell it, you'll report capital gain or loss on the sale equal to the difference between the amount received in the sale and the amount paid for the option. The gain or loss is long-term if you held the option more than a year before the sale.

Writers of Call Options

You can sell a call option even if you don't own one. In this case you're creating a new option, and you're the *writer* of the option. If the purchaser of the option exercises it, you're obligated to sell stock at the strike price.

Although you receive cash at the time you sell the option, you don't report gain or income at that time. Instead, you wait until your option position terminates to report the consequences. There are three ways your option position may terminate:

The call option is exercised. If the option is exercised, you're required to sell stock at the strike price. You don't report any gain or loss on the option, but you increase the amount reported on the sale of the stock by the amount you received when you sold the option.

> **Example:** You sell (write) a call option for 100 shares of XYZ with a strike price of $45, receiving $500 in the sale. The option is exercised, and you're forced to sell the stock at $45. In addition to the $4,500 you received in the sale of the stock, you received $500 in the sale of the option. You'll report that you sold the stock for $5,000.

The call option expires. The holder of the option may permit it to expire unused. If this happens, you get to keep the amount you received when you sold (wrote) the option. You'll report this amount as short-term capital gain on the date the option expired. Note that this gain is short-term even if the option was outstanding more than a year.

> **It ain't true.** There's a persistent myth that if you sell a call option on stock you hold (a *covered call*), you don't report gain when the option expires, but instead merely reduce your basis in the stock. That isn't true, and never has been. See Chapter 19 for more details on covered calls.

Closing transaction. Your option position may terminate because of a *closing transaction.* In essence, you're buying back the option you sold. You'll report a short-term capital gain or loss determined by the difference between the amount you received when you sold (wrote) the option and the amount you paid in the closing transaction.

> **Example:** You sell (write) a call option for 100 shares of XYZ with a strike price of $45, receiving $500 in the sale. Later, when this option is trading at a lower price, you pay $300 to

close your position. You report a capital gain of $200. The gain is short-term, regardless of how long the option was outstanding.

Caution: If you hold stock at the same time you write a call option on the same stock, you've written a *covered call.* Special rules described in Chapter 19 apply to covered calls.

Writers of Put Options

As in the case of a call option, you can sell a put option even if you don't own one. In this case you're creating a new option, and you're the *writer* of the option. If the purchaser of the option exercises it, you're obligated to buy stock at the strike price.

Although you receive cash at the time you sell the option, you don't report gain or income at that time. Instead, you wait until your option position terminates to report the consequences. There are three ways your option position may terminate:

The put option is exercised. If the option is exercised, you're required to buy stock at the strike price. You paid money for the stock, but you received money when you sold the option. You don't report gain or loss at this point, but you reduce your basis in the stock by the amount you received for the put option.

Example: You received $500 when you sold (wrote) a put option permitting the holder to sell 100 shares of XYZ at $45. The holder exercises the option, forcing you to buy the stock for $4,500. You received $500 for the put option, so your net cost for the stock is $4,000. When you sell the stock, you'll report gain or loss relative to a basis of $4,000.

The put option expires. The holder of the option may permit it to expire unused. If this happens, you get to keep the amount you received when you sold (wrote) the option. You'll report this amount as short-term capital gain on the date the option expired. Note that this gain is short-term even if the option was outstanding more than a year.

Closing transaction. As in the case of a call option, you can close your position in the put option, in effect buying it back for the current trading price of the option. You'll report a short-term capital gain or loss determined by the difference between the amount you received when you sold (wrote) the option and the amount you paid in the closing transaction.

> **Example:** You sell (write) a put option for 100 shares of XYZ with a strike price of $45, receiving $500 in the sale. Later, when this option is trading at a higher price, you pay $750 to close the option. You report a capital loss of $250. The loss is short-term, regardless of how long the option was outstanding.

Wash Sales and Options

Chapter 10 covers the wash sale rule in general. Options present two different types of problems in connection with the wash sale rule. First, if you sell stock at a loss, you can turn that sale into a wash sale by trading in options. And second, losses from the options themselves can be wash sales.

Buying call options. If you sell stock at a loss, you don't have to buy replacement stock within the wash sale period to have a wash sale. You can have a wash sale merely by entering into a contract or option to buy replacement stock.

> **Example:** On March 31 you sell 100 shares of XYZ at a loss. On April 10 you buy a call option on XYZ stock. (A *call option* gives you the right to buy 100 shares.) The sale on March 31 is a wash sale.

It doesn't matter whether the call option is in the money. This is an automatic rule. If you buy a call option during the wash sale period (from 30 days before the sale until 30 days after the sale), you have a wash sale. That's true even if you never exercise the option to acquire the stock. The disallowed loss is added to your basis for the call option.

Selling put options. You can also turn a sale of stock into a wash sale by selling put options. This rule is *not* automatic. It applies only if the put option is deep in the money—and there's no precise standard as to when a put option is *deep enough* in the money for the rule to apply. The rule applies if it appears, at the time you sell the put option, that there's no substantial likelihood it will expire unexercised. When that happens, selling the put option can be roughly equivalent to buying the stock.

> **Example:** On March 31 you sell 100 shares of XYZ at a loss. On April 10 you sell a put option giving the holder the right to sell to you 100 shares of XYZ at a price substantially higher than the current market price of the stock. The sale on March 31 is a wash sale.

As seller of a put option that's deep in the money, you participate in the upward and downward movement of the stock price, unless the price moves higher than the strike price. If the strike price is high enough, the chances of that happening are small, and you've simply found a different way to continue your investment in the stock.

Holding period questions. For technical reasons, the law isn't crystal clear how the rules for holding periods work when the wash sale rule applies because of trading in options. One knowledgeable commentator has suggested that the wash sale rule doesn't affect the holding period of a call option. I have my doubts, though, because it would be easy to convert a long-term loss to a short-term loss if you didn't add the holding period of the stock to the holding period of the option. The tax law contains elaborate rules designed to prevent this type of conversion, and all those rules would be pointless if you could defeat them through the use of wash sales involving options.

To prevent this type of conversion, it would be necessary to apply the extended holding period not only to a call option, but also to any stock acquired by exercise of that option. That's contrary to the usual rule for determining the holding period of stock acquired by exercising an option. You would also have to extend the holding period of a short call position, if the wash sale rule applied because you sold a call that was deep in the money. That's a very strange rule because short positions are always considered to be short-term: their holding period is zero because you don't hold an asset.

The IRS has never told us the extended holding period applies in these situations. If you can benefit from converting long-term loss to short-term loss, you may want to consider using stock options and the wash sale rule to accomplish this result.

> **Example:** You have a large, long-term loss on XYZ stock. In the same year you have long-term gains and short-term gains. If you simply sell the stock, the loss will reduce your long-term gains. A short-term loss would be better, because it would reduce your short-term gains.
>
> To get the better result, you sell the stock and immediately buy a call option for the same number of shares of XYZ. Shortly thereafter, you sell the option. The wash sale rule prevents a deduction for the loss on sale of the stock. The loss is added to your basis for the option, and you claim a short-term loss on sale of the option.

Will the IRS accept this result? If not, will you win if you fight the IRS in court? There's no way to know for sure. If you're willing to venture into a gray area, be my guest, but don't say I didn't tell you it was gray.

Losses on options. Congress amended the wash sale rule in 1988 so that it applies directly to contracts or options to buy or sell stock or securities. That means you can have a wash sale when you close an option position at a loss, if you establish a replacement position within the wash sale period. The Treasury has yet to issue regulations under this rule, and a host of questions remain unanswered. Foremost among these is the question of when one option is substantially identical to another option.

Until the Treasury decides to issue regulations or other guidance, neither I nor anyone else can say exactly how the wash sale rule applies to losses on options. But there's a pretty good rule of thumb that should tell you when you're safe and when you're on thin ice. If the positions you acquired within the wash sale period permit you to participate in the same up and down market swings as the position that produced the loss, there's a chance the IRS will say you have a wash sale. If that's not the case, you should be safe.

Suppose you bought a call option and later sold it at a loss. Buying another call option on the same stock within the wash sale period may be viewed as a wash sale even if the new call option has a different expiration or a different strike price. The new option isn't identical, but perhaps it can be considered *substantially* identical, which is enough to invoke the wash sale rule.

The IRS also might assert that you have a wash sale if you buy XYZ *stock* after selling a call option at a loss, especially if the call was in the money when you sold it. Similarly, you could also have a wash sale if you write a deep-in-the-money put option during the wash sale period after selling a deep-in-the-money call at a loss. All of these are ways of continuing to participate in the up and down motions of the price of the same stock.

By contrast, you shouldn't have a wash sale if you sell a call option at a loss and also write a put option that's at the money or out of the money. The long call option and the short put option are both bullish positions, but the short put option doesn't let you participate in the upside of the stock. You haven't preserved your overall position relative to the stock.

These remarks are simply my ideas of how the IRS might interpret the wash sale rule in connection with options. Until we have further guidance, we won't be able to say with certainty what transactions will or will not produce wash sales. Unfortunately, there's no sign that guidance on these issues will be forthcoming in the near future.

17

Section 1256 Contracts

FOR THE MOST PART, the subject of section 1256 contracts is beyond the scope of this book. Most people encounter this subject in connection with trading commodities, and this book doesn't cover rules for commodity trading. Yet there's one category of section 1256 contracts—index options—that's close enough to our subject matter to deserve at least brief coverage.

The tax treatment of section 1256 contracts is different from any other kind of financial asset. There are three special rules:

- Your holdings in section 1256 contracts are *marked to market* at the end of each year.
- Any gain or loss you have from section 1256 contracts is 60% long-term gain or loss and 40% short-term gain or loss, without regard to how long you held them.
- Net losses in this category can be carried back to earlier years.

We'll look at details for these rules in a moment. First, let's look at the one type of section 1256 contract we're interested in here: index options.

Index options

There are several categories of section 1256 contracts, but only one that falls within the scope of this book. *Index options* are a way of making a bet on which way a particular stock index is going to move—or hedging a bet you've already made.

Suppose you think the S&P 500 index is going to rise in the near future. There are various ways you can bet on that result. You can buy shares of the stocks that make up the S&P 500, but that wouldn't usually be practical. A more likely choice would be to buy shares of a mutual fund or ETF that seeks to mimic the performance of the S&P 500 index. An index option provides a third possibility. You could buy an option on the S&P 500 index. If the index is higher than the strike price on the expiration date, you'll receive cash equal to the difference.

Not all index options are section 1256 contracts. Only those that meet certain technical requirements qualify. Generally, they must be considered "broad-based" under criteria of the Securities and Exchange Commission, and they have to *settle in cash*. That means you don't get shares of stock when you exercise the option; instead, you get an amount of cash determined by the difference between the value of the index on the exercise date and the strike price of the option. Further details concerning which index options qualify as section 1256 contracts are available from the exchanges on which the options trade.

> Don't confuse index options with options on exchange-traded index funds. Options on exchange-traded index funds settle in shares of the fund, not in cash, so they aren't section 1256 contracts.

The 60/40 rule

The most remarkable thing about the tax treatment of section 1256 contracts is that gain or loss from short or long positions in these investments will be treated as 60% long-term capital gain or loss and 40% short-term gain or loss. It doesn't matter how long you hold them. You get the long-term part even if you sell the same day you bought them, and you get the short-term part even if you hold them more than a year. In effect, you get a blended tax rate on gain from section 1256 contracts: somewhere between the rate you pay on long-term capital gain and the rate you pay on ordinary income (which is the rate that applies to short-term capital gain).

Mark-to-market rule

Under the mark-to-market rule, you're treated as if you sold (or closed) all your section 1256 contracts for their fair market value on the last day of the year. You'll report gain or loss from that deemed sale just as if it were an actual sale. Your basis for the section 1256 contracts is adjusted to reflect the gain or loss you reported.

> **Example:** At the end of the year, you hold a section 1256 contract you bought for $4,000. The value of the contract at the end of the year is $4,250, so you report gain of $250 ($150 of long-term capital gain and $100 of short-term capital gain). Your basis in the section 1256 contract is adjusted to $4,250. If you later sell it for $4,300, you'll report only $50 of gain ($30 of long-term capital gain and $20 of short-term capital gain).

No wash sales. The wash sale rule (Chapter 10) is designed to prevent you from claiming losses that otherwise wouldn't be allowed while you continue to hold an investment. When it comes to section 1256 contracts, all your gains and losses are reported each year because of the mark-to-market rule. For that reason, the wash sale rule doesn't apply to section 1256 contracts.

Loss carrybacks

Individual taxpayers who aren't able to use all their capital losses because of the $3,000 limitation can carry them forward to later years, but generally cannot carry them back. Losses from section 1256 contracts are an exception: you can carry them back three years, but only to use against gains from section 1256 contracts in those years.

Mixed straddles

When you start combining section 1256 contracts with other investments, you can run into rules for *mixed straddles*. For example, if you hold a put option on the S&P 500 at the same time you hold shares of a mutual fund that mimics the performance of the S&P 500, you have a straddle because one investment position protects you from loss in the other. This is a *mixed* straddle because gain and loss on one part of the straddle is 60/40 gain or loss, while gain or loss on the other position is subject to the normal rules for capital gains and losses.

There isn't room here to go into the technicalities for mixed straddles. I mention them so you'll be aware that such rules exist if you do this kind of trading. These rules may require you to report long-term loss when you would expect to report short-term loss, or you may have to report short-term gain when you would normally report long-term gain. The idea behind these rules is to prevent people from creating unfair tax advantages from combining different types of investment positions, but you can have negative effects from these rules even if you aren't seeking any special tax advantage in your trading.

18

Constructive Sales

THIS CHAPTER COVERS A RULE, ADOPTED IN 1997, under which you may be treated as having sold an asset even when you continue to own it. This *constructive sale* treatment applies when you have other transactions that neutralize your market position. The most common example is a situation where you hold stock and at the same time make a short sale of the same stock—in other words, sell *short against the box.*

The constructive sale rule doesn't apply to all short sales, or even to all sales that are short against the box. For an explanation of short sales, and rules that apply to short sales *other than* constructive sales, see Chapter 15.

Background

What do you do when you make a winning investment? It's a nice problem to have, but a problem nonetheless. If you continue to hold the stock, it may continue its ascent—but it may fall back, eliminating your gains. Yet if you sell it, you're volunteering to pay taxes you could have avoided, at least for the time being, by standing pat.

Until 1997, there was a third alternative. You could make a short sale of that stock while continuing to hold your appreciated shares—a sale *short against the box*. The short sale neutralized your market position without requiring you to report any gain.

> **Example:** You bought XYZ at $24 and it has soared to $68. You believe this stock's run is over and it's time to consolidate your gain. Before 1997 you could accomplish this by making a short sale of XYZ while continuing to hold the stock. You wouldn't report any gain on the sale because you haven't sold the shares that went up in value. You don't lose anything if the stock goes down after you've made the short sale, because your short position gains by the same amount as your long position (the shares of stock) loses.

Congress decided in 1997 that you shouldn't be able to neutralize your position this way without reporting gain. Under the constructive sale rule, you're treated as if you sold the appreciated stock, even though you continue to hold it, if you keep the short sale position open too long. You can also have a constructive sale if you trade options in such a way as to neutralize your stock position.

Constructive sales in general

Selling short against the box doesn't necessarily create a constructive sale. For one thing, the rule applies only to appreciated positions (stock that has a value higher than your basis). If you make a short sale against the box for stock that hasn't gone up in value, the rules described in Chapters 15 and 19 apply.

The rule also doesn't apply if you close the short sale soon enough—and leave it closed long enough while continuing to maintain your position in the appreciated stock. To avoid having a constructive sale, you have to close the short position no later than 30 days after the end of the year, then continue to hold the appreciated stock without protection for at least 60 days. If you establish a new short position within 60 days after closing the first one, you can still avoid having a constructive sale if you meet these requirements for the *second* position. In other words, you would have to close the second position no later than 30 days after the end of the year of the original short sale, and continue to hold the appreciated stock without protection for at least 60 days.

These time periods refer to calendar days, not trading days. For the vast majority of taxpayers—everyone who reports on a year that ends December 31—the deadline for closing a short position to avoid a constructive sale is January 30.

> **Example:** On June 17, while holding shares of XYZ that went up in value, you make a short sale of XYZ stock. You're protected against any loss in the value of this stock for as long as you hold the short position open. On January 10 you buy shares in the market to close the short sale, and continue to hold your shares of XYZ, without making any further short sales or establishing other protective positions, for at least 60 days. You have satisfied the conditions to avoid a constructive sale.

Notice that in this example you're protected against market loss on your stock for an extended period of time, without having a constructive sale.

Effect of a constructive sale

If you have a constructive sale, you're treated as if you sold the appreciated stock on the date of the short sale. That's true even though we don't know whether you have a constructive sale until the following year.

> **Example:** You hold appreciated shares of XYZ and sell short against the box in February. On January 25 of the following

year, you close the short position and continue to hold the XYZ stock. But then on March 10 (several weeks later) you make another short sale against the box.

You have a constructive sale because your second short sale, in March, comes less than 60 days after you closed the first short position. As a result, the short sale that occurred in February of the preceding year, more than a year earlier, is a constructive sale. You have to report gain from that constructive sale on your tax return for the preceding year. The same would be true if you simply sold the XYZ stock (instead of selling short against the box) the following March 10.

When you have a constructive sale, you're treated as if you sold *and repurchased* the stock at its fair market value on the date of the constructive sale. The stock takes a basis equal to the value used for the constructive sale, so you don't get taxed twice on the same gain. The stock also takes a new holding period: you're treated as if you acquired it on the date of the short sale.

> Although you're treated as acquiring the stock on the date of the short sale, the holding period for purposes of determining gain is presumably suspended under the rules explained in Chapters 15 and 19 until such time as you close the short position. You would have to hold the stock at least a year and a day after closing the short position to get a long-term capital gain.

Options and other protective positions

You don't have to sell short against the box to have a constructive sale. You can have the same result if you use stock options or other protective positions to neutralize your position in appreciated stock.

The Treasury hasn't issued regulations telling us exactly what positions (other than short sales against the box) will give rise to a constructive sale. When the regulations come out, they should be prospective, applying only to transactions that occur after the regulations are issued. The Treasury has informally indicated, however, that the regulations may apply retroactively to transactions that obviously fall within the intended reach of the constructive sale rule.

Meanwhile, we can glean some guidance from the legislative history of the constructive sale rule. It's clear that you don't have a constructive sale if you establish a position that provides only "one-way" protection for your stock position. For example, if you buy a put option on shares you own, you're protected against a decline in the value of your stock, but you can still benefit from further appreciation. Likewise, if you sell a call option, you lose the benefit of further appreciation in the stock price, but you can still suffer from a decline in value.

Buying a put option or selling a call option would not be safe from application of the constructive sale rule, however, if the option is deep in the money at the time of the transaction. For example, if you hold appreciated shares of XYZ and buy a put option at $150 when the stock is trading at $110, it's likely that you'll be treated as if you made a short sale for purposes of this rule. The wide disparity between the value of the stock and the strike price of the option creates a situation where you have not only protected yourself against loss if the market price of the stock declines, but also transferred to the writer of the option the economic benefit of any appreciation in the value of the stock up to a price of $150.

Similarly, you can have a constructive sale from a *combination* of options, where either one of the options by itself would not cause a constructive sale. For example, if your appreciated XYZ stock is trading at $98, you could buy a put option at $95 and simultaneously sell a call option at $100. This combination of option positions is called a *collar*, because it limits both your profit and loss from the stock position. A collar this "tight" is almost certain to be considered equivalent to a short sale for purposes of the constructive sale rule.

A "looser" collar should be permitted without a constructive sale, however. Some have suggested, based on vague support in the legislative history of the relevant tax law, that a collar is loose enough if the spread between the strike prices of the put and call options is at least 15% of the current value of the stock. More conservative commentators suggest using a 20% rule.

In short

The constructive sale rule does not entirely deprive us of opportunities to control risk without reporting gain. We can eliminate all risk for a limited period of time by selling short against the box. If we need protection for a longer period of time but can accept risk within certain limits, we can use a collar that meets the standards mentioned above. The constructive sale rule doesn't do away with tax-wise risk management, but success now depends on the planner's ability to adopt more sophisticated tax planning approaches.

19

Straddles

WE COME NOW TO AN INTRICATE AND ESOTERIC SUBJECT, but one you can easily bump up against if you buy and sell stock options. A *straddle* is a set of two or more *offsetting positions*—that is, positions that reduce risk because they normally move in opposite directions. There's nothing wrong with trading in such a way as to create straddles. If you do, though, you'll encounter rules designed to prevent people from using straddles to obtain unfair tax advantages. These rules apply even if you created the straddle without any improper tax motive. The rules for straddles have three main effects:

- They may require you to delay claiming some or all of your loss from selling or closing one position in the straddle.
- They may turn a long-term gain into a short-term gain, or turn a short-term loss into a long-term loss.
- They may require you to treat certain expenses as part of the cost of the straddle instead of claiming an ordinary deduction.

This chapter falls short of being a complete explanation of the straddle rules. The subject is simply too large—and too technical—for a full explanation here. Yet you'll learn enough to identify straddle issues and handle the situations that are most likely to arise. We'll also explain how you can avoid some of the straddle rules if you write *qualified covered calls.*

Definition of straddle

The term *straddle* comes from the notion of someone who can't make up his mind which side he wants to be on. He has one leg on one side of the fence and one leg on the other, so he straddles the issue. In fact, we sometimes refer to a pair of financial positions as the *legs* of a straddle. The straddle rules apply to many types of financial positions, including futures contracts, forward contracts, and options on currencies and commodities. In this book we're concerned only with positions in stocks, and in options on stocks.

> The term *straddle* has a specific meaning to option traders. The definition in the tax law is broader. It includes combinations of positions an option trader might call a *spread* rather than a straddle, for example.

Position. You hold a *position* if you have an interest in the stock or option, which may be a positive or negative interest. If you hold shares of XYZ stock, you have a position (specifically, a *long* position) in that stock. You also have a position in that stock if you don't hold any shares, but you have sold the stock short. Likewise, you can establish a position by buying or selling a call option or a put option.

Straddle. Generally speaking, the term *straddle* is used in the tax law to refer to a combination of two or more financial positions that offset one another. When one position goes down in value, the other one will rise. It isn't necessary to have a perfect correlation, though. It's enough if one position protects, at least partially, against loss from another position. Positions are *presumed* to create a straddle if they relate to the same stock, and the value of one or more positions ordinarily varies inversely with the value of the other. In other words, if one goes down, you expect the other to rise.

> **Example:** You hold 100 shares of XYZ, and you buy an option to sell 100 shares of XYZ (a *put* option). When the value of the stock rises, the value of the put option will normally fall. This combination of positions is a straddle.

Straddles often consist of a stock position and a position in options on that stock. A straddle may also be made up entirely of options.

> **Example:** A straddle might consist of a short position in January calls on XYZ and a long position in April calls on the same stock. Another possible straddle would be a long position in puts at $95 and a short position in puts at $105.

Short against the box. Prior to 2004, selling stock short against the box did not create a straddle, even though the stock and the short position are obviously offsetting positions. There was no particular logic to that result; it was simply a rule in the tax law. In 2004 Congress changed that rule, so the straddle rules now generally apply if you make a short sale of any actively traded stock. Somewhat different rules, described in Chapter 15, apply if you established offsetting positions before October 22, 2004.

Covered calls. We'll see below that if you engage in the common practice of selling calls on stock you own, these *covered calls* may or may not result in straddles. Even if they don't result in straddles, you may be subject to some of the rules that apply to straddles.

Interests owned by others. You can have a straddle because of an offsetting position owned by your spouse, or by a partnership or other entity you own. For example, if you hold shares of XYZ and your spouse holds an option to sell XYZ (a *put* option), the two of you collectively hold a straddle, and the rules described here will apply.

Loss deferral

If you have a loss from selling or closing one position of a straddle, you have to determine whether that loss is allowed under the special rules that apply to straddles. The first step is to apply the wash sale rule explained in Chapter 10. If the regular wash sale rule disallows your loss, then that's the rule that applies and you don't have to go any further. You look at the special rule for straddles only if you have a loss that isn't disallowed by the regular wash sale rule.

The special rule reduces your remaining loss deduction (the part that isn't affected by the regular wash sale rule) by the amount of unrecognized gain you have in certain other positions as of the end of the year. You have *unrecognized gain* if selling or closing the position at fair market value would produce a gain. For example, if you made a short sale of XYZ at $60 and the stock is trading at $50 at the end of the year, you have unrecognized gain of $10 per share in your short position if it remains open.

There are three types of positions that can have unrecognized gain:

- Offsetting positions,
- Successor positions, and
- Offsetting positions to successor positions.

Offsetting positions are the positions that caused you to have a straddle in the first place. These are positions you held at the same time as the position that produced the loss, where the value of the position normally changes in the opposite direction to the position that produced the loss.

> **Example:** You sold short 100 shares of XYZ and also bought a call option permitting you to buy 100 shares of XYZ. You close the short position at a loss of $800. The value of the call option normally changes in the opposite direction of the short stock position, so it's an offsetting position.

At the end of the year you still hold the call option and it's trading at $5 per share more than the amount you paid. That means the call option has $500 of unrecognized gain. You can report only $300 of your loss from the short position. The rest is deferred until next year.

Here's where things get really technical. A *successor position* is a position (P) that meets all of the following requirements:

- P was at any time offsetting to another position (the "second position").
- The second position was offsetting to any position you sold or closed at a loss.
- You entered into P within 30 days before or after you sold or closed the loss position.
- You entered into P no later than 30 days after the loss position was no longer included in a straddle.

If you're an ordinary mortal, that's enough to make your head swim. The basic idea, though, is to extend the wash sale rule to cover situations where you trade in and out of positions that offset the same position.

Example: You hold 100 shares of XYZ stock, and also hold an option to sell 100 shares of XYZ stock (a put option). These are offsetting positions, so you hold a straddle.

You sell your put option at a loss and, within 30 days after that sale, sell a call option on your XYZ stock. As the seller of a call option, you once again hold a position that is offsetting to the stock, which you continue to hold.

If you still have the position in the call option at the end of the year, and you have unrecognized gain in that position, the loss you can claim from selling the put option will be reduced by the unrecognized gain in this position.

The third situation where your loss is reduced or eliminated is when you have a unrecognized gain in a position that's offsetting to a successor position. The definitions above for offsetting and successor positions apply to this rule.

> **Example:** You hold shares of XYZ and also an option to sell XYZ, creating a straddle. You sell the put option at a loss on June 10. On June 20 you sell the stock at a gain. On June 30, you again buy stock in XYZ. The stock purchase doesn't create a wash sale because your previous sale of the stock was at a gain, not a loss. Yet the new stock position is a *successor position* to the previous stock position—and that position was offsetting to the put option, which created the loss. As a result, your loss will be reduced or eliminated if you have an unrecognized gain in the new stock position at the end of the year.

Treatment of disallowed loss. If you have a loss that's disallowed under this rule, the tax treatment depends on whether you have an *identified straddle* as described next. If the straddle isn't identified, the loss is carried over to the next year. To claim the loss, you have to dispose of the position that caused it to be disallowed. You also have to apply the rule described above to make sure the loss you carried over isn't disallowed because of unrecognized gain at the end of the second year in an offsetting position, a successor position, or a position that's offsetting to a successor position.

Identified straddles

If your trading creates straddles, you may be able to improve your tax situation if you *identify* your straddles. To be an identified straddle, a straddle must meet the following requirements:

- You clearly identified the straddle on your records before the close of the day on which you acquired it.
- For straddles acquired after December 29, 2007, you identified the positions in the straddle that are offsetting with respect to one another.

- The straddle is not part of a larger straddle.

As to the first two requirements, you don't have to send anything to the IRS. You don't even have to notify your broker, the way you do when identifying shares as described in Chapter 8. You simply put an entry in your personal records clearly indicating that two or more positions are to be treated as an identified straddle for federal tax purposes.

Prior to a 2004 change in the law, you had to acquire all positions of a straddle on the same day to have it treated as an identified straddle. The current rules allow you to identify a straddle when you "leg into" it. For example, you may have shares of stock you've held for some time, and decide to protect that position by purchasing a put option. The put option is an offsetting position, so this creates a straddle. Under the old law, you could not treat this as an identified straddle, but this is now permitted.

Effect of identified straddle. When you identify a straddle, any loss you have from one position is disallowed and added to the basis of the remaining position(s) in your straddle. This happens regardless of whether you have unrecognized gain in the remaining position(s) at the end of the year. If you have more than one remaining position, the disallowed loss is allocated among them in proportion to the amount of unrecognized gain in those positions, determined as of the time the loss is incurred rather than at the end of the year. You'll get the benefit of the disallowed loss, in the form of a smaller amount of gain or larger amount of loss, when you sell or close those positions with the increased basis.

> In many situations the result is the same as if the loss had been suspended under the rule for unidentified straddles, but sometimes you're better off with the basis adjustment.

Loss treated as long-term

Even if your loss isn't disallowed under the rules described above, the straddle rules may require you to treat a short-term loss as a long-term loss. This rule applies to any loss from disposition of a position in a straddle if both of the following are true:

- You held one or more offsetting positions when you acquired the position that produced the loss, and
- You would have had long-term gain or loss if you sold any offsetting position on the day you acquired the position that produced the loss.

Example: You've held XYZ stock more than a year when you buy an option to sell XYZ stock. Two months later you sell the put option at a loss. Although you held the put option less than a year, you have to treat the loss as a long-term loss, because you held an offsetting position (the stock) more than a year before you acquired the put option.

Holding period rule

Here's a rule that trips people up fairly often. If you hold a position as part of a straddle, and you didn't have a long-term holding period for the position before it became part of a straddle, your holding period for that position doesn't begin until you no longer hold an offsetting position. In other words, if you want long-term gain when you sell a position that was part of a straddle, you have to hold it for at least a year and a day after you terminate the straddle.

Example: You made a good investment when you bought XYZ stock ten months ago: it has doubled in value. You want to hold the stock long enough for a long-term gain, but you're afraid the market in this stock is ready to pull back. If you aren't aware of the straddle rules, you might buy a put option, to protect against a decline in the price of the stock, then sell both positions when you've held the stock more than a year.

The put option creates a straddle, so this strategy leaves you with a short-term capital gain.

What's more, if you sell the put option and continue to hold the stock, you won't get credit for the 10 months you held the stock before you created the straddle. To get a long-term gain, you have to start over again, holding the stock more than a year after you sold the put option.

Carrying charges

If you incur interest or other costs with respect to a position in a straddle, in excess of any taxable income you have from a straddle (such as dividends on stock that's part of the straddle), you aren't allowed to deduct that amount. Instead, you have to add it to the basis of the straddle position.

Example: You take out a margin loan to buy XYZ stock, and you also buy an option to sell that stock, creating a straddle. Interest on the margin loan (reduced by dividends paid by this stock, if any) is not deductible. Instead, you have to add the interest expense to the amount you paid for the stock when you sell it.

Covered call options

There's one straddle-like transaction that's often used by professional investment managers and others: covered call options. The idea is to sell call options on stock you already own. You receive a cash payment—the option *premium*—when you sell the call option. If the option expires unexercised, as is often the case, you get to keep the premium, which increases your overall investment return. At the same time, you set the strike price of the option high enough so that if it *is* exercised, you'll be happy with the profit you receive on the sale.

This brief description may make it sound as if it's easy to enhance your investment return by selling covered calls. The contrary is true, and this technique is best left to the experts.

The people who wrote the straddle rules were aware that there's a legitimate investment practice that involves selling covered calls. They didn't want the straddle rules to punish people who engaged in that practice, so they wrote an exception for *qualified covered calls*. This exception doesn't apply to *all* covered calls. It applies only to *qualified* covered calls, as defined below. What's more, even if you sell only qualified covered calls, some aspects of the straddle rules described above may apply to you.

General rule. In general, your positions aren't treated as a straddle if you sell options that are *qualified covered call options* on stock you hold, provided that those positions aren't part of a larger straddle. Subject to exceptions below, this rule for qualified covered calls avoids all the problems described above: loss deferral, loss treated as long-term, the holding period rule and the rule for carrying charges.

Special year-end rule. There's one situation where the loss deferral rule described above applies, even if your investment positions consist of stock and qualified covered calls. It's designed to prevent you from claiming a loss from one position just before the end of the year, when you plan to dispose of the other position just after the end of the year. The loss deferral rule applies to a straddle that consists of stock and a qualified covered call if all of the following are true:

- You dispose of either position (the stock or the call position) at a loss.
- You have gain on the other position in a different taxable year.
- You held the other position less than 30 days after disposing of the loss position.

Definition of qualified covered call. There are three main requirements for an option position to be a qualified covered call:

1. You sell the option more than 30 days before its expiration date,
2. You grant the option with a year or less until it expires, and
3. The option is not *deep in the money.*

The first two are easy, but the definition of *deep in the money* is highly technical. What's more, we'll see at the end of this section that even if the option you sell isn't deep in the money, certain aspects of the straddle rules can apply if your option is even *slightly* in the money.

First you have to know what we mean when we say an option is in the money. There's a very precise definition that applies just for purposes of these rules. An option is in the money if the strike price is lower than the *applicable stock price.*

Generally, the *applicable stock price* is the closing price on the day before you sold the option. But if the stock opened on the day you sold the option at a price greater than 110% percent of the previous day's closing price, then the opening price is the applicable stock price.

Before we go on, let me point out that you'll save yourself a lot of brain damage if you never sell call options with a strike price below the applicable stock price. When you do that, you don't have to worry about whether your option is deep in the money, because it isn't in the money at all. You also don't have to worry about the special rules, described later, for qualified covered calls that are in the money when issued.

Deep in the money. Unless you have a perverse love of complexity, you're going to just *hate* the definition of *deep in the money.* Here it is, in all its glory:

> An option is deep in the money if its strike price is lower then the lowest qualified benchmark. Generally, the lowest qualified benchmark is the highest available strike price that's

less than the applicable stock price (as defined above). However, the lowest qualified benchmark for an option with a term of more than 90 days and a strike price of more than $50 is the *second* highest available strike price that's less than the applicable stock price. Also, if the applicable stock price is $25 or less, the lowest qualified benchmark can't be less than 85% of the applicable stock price. Furthermore, if the applicable stock price is $150 or less, the lowest qualified benchmark can't be more than $10 below the applicable stock price.

Got that? We'll have a quiz in the morning.

Qualified covered calls that are in the money. Apart from avoiding having to deal with that horrible definition, there's another reason to avoid selling call options that are in the money. Two special rules apply to qualified covered call options that are in the money when issued:

- If you held the stock long-term before selling the call option, then any loss you have on the option will be long-term capital loss. This is the same rule that applies to straddles in general.
- Your holding period for the stock doesn't include the time the option was outstanding. This is *not* the same as the usual rule for straddles. Under the usual rule, your holding period *starts over* when you no longer have a straddle. In this case, the holding period is interrupted while the straddle is in place, but then resumes.

Part V
Asset Transfers

20

Tax Rules for Gifts

This chapter tells what you need to know if you make or receive what I call *financial gifts*—in other words, gifts of cash, stock or other financial assets. Actually, the rules here apply to non-financial gifts as well. For example, you may have to file a gift tax return if you give your child an automobile. In this chapter you'll learn:

- How gifts are treated under the income tax.
- How the "unified transfer tax" applies to gifts and estates.
- How the annual gift tax exclusion works, and what other exclusions are available.

Gifts and income tax

Before we turn to gift tax, let's take a look at how gifts affect your income tax.

Recipient doesn't report income. Gifts you receive aren't considered income. You don't report them on your income tax return in any way. There are two important qualifications on this simple rule.

- **True gifts.** This rule applies only to true gifts. You can't avoid paying income tax by calling something a gift when it isn't. For example, a "gift" you receive in exchange for services or some other consideration isn't a gift.
- **Income after gift.** If you receive a gift of property that produces income, you must report any income produced after the gift. For example, if you receive stock as a gift, you must report any dividends paid on that stock after the gift.

No deduction except for charitable gifts. Some people hear that you can make an annual gift to a child "tax-free" and wonder if this means they can claim a deduction for such gifts. I'm afraid the answer is no. There is no deduction for gifts—except gifts to qualifying charities as explained in Chapter 22. The annual exclusion allows you to avoid paying *gift tax*. It does not affect your *income tax*.

Basis and holding period. If the gift consists of property other than cash, it's important for the recipient to know the basis and holding period of the property. That way the recipient knows how much gain or loss to report on a sale, and whether the gain or loss is short-term or long-term. Chapter 11 provides an explanation of the rules for determining basis and holding period for property received as a gift.

The unified transfer tax

Federal estate and gift tax work hand in hand. Gifts you make during your lifetime can affect the amount of estate tax that's owed at your death.

To understand this, begin with the estate tax. This tax generally doesn't kick in until you leave a total of more than $12,920,000 (as of 2023) to people other than your spouse or a charity. The way this works is there is a *credit* that applies against the estate tax, to wipe out the tax that would otherwise apply to this much of your taxable estate.

This same credit is used against the gift tax. If you make a taxable gift, you don't actually pay tax on the gift unless the total amount of taxable gifts in your lifetime is greater than the amount that's exempt from estate tax. Because the same credit is used for both taxes—it's called the *unified credit*—any part of the credit that gets used up because of taxable gifts will reduce the amount of credit that's available for your estate when you die.

For wealthier individuals, it often makes sense to use the unified credit during their lifetime. But you don't want to use it unnecessarily if you think there's any chance your taxable estate will be large enough so the estate tax will apply. That's where the gift tax annual exclusion comes in.

Gifts tax annual exclusion

Under the gift tax you can give an annual amount to each donee each year without reporting a taxable gift. The amount is adjusted for inflation in $1,000 increments. As of 2023 the annual amount is $17,000. If you're married, you and your spouse can jointly give twice that amount per donee each year, even if the entire gift comes from just one of you. (To do this, you and your spouse must file gift tax returns and elect "gift-splitting.") You can use this rule to remove a large dollar amount of assets from your estate without incurring any gift tax or reducing your unified credit.

> **Example:** Suppose you're married and have three adult children, each of whom is married. Each year, you can give double the annual exclusion amount to each child, and to the spouse of each child, for total gifts of twelve times the annual exclusion amount per year without any gift tax implications.

This exclusion applies only to gifts that take effect right away, called gifts of *present interests*. If you want to make your gift through a trust, you need to have an expert make certain the trust contains provisions that will prevent your gift from being a *future interest*. Trusts that meet this requirement are often called *Crummey trusts*, named after a case that clarified the tax treatment of this type of trust.

You can also make gifts of present interests through a custodial account under the Uniform Transfers to Minors Act. These gifts are considered present interests (and therefore qualify for the annual gift tax exclusion) even though the minor does not gain control until age 18 or 21. See Chapter 21 for more about custodial accounts.

Other exclusions

The annual exclusion isn't the only way to make gifts without incurring gift tax. There's an unlimited exclusion for gifts to your spouse. (An annual limit applies if your spouse is not a United States citizen, but it's about ten times the usual gift tax exclusion.) There's also an unlimited exclusion for the payment of medical expenses or educational costs, provided you make these payments directly to the service provider or educational institution.

21

Custodial Accounts for Minors

PEOPLE WITH CHILDREN (or other young relatives) sometimes think of setting up investment accounts for kids. State laws make it easy to set up *custodial accounts* for minors and relatively simple to administer them. A custodial account can be an excellent way of introducing a minor to the world of investing, or establishing a fund that helps a young adult get started. These accounts have drawbacks, however, so you should make sure you understand what you're getting into before putting a lot of money in a custodial account.

Custodial account basics

A minor child can't maintain a brokerage account, even with the permission of his or her parents. Only persons who have reached the *age of majority*—18 in most states—can buy and sell stocks. Many years ago, the only way to transfer stock ownership to a child was to establish a trust. Custodial accounts are designed to provide a simpler and less costly way of transferring stock and other assets to a child.

Each state has its own law for custodial accounts. The laws are based on a model called the Uniform Transfers to Minors Act, and custodial accounts are often called UTMA accounts. The laws are uniform in the sense of being based on the same model, but they differ in various details. In particular, not all states use the same age of maturity to transfer control of assets to the child. In some states, the child gets the assets at age 18, in others at age 21, and in some states the person who sets up the account can choose between these two ages. Comments here about the "Act" refer to the model on which the state laws are based. Your own state's law may differ.

> Nearly all states have replaced the earlier Uniform *Gifts* to Minors Act with the more modern Uniform *Transfers* to Minors Act, but some people still refer to *UGMA* accounts from force of habit.

Ownership. The first important thing to understand about custodial accounts is that *the child owns the assets.* Even though control of the assets has not yet passed to the child, *ownership* has passed as soon as you put money or other assets into a custodial account. *Custodial assets belong to the child.* That simple fact answers many of the questions people have about custodial accounts:

Q: *Can I take back the money I transferred to the account?*

A: No, the child owns that money now.

Q: *Can I move money from an account set up for one child to another child's account?*

A: No, because the money in a child's account belongs to that child.

Q: *Who pays tax on the account's income and gains?*

A: The child does, because the child is the owner of the account's assets.

Custodian. Although the child is owner of the account, control of the assets is in the hands of the *custodian*. The custodian can be, but doesn't have to be, the person who transferred cash or other property to the account. The custodian has several responsibilities:

- The custodian must prudently invest the custodial assets.
- The custodian must maintain records of all transactions and provide tax information to the child or, if the child is too young, to the person responsible for filing the child's tax return.
- The custodian determines what expenditures to make on behalf of the child from account assets.
- When the child reaches the age specified by the relevant state law, the custodian must turn the account over to the child.

When custodial accounts are suitable

Custodial accounts are a wonderful convenience when used for suitable purposes. Yet many people who set up these accounts end up regretting that they did. Here are some of the main reasons for what I call *UTMA regret*:

- The account was intended for the child's education, but the child has other ideas about how to use it, and will obtain full control at age 18.
- Parents who contributed to the account find that they need cash to buy a new house or for some other reason, but can't use this account because it belongs to their child.
- The account established for the first child made some fortunate investments and is now far larger than the account established years later for a younger sibling, and there's no way to equalize the accounts.
- The account reduces the amount of student financial aid the child qualifies for in college, to a much greater extent than if the parents held the same assets.

Before you set up a custodial account, ask yourself *why*. There are certainly some good reasons to do this. You may want to introduce the child to principles of investing by letting him or her participate in investment decisions and see how the account grows. You may want to provide the child with a nest egg with which to be "launched" into adulthood—bearing in mind that the child may not be mature enough to handle this sum of money well, and may have to chalk up a waste of these funds to experience.

What's more, custodial accounts can produce tax savings by shifting income into the child's tax bracket. You can shift capital gains to the child, too, even when the property increased in value before you made the gift. We'll see in Chapter 33 that the tax savings from shifting income and capital gains are quite limited for children under age 24, however.

You should think twice before accumulating large amounts of money in a custodial account. These accounts are not well designed for estate planning. They adversely affect eligibility for student financial aid. They place the child in complete control of financial assets at an age when the child may have foolish ideas about how to handle them.

There are better alternatives for setting aside larger dollar amounts. Trusts are a little more complicated than custodial accounts but provide protections in terms of how and when the money is used, and also can be far better vehicles for estate planning. If you simply want to save for college in a way that makes more sense than using a custodial account, consider using a 529 plan or a Coverdell education savings account. Then again, you can simply keep the assets in your own name, perhaps in a separate account that you intend to turn over to your child or use for the child's benefit.

Let me emphasize that I'm not *anti-UTMA*. I had custodial accounts for my own children. Yet I'm amazed at the number of messages received at my web site from people who regret setting up these accounts. It's a lot easier to get into that situation than to get out of it.

Using custodial accounts

UTMA accounts are not just for investing. The custodian is allowed to use money in the account for the benefit of the minor. Specifically, the Uniform Act says:

> A custodian may deliver or pay to the minor or expend for the minor's benefit so much of the custodial property as the custodian considers advisable for the use and benefit of the minor, without court order and without regard to (i) the duty or ability of the custodian personally or of any other person to support the minor, or (ii) any other income or property of the minor which may be applicable or available for that purpose.

That's a pretty liberal standard! An earlier version of the Act contained the words, "for the support, maintenance, education and benefit of the minor," leading some people to believe custodial property could be used only for items that would constitute *support.* The current version, which is in effect in nearly all states, uses the more generous words, "for the use and benefit of the minor." Official commentary on the Act says this change was "intended to avoid the implication that the custodial property can be used only for the required support of the minor."

> **Note:** As custodian, you're supposed to be able to account for where the money went. If you pulled money from the account to buy a computer for your child, make a permanent record of this fact.

Here are some of the questions that come up most often:

Support. Some people have the idea you can't use a custodial account to cover expenses that fall within a parent's support obligation. If you read the language quoted above, you'll see that it clearly permits use of the account *without regard to the duty of any person to support the child.* We'll see below that there's at least a theoretical tax issue if you use the account to satisfy a support obligation, but the Uniform Act says that if the custodian uses the account for the minor's benefit, it doesn't matter if the custodian or someone else has a support obligation.

> This is not to say that a divorced parent can draw from the account to make child support payments to a former spouse. In this case the account is being used for the benefit of the parent with the obligation rather than being used for the benefit of the child.

Costs of education. *Of course* you can use these accounts to pay for the child's education. That's probably the biggest single use. For reasons explained above, this isn't likely to be the best way to save for college, but if you want to use a custodial account for college costs (or costs of primary or secondary education) that's clearly proper.

Car for the child. Your child needs an auto? Why not? It's an expenditure for the benefit of the child. A car for your own use, which may include driving the child to soccer practice, is another question, though.

Paying taxes on the child's income. The child owns the account, and is liable for tax on any income the account generates. Since the child owes the tax, a withdrawal from the account to pay the tax is a payment for the benefit of the child.

Transfer to another child. Sometimes one child ends up with an account that's larger than the parent can provide for a sibling, due to a later start or a difference in the way the account was invested. Can you make a transfer from one account to the other to "even things up"? As a parent I sympathize with the motive, but I can't see how that's proper under the Act. The child with the larger account *owns* the account. Taking money from that account to transfer to a sibling's account may, in some philosophical way, be for the benefit of both children. Yet I believe the Act requires a more direct benefit to the child who owns the account.

Paying family expenses. You can get into some tough issues here. Suppose tapping the account is the only way the parent can afford to live in a nice neighborhood. Suppose further that the reason the parent wants to live in the nice neighborhood is better schools and environment for the child. Can you charge rent from the child and pay it from the account? Use the account for part of the down payment on a home? If push came to shove I would have to say these types of expenditures are probably improper under the Act, but others may disagree.

Tax treatment of custodial accounts

In nearly all cases, a transfer to a custodial account is a gift, although a custodial account may also be used to hold assets the child inherits, or even money the child earns. The tax treatment of gifts is discussed in Chapters 11 and 20. Apart from tax consequences that apply to gifts in general, there are no special tax rules for transfers to custodial accounts. There is no limit on the amount that can be transferred in this way.

As mentioned briefly earlier, you have to report income and gains from custodial accounts as income of the minor. The tax law treats the child exactly as if he or she had direct control of the assets, with no custodian intervening.

Generally, withdrawals from custodial accounts have no significance at all. Of course, if you sell assets to make the withdrawal, gain or loss from the sale will appear on the child's tax return for the year of the sale. Also, the custodian should maintain records of all amounts withdrawn from the account and how those amounts were used. There's no tax reporting for the withdrawals per se, though.

Many years ago, the IRS issued a ruling saying that if custodial assets are used to satisfy a support obligation, income of the account is taxable to the person having the support obligation. How much do you need to worry about this? It's unclear. The Act specifically says that payments made from a custodial account for the benefit of the minor don't affect the support obligation of any person. This language was included specifically to prevent attribution of income. While the issue hasn't been tested in court, there is some question whether income from a custodial account would be taxed to a person other than the minor under this old ruling.

22

Charitable Gifts of Stock

AT SOME POINT YOU'RE LIKELY TO HEAR that charitable gifts of stock can provide better tax benefits than charitable gifts of cash. (I hear this all the time from my law school alumni association.) There are a few things you should know if you're planning such a gift.

Overview

If you give cash to a qualified charity, and you choose to claim itemized deductions on your tax return, you can deduct your charitable contribution up to a limit, which the Tax Cuts and Jobs Act increase from 50% to 60% of adjusted gross income.

> **Example:** You contribute $24,000 to charity this year. Assuming your adjusted gross income is greater than $40,000, you can claim the entire $24,000 as a deduction. If your adjusted gross income for the year turned out to be $36,000, you would deduct $21,600 this year and carry the remaining $2,400 forward as a possible deduction the following year.

If you give stock instead of cash, you may be able to deduct the full value of the stock, even though you bought the stock at a lower value and never paid tax on the gain.

> **Example:** You bought 200 shares of XYZ in 2008 for $8,000. The shares are now worth $20,000. If you contribute the shares to charity, you can claim a charitable contribution deduction of $20,000 even though you never paid tax on your $12,000 gain.

That's an important advantage. If you sold the stock instead of contributing it to charity, you would pay federal income tax on the gain. At the 15% rate, for example, you would pay $1,800. Then you would have only $18,200 left to contribute to charity. You would contribute a smaller amount to charity, and receive a smaller charitable contribution deduction. Giving the stock allows you to provide a larger benefit to the charity *and* claim a larger tax deduction.

Important details

Giving shares of stock to charity is a perfectly legitimate way of obtaining a tax benefit from your contributions. In planning such a contribution, keep the following points in mind:

- **It's still a contribution.** This form of contribution gives you more bang for your charitable buck—but the tax benefits are not so great that you come out ahead of where you would be if you didn't make the contribution. If you're inclined to make a charitable contribution, it makes sense to get the best possible tax result from that contribution, but don't forget the value of what you're giving away is still greater than the tax benefits.
- **Appreciated stock only.** There's no special tax advantage in giving away stock that hasn't gone up in value. In fact, if stock has gone down in value, it's generally better to sell the stock

and make a gift of the proceeds. That way you can claim a deduction for your capital loss on the stock.

- **Long-term shares only.** This is an important point that some financial advisors forget: you get a tax benefit only if you held the stock more than a year before making the contribution. In the example above where you bought the stock for $8,000 and contributed it when it was worth $20,000, your deduction would be only $8,000 if you held the stock a year or less at the time of the contribution.
- **Stock from options.** If you acquired stock by exercising an incentive stock option, a charitable gift of this stock may not be good tax planning, even after you've satisfied the special holding period for this type of stock. The reason is that tax on a sale of this stock may be offset by a credit for the AMT you paid when you exercised the option.
- **Lower limit applies.** The limit on charitable contribution deductions is lower for property than for cash. As mentioned earlier, your deduction for cash gifts is limited to 60% of your adjusted gross income. For gifts of property, the limit is 30% of your adjusted gross income. If you make $100,000 and give more than $30,000 worth of stock or other property, you'll have to claim only part of your contribution as a deduction and carry the rest forward for possible deduction in a later year.

Unfortunately, the tax rules for charitable contributions are just as complicated as tax rules for anything else. The summary above would change, for example, if you were making a contribution to a *private foundation* instead of a public charity. There are many other rules relating to charitable contributions. If you're planning to make a very substantial gift, it may pay to have a tax professional with expertise in this area review your plans.

Part VI
Taxation of Traders

23

Introduction to Trader Status

ALMOST FROM THE VERY BEGINNING OF THE INCOME TAX, the courts and the IRS have divided taxpayers who buy and sell stocks into three categories: investors, dealers and traders. *Investors* generally seek to profit by *holding* stocks: they look for dividends or rising stock prices, or both. *Dealers* seek to profit from transactions in which they sell securities to customers: they buy stock to sell it as inventory, not for the purpose of obtaining investment returns.

Traders make up the third category. They seek their profits in short-term price swings. They may have little or no interest in the outlook for the company they're trading because they don't hold shares for long periods. Traders have been known to trade a stock without knowing anything at all about a company except the stock symbol and the recent trading patterns. Yet traders aren't dealers because they don't have customers. They buy and sell to secure the profits they can from the stock market's zigs and zags.

Trader definition

You're a trader if your activity of buying and selling stocks meets two requirements. First is the *trading activity test.* This test looks at the type of buying and selling you do. As outlined above, you pass this test if your trading approach is designed to capture short-term swings in stock prices. See Chapter 25 for more details on this test.

The second requirement is the *substantial activity test.* Here we're looking at how serious you are about trading. Do you consistently do enough trading over a long enough period of time so we can consider your activity a business? Or is it merely something you do on the side, albeit with a hope of scoring some big profits? Chapter 26 provides details on this test.

You aren't a trader unless you pass both tests. We'll see later that there are a number of cases where taxpayers engaged in very substantial market activity, yet failed to qualify as traders because their activity was investing, not trading. Likewise, there are cases where the taxpayer may have done some trading, looking for short-term market swings, but wasn't considered a trader because the volume of trading wasn't large enough over a long enough period of time.

Someone who fails either test is considered an *investor.* The term makes sense when you fail the trading activity test, because that means you're seeking investment returns, usually by making relatively long-term investments. Yet the term also applies when you fail the substantial activity test. This is a strange use of the term, because it may apply to someone who never holds stock more than an hour at a time. If that's your approach, you're not much of an investor in the normal sense of that word. Under the tax law, though, if you don't pass the substantial activity test you're not a trader, and that means you're treated as an investor.

Tax treatment of traders

The tax law treats traders in some ways the same as investors, and in other ways better than investors. They are the same as investors in the following respects:

- Profits and losses from buying and selling stocks are capital gain or loss, not ordinary income or loss.
- Brokerage commissions are used in computing gains and losses, not as a separate business deduction.
- Traders are subject to the wash sale rule.
- Traders don't pay self-employment tax on profits from trading stocks.

Yet there are important ways in which traders are treated differently from investors:

- Interest expense (usually margin interest) is a business expense, so it isn't subject to the investment interest limitation.
- For investors, many other investment expenses are limited or not allowed at all as a deduction. Traders may be able to claim these expenses as business deductions.

See Chapter 27 for more details on the tax rules for traders.

Mark-to-market

Beginning in 1997, securities traders have been allowed to elect a special tax treatment called "mark-to-market" accounting. *You don't have to make this election to be considered a trader.* If you make the election, the following special tax rules apply:

- Any shares you hold at the end of the year are treated as sold on that date for an amount equal to the fair market value of the shares. You report any gain or loss that results from this deemed sale.

- The wash sale rule doesn't apply to your trading activity.
- Profits and losses from your trading activity are treated as ordinary income and loss, not capital gain and loss. Although your trading profits are ordinary income, they still are not subject to self-employment tax.

Chapter 28 provides details on the consequences of this election and how you make it.

Explaining trader taxation

The tax treatment of traders is unusual to the point of being almost unbelievable. Knowledgeable tax professionals who have never studied trader taxation are likely to look at the tax treatment described above and say it simply can't be right. So before we get into details of what the rules are, we'll look at details of how the rules came to be. Chapter 24 provides a complete explanation, and legal citations tax professionals can use to confirm that the treatment described here is correct.

24

The Trader and the Platypus

WHEN THE FIRST PLATYPUS WAS BROUGHT FROM AUSTRALIA to England, people figured it had to be a hoax. Here was an animal that had to be considered a mammal because it had fur and fed its young on breast milk—yet it had a flat bill and webbed feet like a duck, and laid eggs. The idea was preposterous, and the more you knew about biology, the more likely it was you would refuse to believe such an animal existed.

At the risk of offending traders, I compare them to the duck-billed platypus, at least when it comes to taxes. The tax treatment of traders is a unique mixture of rules for investors and rules for businesses:

- Traders don't sell goods or services to customers, yet they're considered to have a business.
- Despite having a business, traders don't pay self-employment tax on their income.
- Traders report deductions on Schedule C (used for businesses) but report their trading income on Schedule D (used for

capital gains and losses). As a result, Schedule C nearly always shows a loss, even when the trading activity is profitable.

The more you know about taxes, the stranger these characteristics seem. Like a mammal that lays eggs, trader taxation simply doesn't fit anything we know about the world. Many experienced tax professionals who lack specific knowledge of trader taxation simply refuse to believe the statements above can possibly be true.

A willingness to understand and accept these rules has become more widespread as the IRS has included information about the general characteristics of trader taxation in its instructions for Schedule D and in Publication 550. Nevertheless, you may encounter misinformation on this subject, even from sources that are normally quite reliable:

- For many years, the web site of one of the top accounting firms included a statement that "according to recent cases" you can't be a trader unless you perform transactions for others. In reality the opposite is true: if you perform transactions for others, you aren't a trader as that term is used in the tax law.
- An individual who had many years of experience hosting the tax message board of a popular investment web site insisted the income of traders should be treated as ordinary income, not capital gain. Yet the law for more than 60 years has been that trading profits and losses are capital.
- A tax professional in New York City requested clarification of trader taxation from the IRS. The request went to someone who lacked knowledge of trader taxation, and a letter came back saying traders can't report gains and losses on Schedule D while taking expense deductions on Schedule C. According to this letter, "Such 'best of both worlds' treatment is clearly not allowed under the [Internal Revenue] Code and Regulations." At the same time the IRS was preparing this letter, another group within the IRS was preparing form instructions correctly stating that trader gains and losses go on Schedule D, while trader expenses go on Schedule C.

The people who made these blunders are not fools. In fact, they're professionals who normally provide accurate information—just like the biologists who confidently proclaimed that an egg-laying mammal must be a hoax. They are reacting to claims that seem absurd in light of their training.

Endangered species

One reason for so much neglect of this subject is that most of the rules of trader taxation don't appear in the Internal Revenue Code and regulations. Instead, they appear in opinions issued by judges who decided scores of cases involving trader classification. When you need an answer about trader taxation, there's no convenient way to look it up.

There's another reason so few people have knowledge of trader taxation. Until recently, very few people were traders. In fact, it was almost impossible to be a trader without trading on the floor of an exchange. By definition, traders are people who buy and sell rapidly. That's a recipe to go broke in a hurry if you're paying high commissions, burdened with large spreads, and relying on outdated information, all of which were likely not long ago.

In recent years we've seen commissions fall to a small fraction of what they once were. The bid-ask spread is also much smaller than it was at one time. Real-time quotes and other current information are as close as the nearest Internet connection. It's still hard for someone other than a floor trader to make money trading in and out of stocks rapidly, but it's no longer impossible.

The result was an explosion in the number of people engaged in short-term trading during the bull market of the late 1990's. Not all of these people qualify as traders, but it's a safe bet that the number of people with a legitimate claim to that status in 2000 was many times the number in 1990. The IRS has provided us with some basic guidance in the instructions for tax forms, beginning in the year 2000.

Yet we're still faced with a situation where many skilled tax practitioners are puzzled by the seemingly bizarre tax rules that apply to traders. The remainder of this chapter explains how these rules came to be as they are. We'll also look at the frequently made comment that these rules can't be correct because they're "too good to be true."

The bike man cometh

From the very beginning of the income tax we've had to distinguish between business activities and non-business activities. For example, you can deduct expenses if you raise dogs as a business, but if you raise dogs as a hobby your deductions are limited to income from that activity. Sometimes it's hard to draw the line between business and non-business, but the line must be drawn because it determines how much tax you pay.

Early decisions by the Board of Tax Appeals (predecessor of today's Tax Court) established that buying and selling stock for your own account can be a business. A good example is the *Ignaz Schwinn* case [9 BTA 1304 (1928)]. Schwinn's last name is well known because he organized a successful bicycle manufacturing company. Yet during a number of years when that business was in low gear he spent more time playing the market (both stocks and commodities) than running the bicycle business. In 1924 he had a loss of nearly $70,000 on a sale of 2,300 shares of Anaconda Copper stock he bought in 1919. Under the law then in effect, Schwinn was entitled to a full deduction for this loss if it was connected with a business. The loss wasn't connected with the bicycle business, but the court found that Schwinn's trading activities were a business and allowed the loss.

Schwinn's loss wouldn't be allowed today. For one thing, he probably wouldn't be considered a trader, because his trading wasn't short-term (see Chapter 25). In addition, traders are now subject to the same capital loss limitations as investors, unless they make the mark-to-market election. We'll return to capital gain in a few moments. First, though, let's focus on an issue that gives fits to many tax professionals.

Trading for your own account

The Board of Tax Appeals found that Ignaz Schwinn's market activity was a business, even though he was trading for his own account—in other words, not on behalf of his bicycle company or anyone else. He wasn't providing goods or services to anyone else: he was simply trying to make trading profits for himself. Some tax professionals will tell you this type of activity can't be a business. They believe you must have *customers*, or trade for others, to have a business.

Perhaps that notion comes from *Deputy v. DuPont* [308 US 488 (1940)], a famous tax case in which the United States Supreme Court denied deductions connected with the stock dealings of Pierre duPont. The Court said duPont incurred the expenses for the benefit of the corporation (not for his own benefit) and also that they weren't "ordinary and necessary" expenses, as required to claim a business deduction. In a concurring opinion, though, Justice Frankfurter said there was another, simpler reason to deny the deduction: to have a business, you must "hold [yourself] out to others as engaged in the selling of goods or services."

Justice Frankfurter's comment was strange because it was already firmly established, in cases like *Schwinn*, that trading for your own account can be a business. It doesn't seem likely that he intended his brief remarks to suggest that all those cases were incorrect. As we'll see shortly, Congress had recognized six years earlier, in connection with a change in the definition of capital assets, that a "stock speculator" may have a business for tax purposes. In any event, the courts never adopted the approach Justice Frankfurter suggested in his concurring opinion.

The IRS made at least one attempt to apply the Frankfurter approach to a trader, but seemed to abandon that effort after losing the *Fuld* case [139 F2d 465 (2d Cir 1943)]. Some years later, the IRS tried to use this theory on professional gamblers, saying they can't claim business deductions because gamblers don't provide goods or services to customers. The IRS won some of these cases but lost others, and in 1987 the United States Supreme Court decided the *Groetzinger* case [480 US 23 (1987)] to resolve the issue. The result was a resounding defeat for the IRS.

The opinion pointed out that the Supreme Court as a whole had never endorsed Justice Frankfurter's idea that a business had to have customers. Furthermore—and most important for our purposes—the opinion noted that traders, like gamblers, have no customers, yet they have long been considered to have a business. In fact, the IRS conceded as much in oral argument. The Court decided to "formally reject the Frankfurter gloss which the Court has never adopted anyway."

The *Groetzinger* case eliminates all argument on this issue. The Supreme Court could not have been more definitive in concluding that you can have a trade or business without having customers. What's more, although the case involved a gambler rather than a trader, it discusses trader cases and cites them with approval.

Too good to be true? What all this means is that traders—individuals who meet the requirements described in the following chapters—treat their expenses as business deductions. The "miscellaneous" deductions that for investors were previously subject to a 2% floor, and now are entirely disallowed, are deductible for a trader. To some tax professionals this seems too good to be true, if a trader is simply someone who buys and sells stock for his own account, as an investor does.

Yet that's what it *means* to be a trader. A trader is someone whose activity qualifies as a business under the tax law. That means a trader's expenses are business deductions, not investment deductions.

If you believe traders shouldn't be permitted to claim business deductions, you're missing the entire point of trader classification: determining that the activity should be treated as a business.

Traders and capital gain

Tax professionals are used to the idea that business profits are ordinary income, not capital gain. If trading is a business, then the profits from trading can't be capital gain, right? Wrong.

In the early days, traders (or "speculators," as they were usually called then) did *not* have capital gains and losses. That was the point of the *Schwinn* case discussed earlier: the taxpayer wanted to avoid the limitation on capital losses. By establishing that his trading activity was a business, Ignaz Schwinn was able to claim a business deduction, not a capital loss, on his stock sale.

Congress decided the capital loss limitation should apply to traders, and accomplished this by changing the definition of *capital asset*. Before 1934, capital assets did not include "property held by the taxpayer primarily for sale in the course of his trade or business." The new definition used almost the same words, but now an asset was excluded only if it was held for sale *to customers*. The specific purpose of this change, as explained in the *Fuld* case discussed earlier, was to prevent stock speculators from avoiding the capital loss limitation.

In making this change, Congress recognized that stock speculation—trading—can be a business, but specified that the profits and losses from the business would be treated as capital gains and losses. That fundamental approach to trader taxation remained unchanged for more than six decades, and is still in force except for traders who make the mark-to-market election as explained in Chapter 28.

Too good to be true? Traders are treated as having a business, so they can claim business deductions, yet their profits are treated as capital gain. At first blush, this result seems too good to be true. If you stop and think for a moment you'll see that this isn't so. Trader profits are nearly all *short-term* capital gain, taxed at the same rates as ordinary income, so there's no benefit there. Yet trader losses are subject to the $3,000 per year capital loss limitation—a limitation that doesn't apply to other types of business losses. Capital gain treatment of trader profits is more harm than benefit because of the capital loss limitation. Avoiding this disadvantage is one of the main reasons for making the mark-to-market election (Chapter 28).

Self-employment income

Here's another place tax professionals—including some of the tax professionals who work for the IRS—sometimes go wrong. Normally, if you carry on a business, the net income from that business is subject to self-employment tax. This tax replaces the usual social security tax that applies when you work as an employee. It can be a heavy hit, because employers and employees each pay half of the social security tax. When you're self-employed, you're both the employer and the employee, so the self-employment tax is roughly double the social security tax you would pay as an employee. It would potentially be a significant disadvantage of trader status if you had to pay that tax.

Yet the self-employment tax doesn't apply to trader income. This has always been true for traders whose income consists of capital gain, because the law quite plainly excludes capital gain from the definition of self-employment income. It's possible that a trader could have some incidental income that isn't capital gain. In the rare case where such income exceeds deductible expenses, the net amount would be subject to self-employment tax.

When Congress changed the law to provide the mark-to-market election for securities traders, there was some question as to whether traders who made the election would be subject to self-employment tax. That's because the election converts trading profits and losses into ordinary income or loss. Yet Congress didn't intend the self-employment tax to apply, even when traders make the mark-to-market election, so an amendment was adopted (see section 475(f)(1)(D)) to clarify that even in this case, the income of a trader is not self-employment income.

Too good to be true? The law is now perfectly clear that traders don't pay self-employment tax on their trading profits, regardless of whether they made the mark-to-market election. To many people it will seem as if traders are getting away with something. Yet there's a flip side to this rule. If trading profits aren't self-employment income, then traders can't use those profits to qualify for social security benefits. Those benefits are determined in part by the number of years worked and the amount paid in social security tax or self-employment tax, so a trader may end up with lower benefits than someone in a different type of business.

Perhaps more important, a trader can't use his or her trading profits as a basis for contributing to IRAs and other retirement plans. The generous tax treatment of retirement savings is one of the best deals available under the tax law. Many traders would be much better off if they could treat their trading profits as self-employment income and sock away money in a tax-qualified retirement plan. That's an opportunity traders simply don't have.

25

The Trading Activity Test

MANY BOOKS ON INVESTING WILL TELL YOU the best way to accumulate wealth is to buy good stocks and hold them long-term. Avoid "churning"—the frequent buying and selling that eats away at investment accounts. When you hold long-term, your expenses are lower, your taxes are lower, and you make a lot fewer mistakes.

If that's the way you operate, you may be a good investor but you aren't a trader under the tax law. The cases firmly establish that trader status is available only if your primary focus is the small zigs and zags that happen over minutes, hours and days. If your goal is to benefit from price changes that occur over months and years—or from other forms of investment income, such as interest and dividends—then you're an investor, not a trader. That's true no matter how much time you devote to your investments.

History

In the earliest cases, courts didn't always apply the trading activity test. The *Schwinn* case, described in Chapter 24, is a good example. The court found that the taxpayer's buying and selling of stocks and commodities was a business without seeming to focus on whether the trading was short-term. In fact, the issue in that case was how to treat a loss from stock held more than two years.

Not long after these early cases, the IRS began to assert that the activity of investing should not be considered a business even when people devote a great deal of time and energy to that activity. Taxpayers won some cases and lost others. In 1941, the Supreme Court decided to clear the air.

Eugene Higgins [312 US 212 (1941)] had extensive investments in real estate, bonds and stocks, and devoted "a considerable portion of his time" to the oversight of these financial interests. In fact, he rented offices and hired others to help him by keeping records, receiving securities, interest and dividend checks, making deposits and so forth. The IRS said Higgins should not be allowed to deduct these expenses because they didn't arise in a business. The Supreme Court agreed:

> The petitioner merely kept records and collected interest and dividends from his securities, through managerial attention for his investments. No matter how large the estate or how continuous or extended the work required may be, such facts are not sufficient as a matter of law to permit the courts to reverse the decision [against the taxpayer].

After *Higgins*, it was reasonably clear that long-term investors could not qualify as traders. Every now and then someone would try to get around this requirement, but the courts stood firm.

The *Yaeger* case [889 F2d 29 (2d Cir 1989)] provides a good example. Louis Yaeger's stock trading was so extensive that he maintained an office at his brokerage firm. He spent a full day at the office, then "returned home to read more financial reports late into the night," working every day of the week, right up until the day before he died.

Yet his activity was clearly investing, not trading. He had over 1,000 securities transactions per year, but nearly all of them were purchases with only a few sales. His investment strategy involved the purchase of distressed companies whose underlying value was not recognized. He had some short-term capital gains, but a far greater portion of his income was from dividends and long-term capital gains. Under the rule established in the *Higgins* case, Yaeger couldn't be considered a trader, so the court ruled for the IRS.

The more recent *Endicott* case [T.C. Memo. 2013-199] offers another example. The taxpayer pursued (with painful results) a covered call strategy, simultaneously acquiring stock and selling options against those shares. The Tax Court found that this strategy was inconsistent with a trading activity geared toward profiting from short-term swings in market prices.

How short is short?

Many day traders sell all their holdings at the end of the day. Clearly their activity is trading, not investing. Yet you don't have to be a day trader to be a trader. Someone who often holds stocks several days at a time should still be considered a trader, not an investor.

Beyond this, though, there isn't a lot of guidance in the cases. The courts sometimes look at how much gain is long-term (more than a year), but my sense is that this is simply a convenient fact to mention in the opinion. I doubt that someone with an average holding period of nine months would be considered a trader, even though that's less than a year. A court is likely to conclude that when you hold stock that long, you're looking for an investment return, not a trading profit.

Does Strategy Matter?

In a doubtful case, the court might look beyond the holding period to consider the strategy. An average holding period of six weeks might come from following a short-term trading strategy based on technical analysis—or simply be the result of impatience or market turbulence affecting someone who is engaged in investing, not trading. Until we see cases of this nature, though, we can't be certain how the courts will approach them.

Other investment income

Some courts have noted the amount of other investment income the taxpayer had, as a way of indicating that his activity was investing, not trading. If the income from an activity was mostly interest, dividends and long-term capital gain, it might seem reasonable to conclude that the activity was investing, not trading.

I would suggest, though, that courts should distinguish between the amount of short-term capital gain and the amount of short-term *trading activity*. It's possible for a trader to end up with a very small profit (or even a loss) despite making over a hundred million dollars in trades. In this situation, the fact that interest income happened to be greater than the income from short-term trades should not be viewed as an indication that the individual is primarily an investor.

Traders as investors

Can you be *both* an investor and a trader? There's no question that you can. It would be perfectly reasonable to set aside some of your assets as an investment fund that isn't part of your trading activity. If you otherwise qualify as a trader, you shouldn't lose that status because you also hold stocks as an investment.

If you fail to keep the two activities separate, though, you could cast doubt on whether you qualify as a trader. It might appear that your short-term trading is part of your investing, rather than a distinct activity. Furthermore, if you commingle the activities it may be difficult to allocate your expenses between investing and trading in a way that will satisfy the IRS.

For that reason, if you maintain investments at the same time you're trading, you should take care to keep the two activities separate. Your investments should not be in the same account you use for trading, and any expenses relating to your investment activity should be recorded as investment expenses, not trading expenses. If you make the mark-to-market election, you're required to *identify* your investment securities, as described in Chapter 28.

26

The Substantial Activity Test

THE LATE 1990'S SAW AN EXPLOSION OF INTEREST in day trading: buying and selling stock within the same day, often within the same hour, in the hope of capturing very short-term movements in stock prices. There should be little doubt that day traders pass the trading activity test described in the preceding chapter. Yet they aren't considered traders for tax purposes unless they also pass the *substantial activity test.*

Frequent, regular and continuous

The substantial activity test is most often stated as a requirement that the trading activity be *frequent, regular and continuous.* These words don't establish a precise standard. Most of the cases dealing with this test are no-brainers—for example, situations where the taxpayer was obviously not a trader because he made fewer than 20 sale transactions per year. These cases give us only a limited amount of help in deciding where to draw the line between trading activity that does or does not qualify you as a trader. I've studied the cases, and here's what I make of them.

Number of trades

Probably the most important factor in this test is the number of trades. If you trade only a few times per month, your trading probably isn't frequent enough to qualify you as a trader. For example, in the *Boatner* case [TC Memo 1997-379], 75 trades in a year fell short of this standard.

How many trades are enough? There's no way to say with certainty. I imagine that 75 trades per *month* would easily qualify, although I can't point to a case that establishes this as a "safe" level for a trader. Assuming we could all agree that 75 trades per month qualifies as "frequent" trading, what about 50? Or 30? The cases provide no guidance on where to draw the line.

I heard one tax lawyer say that even a thousand trades per year probably isn't enough. She was probably thinking of the *Yaeger* case mentioned in the previous chapter. The taxpayer in that case wasn't a trader even though he had more than a thousand trades per year. Yet he failed to qualify because his primary activity was long-term investing. More than 90% of his trades were purchases. If he had made over a thousand short-term trades, I'm confident he would have been considered a trader. Don't confuse the trading activity test with the substantial activity test!

Consistent activity

Remember that "frequent" is only one of the words used to describe activity that passes this test. Even if your trading is frequent, you may not qualify as a trader if your activity isn't "regular and continuous."

Although the courts have used these words repeatedly, I'm aware of only one case that illustrates how they may be applied. In the *Paoli* case [TC Memo 1991-351], the taxpayer made over 300 sales within a year. Most of the sales were stock held less than a month, and more than 100 were day trades: stock bought and sold the same day.

Possibly this level of activity would have qualified the taxpayer as a trader if he traded consistently throughout the year. Yet nearly 40% of the trades occurred in a one-month period, and the number of trades per month fell off sharply in the following months, with only one trade occurring in the last quarter of the year. The court concluded that this pattern of trading was inconsistent with trader status.

The *Paoli* case is important because it reflects a pattern that arises frequently. Many would-be traders launch their activity with gusto, engaging in a large number of trades only to find that they are rapidly losing money. A trader in this position may pull back and regroup, perhaps trying to trade more selectively in hopes of finding a more profitable approach. Eventually this person may drop out of the game altogether, and wonder whether he or she can at least salvage a good tax result by filing as a trader.

Arguably it would have been more appropriate in *Paoli* to conclude that the taxpayer was a trader *for part of the year*. In the *Vines* case [126 TC No. 15 (2006)], the taxpayer was considered a trader even though he stopped trading shortly after he started (but not before losing over $25,000,000). The issue in this case was not whether he was a trader, but instead whether he should be allowed an extension of time to make the mark-to-market election.

Part-time traders

It's hard to imagine someone failing the substantial activity test while trading on a full-time basis. Yet many people trade during only part of the day, while holding a full-time job that does not involve trading. Some people seem to believe it isn't possible to qualify for trader status without trading full-time, but that's incorrect. We can point to only one case [*Carmel*, 134 BR 890 (Bkcy Ct ND Ill. 1991)], where a part-timer was found to be a trader, but there are others, such as the *Paoli* and *Boatner* cases cited earlier, in which the courts considered other factors before concluding that individuals who bought and sold on a part-time basis were not traders. If you can't be a trader without engaging in the activity full-time, these cases wasted a lot of time looking at other issues.

Although it's clear that you can be a trader on a part-time basis, you have to expect greater skepticism regarding your status if trading isn't your main activity. To overcome that skepticism, you need to show you spend enough time at trading to indicate that you take the activity seriously as a business. I can imagine someone failing to qualify as a trader despite frequent trading if the amount of time devoted to the activity was negligible, perhaps because all trades were based on a tip sheet to which that person subscribes. Success in establishing trader status may depend on your ability to make a plausible claim to have devoted many hours to the activity.

Dollar amount

A large dollar amount of trading isn't likely to qualify you as a trader if your trades are infrequent. This is likely to be a minor factor if it is considered at all. Yet a small dollar amount may indicate that you aren't serious about trading as a business, and could be a negative factor in a borderline case.

Professional approach

You have a better shot at qualifying as a trader if you take a professional approach to the activity. It should be helpful if you can show that you made a careful study of trading before plunging in; that you keep good records; that you trade based on analysis of some kind, not mere hunches. Of course these factors are also likely to contribute to your success as a trader, so you should follow these procedures in any event.

27

How Traders Are Taxed

THE TAX RULES FOR TRADERS ARE UNUSUAL—unique, in fact. Yet for the most part they follow from two simple principles:

- A trader is considered to be carrying on a business, so traders are entitled to business deductions (rather than the deductions allowed for investors).
- Although traders carry on a business, their trading profits and losses are capital gain and loss, not ordinary business income and loss.

Chapter 28 describes the mark-to-market election, which changes some of the rules described here. Be sure to read that chapter if you've made this election. Chapter 24 explains how the rules described here came to be as they are and provides references tax professionals can use to confirm that the rules stated here are correct.

Declaring trader status

People ask how they declare to the IRS that they intend to be taxed as a trader. Sometimes they ask how they *elect* to be a trader for tax purposes. Actually, no election is required. In effect, you declare that you're a trader by filing a Schedule C (used to report business income and expenses), and indicating the type of business as "securities trader."

Business deductions

When we call someone a trader, we're really saying his or her activity of buying and selling stock is a business. This is a simple point, but it's one where a lot of people, including knowledgeable tax professionals, get hung up. To some people it simply seems illogical that this type of activity can qualify as a business. Yet that's exactly what we're looking at when we determine whether someone is a trader. *By definition*, a trader is someone whose trading activity is considered a business for tax purposes.

Investment expenses were formerly allowed as a deduction only if you claimed itemized deductions on Schedule A and satisfied a threshold requirement. Beginning in 2018, with exceptions noted in Chapter 14, they are entirely nondeductible.

These rules don't apply to the deductions a trader incurs in his or her trading activity. This activity is a business, so the trader claims business deductions on Schedule C. Some important restrictions that apply to investment expense deductions don't apply to business deductions:

- Expenses that were, for investors, previously subject to the "2% floor" and now disallowed, can be claimed as business deductions.
- A trader can claim these deductions without itemizing.

- A trader's interest expense isn't subject to the investment interest limitation described in Chapter 14.
- A rule against deducting investment seminar expenses does not apply to trading seminars if you're a trader.
- A trader who uses a computer or other equipment mainly for his or her trading business may be entitled to a deduction for the cost of that equipment.
- If a trader devotes part of his or her home to the trading activity, a home office deduction may be allowed.

Except in the area of retirement benefits (see below), the rules for claiming deductions as a trader are generally the same as for any other small business. Bear in mind that brokerage commissions and other costs of buying and selling shares are not considered business expenses. Instead, these costs figure into the gain or loss you have when you sell shares.

Trading profits and losses

Your trading profits and losses are treated as capital gain or loss, even though your trading activity is a business. Way back in 1934 Congress changed the law to require this result, and it holds to this day unless you make the mark-to-market election as discussed in the following chapter. That means you report gains and losses from stock sales on Schedule D.

As a trader who hasn't made the mark-to-market election, you also have to deal with the wash sale rule (Chapter 10). At one time the wash sale rule didn't apply to individual traders. Unfortunately, Congress decided to change the law. The regulations still reflect the old law, but that's because they're out of date. It's clear that the wash sale rule applies.

Some traders engage in thousands of transactions per year, often trading the same stocks over and over again. The burden of reporting each individual trade, and working through the application of the wash sale rule in each instance, now falls on brokers. Their records and calculations may not always be accurate, and with a large volume of trades, it may not be possible as a practical matter to check their work. The mark-to-market election provides a partial solution because it eliminates the wash sale rule. The only other solution I'm aware of is to maintain good records and use the best available software.

Self-employment income

Traders don't pay self-employment tax on their trading income because this tax doesn't apply to capital gains. In theory, a trader could generate enough incidental income other than trading gains to incur some self-employment tax liability, but I've never seen that happen. This is one of the unique and surprising aspects of trader taxation: although your activity is a business, the income isn't considered self-employment income.

IRAs and retirement plans

You may be happy about avoiding self-employment tax, but there's a flip side you won't like as much. You can't contribute to an IRA or a retirement plan unless you have compensation income or self-employment income. Your trading income isn't self-employment income, so you can't use it to support an IRA or retirement plan contribution. Unless you have some other source of compensation income, you'll have to save for retirement without the benefit of one of these arrangements.

28

The Mark-to-Market Election

SINCE 1993, SECURITIES DEALERS have been required to use the *mark-to-market* system of accounting. Beginning in 1997, securities *traders* have been *permitted to elect* to use this system. If you're a trader and you make this election, your tax treatment will change:

- Any trading positions you hold at the end of the year will be treated as sold at fair market value on the last business day of the year, with the gain or loss reported just as if an actual sale occurred. This is what is meant by the term "mark-to-market."
- Gains and losses from your trading activity are treated as ordinary income and loss, not capital gain or loss.
- The wash sale rule does not apply to losses incurred in your trading activity.

You can probably tell right away that there are advantages and disadvantages to making the election. Avoiding the wash sale rule is certainly an advantage. What about the other two points?

Marking to market

For a true day trader, the requirement to treat year-end positions as sold is meaningless. If you sell all your positions at the end of each day, you certainly aren't going to be holding any positions at the end of the year. Day traders should consider the mark-to-market election because of the other tax consequences, but the actual process of marking to market won't apply to them.

You don't have to be a day trader to be a trader under the tax law, however. If you make this election and hold positions at the end of the year, this rule will affect you. In particular, you lose the ability to defer the gain from a winning position into the following year by delaying a sale of that position. Losing this flexibility can be a disadvantage for some traders, but for most traders this rule is of little or no consequence.

Ordinary income and loss

The mark-to-market election changes the character of your profit and loss from capital gain or loss to ordinary income or loss. This can have powerful tax consequences, both good and bad.

Trapping capital losses. An important point to consider in making the election is whether you'll end up trapping capital losses you had from an earlier year. Suppose, for example, you lost $30,000 during your first year as a trader. Because of the capital loss limitation, you were able to deduct only $3,000 of that loss. The remaining $27,000 carried forward to the present year. Now you're trading profitably, and considering the mark-to-market election for this year.

If your profitable trading continues, you might be better off *not* making the election. That way your profits will be capital gain, and you can absorb the $27,000 loss that was carried forward from the previous year. If you make the election, your profits will be ordinary income, and you'll be able to use only $3,000 of your loss carryover.

You'll carry the remaining $24,000 to the next year, but it may take another eight years to use the entire loss.

Of course, at the time you make the election you can't be certain how your year will turn out. (As you'll see below, you have to make the election early in the year.) If you have further losses, you may be glad you made the election, because it's easier to use ordinary losses than capital losses.

New losses. The mark-to-market election can provide more favorable treatment of any losses you may incur after the election takes effect. Changes in the law that took effect in 2018 curtail these benefits in some ways, but they can still provide substantial tax savings.

Under the mark-to-market election a trading loss is ordinary, not capital, which means it can offset ordinary income from another source without regard to the $3,000 capital loss limitation. Beginning in 2018, *excess business losses* are not allowed, but the threshold for this limitation is a generous $289,000 (for 2023), or double that amount if married filing jointly.

Ordinary business losses that exceed the amount you can deduct, either because of the excess business loss limitation or simply because you don't have enough income to absorb the loss, becomes a *net operating loss.* Beginning in 2018, these losses are no longer eligible to be carried back to years before the losses occurred. Yet they can be carried forward, and used to offset up to 80% of your income in a future year. Often this will be an advantage, but note that if you have a capital loss carryover, this 80% limitation wouldn't apply, which could be meaningful in a situation where you carry the loss forward to a year when all your income is capital gain.

Qualified business income deduction. Beginning in 2018, taxpayers can deduct 20% of their *qualified business income.* This term doesn't include capital gain, so trading profits of non-electing traders are not eligible. When you make the mark-to-market election, your capital gain is transformed into ordinary income, potentially eligible for this deduction.

The business of trading in securities is a *specified service trade or business* under the QBI rules. That means the deduction will be reduced or eliminated if your taxable income exceeds a threshold amount. For 2023, that figure is $364,200 for couples filing joint returns and half that amount for singles. With taxable income below the threshold, the mark-to-market election allows you to pay tax on only 80% of your trading profit, whereas the capital gain of a non-electing trader is fully taxable—and generally taxable at the highest rates because the gains are short-term.

Net investment income tax. Converting capital gain to ordinary income via the mark-to-market election does not allow traders to escape net investment income tax on their profits. For purposes of this additional tax (Chapter 30), trading profits continue to be treated as investment income.

Self-employment tax. Similarly, although the election converts your trading profits to ordinary income, you still don't have self-employment income. Congress felt that traders should be able to make this election without changing the status of their income for purposes of the self-employment tax, so a special exception provides that trading gains aren't self-employment income even if the trader makes this election and converts those gains to ordinary income.

Of course this means a trader who makes the election still can't use trading profits to support a contribution to an IRA or retirement plan. The two concepts go hand in hand. You avoid self-employment tax, but also lose the tax advantages of retirement plans.

Terminating the election

The mark-to-market election applies for the year you make the election *and all subsequent years*, unless the IRS grants permission to change the election. There may be some difficulty in obtaining that permission while your trading activity continues. Informal guidance from the IRS indicates, however, that they will generally grant a request to terminate the election if you are no longer engaged in trading.

Making the election

There are two important things to know: *when* to make the election, and *how* to make the election.

Timing. Most accounting elections are permitted at the time you file your tax return for the year of the election. That means you're making the election after the end of the year, when you know what effect the election will have on your results. That's not the case for the mark-to-market election, though. The IRS requires this election by the due date, *without extensions*, of the tax return for *the year before* the year for which the election is effective. In other words, you have to make it by April 15 of the year to which it applies, which is the due date for your tax return for the previous year. *If you miss this deadline, you have to wait until the next year to file the mark-to-market election.*

> If you have a good enough excuse for missing the deadline, you may be able to obtain an extension of time to file it. See *Vines v. Commissioner*, 126 TC No. 15 (2006).

What if you begin trading in August? Unless you had the foresight to make the election in the previous April, before you even started trading, the apparent position of the IRS is that you can't make the election until the following year. If you have losses in your first months of trading (as most traders do), there's no way to convert them from capital losses to ordinary losses. For this reason, if you're thinking of getting into trading in a big way, and it's late in the year, it might be a good idea to wait until January so any losses you incur at the outset can be covered by the mark-to-market election.

Corporations and other entities can make the mark-to-market election within two months and fifteen days after the start of their first tax year. Chapter 36 discusses trading through an entity.

Filing the election. If you file Form 1040 by April 15 (in other words, you don't file for an extension of time to file), your election must be attached to Form 1040. If you file for an extension, you can't wait until Form 1040 is ready, because the election must be filed by the *unextended* deadline for filing the return. So in this case the IRS requires you to attach the election to Form 4868, the form used to file for an extension. In either case, the election should look something like this:

> John Doe
> SSN 123-45-6789
> 2023 Form 1040
>
> The taxpayer elects under section 475(f) of the Internal Revenue Code to use the mark-to-market method of accounting for his securities trading business beginning with the tax year commencing January 1, 2024.

The identifying information at the top should include your name and social security number, and the form number and year. If you file the election with your extension request, the form number is 4868, not 1040.

Reporting change of accounting method

In addition to filing the election as indicated, you may have to file Form 3115. This form is used to show a change of accounting. You don't file this form at the time you make the election, though. You have to make the election by the due date of the *previous* year's return, but you file Form 3115 with the return for the *current* year. For example, if you're making the election for the year 2024, you file the election by April 15, 2024 (the unextended due date of your 2023 tax return) and you file Form 3115 with your 2024 tax return in April, 2025.

Form 3115 is a confusing array of arcane questions, many of which deal with accounting rules that are completely unrelated to the mark-to-market election. Be sure to read the instructions with careful attention to any part of the form relevant to this election.

Section 481(a) adjustment. The section 481(a) adjustment (Part IV of Form 3115) is the amount necessary to eliminate duplications or omissions that result from a change in methods of accounting. It appears that the IRS interprets the adjustment as follows. For the year before the election is effective, you account for your trades in the normal way. For the first year the election is effective, you account for your trades as if you had been using the mark-to-market method all along. As a result, when you sell or close any trading positions you held at the end of the last year before the mark-to-market election took effect, you treat them as if they had been marked to market the previous year (with basis equal to the year-end value). The difference between the actual basis of these positions and the year-end value is the amount of the adjustment.

> **Example:** At the end of the last year before the election took effect you held shares with $24,000 basis but value of $26,000. During the first year the election was effective you sold these shares for $30,000. You report $4,000 of gain on the sale of the shares (as if they had been marked to market, even though they were not), and in addition you have a $2,000 section 481(a) adjustment.

If the adjustment is under $25,000 you can elect to take it in a single year; otherwise you spread it over four years beginning with the year the election took effect. If you didn't hold any trading positions on December 31 of the year before the election took effect, the section 481(a) adjustment is zero.

Attach a statement. You should attach a statement something like this:

> John Doe
> SSN 123-45-6789
> Attachment to Form 3115
>
> In accordance with Rev. Proc. 99-17 and section 475(f) of the Internal Revenue Code, the taxpayer filed an election with his 2023 income tax return to use the mark-to-market method of accounting in connection with his trade or business of trading securities, effective beginning with the taxable year commencing January 1, 2024. This method of accounting will be used for the taxpayer's books and records and financial statements.

Sign the form and attach it to your tax return. In addition, *no later than the date you file your tax return*, send a *copy* of Form 3115 and the attached statement to the national office of the IRS at the address provided in the instructions for Form 3115.

Reporting gains and losses

For any year the mark-to-market election is in effect, you don't report trading gains and losses on Schedule D. Instead, you are to report these gains and losses on line 10 of Form 4797. This makes sense because Form 4797 is used to report sales that produce ordinary income or loss rather than capital gain or loss.

There's one point on which many traders will be disappointed. As of the 2014 tax year, the IRS says they want all transactions listed on an attachment to this form. It isn't good enough to put an aggregate number on the form. If you have 5,000 trades in the course of the year, the IRS wants a listing showing gain or loss from each individual trade! The listing doesn't have to be on a particular form, so it can be a computer spreadsheet that provides the necessary information. The mark-to-market election saves you plenty of paperwork by eliminating the wash sale rule, but it doesn't eliminate the need to report individual trades.

For taxpayers *other than* mark-to-market traders, the IRS eliminated the requirement to report individual transactions if basis is reported by brokers and there are no adjustments. We've proposed to the IRS that they adopt the same approach for MTM traders, but as of this writing, instructions for Form 4797 still ask for details of every transaction.

Identifying investment securities

Before you make the mark-to-market election, you need to think about identifying any stocks you hold as an investment (in other words, not as part of your trading). Failure to do so could be costly.

What's at stake. Suppose you're a trader and you make the mark-to-market election. In addition to stocks you trade, you have some stocks you hold as investments. You've held some of these stocks for years, and they've gone up in value a great deal. If these stocks are considered part of your trading business, you'll report ordinary income, not capital gain, when you sell them. Even if you don't sell them, the gain will be treated as ordinary income when you mark to market on December 31. Depending on how much gain you have in your investment stocks, this could be a real disaster.

What you can do. The rules permit you to maintain investments that are not part of your trading business. To do this, though, you have to identify those investments. In other words, you have to make it clear, up front, which stocks are part of your trading business and which are not. You can't decide later to treat the losers as trading stocks (for ordinary losses) and the winners as investment stocks (to avoid marking to market and get capital gain treatment).

Early in 1999, the Treasury Department issued proposed regulations addressing the identification issue. As of this writing, final regulations have still not been issued. Here is what the proposed regulations tell us:

- If you make the mark-to-market election, you must identify any securities held other than in connection with your trading business.
- Your identification isn't effective unless you can demonstrate by clear and convincing evidence that the securities have no connection to your trading business.
- If you hold an investment security and also trade the same security, or substantially similar securities, your identification isn't effective unless you hold the investment securities in a separate, non-trading account maintained with a third party.

The Treasury asked for commentary on whether these proposed rules are too strict, so it's possible the final regulations will soften these rules somewhat. Until that happens, you should assume that these strict rules will apply.

When to identify. The proposed regulations provide that if you want to identify securities as not being part of your trading business, you must do so on the same day you acquire the security (or enter into or originate your position in the security, in the case of short positions or options). If you hold any investment securities at the time the mark-to-market election becomes effective, presumably you can identify them at that time.

How to identify. Regulations for securities dealers provide two ways to identify securities for purposes of these rules. One is to establish a separate account for investment securities, and the other is to clearly indicate on your own records which securities are not part of your trading business.

These rules also apparently apply to securities traders. There's some question in my mind, however, whether the procedure of identifying shares on internal records makes sense for an individual trader. It will be difficult to establish factually that the identification occurred at the proper time, rather than being made up later. For this reason, I recommend that anyone who makes the mark-to-market election and holds some securities for investment should establish separate accounts for trading and investment activities, taking care never to mix the activities of the two accounts.

No connection to trading business. Even if you identify securities as investment securities, the IRS can disregard your identification unless you demonstrate by "clear and convincing evidence" that the security has "no connection" to your trading activity. If the IRS rejects your identification, you'll be required to mark the securities to market at the end of the year, and report any gain as ordinary income. It isn't entirely clear what is meant by "no connection" to the trading business. In particular, it isn't clear whether investment securities can be used as collateral for trading margin without being drawn into the mark-to-market regime.

Until we receive further clarification from the Treasury or the IRS, the only sure way to avoid problems is to keep your investment securities in a separate account from your trading securities, and avoid using the investment securities as collateral for margin in the trading account. If it's important for you to use your investment securities as collateral in connection with your trading activities, you should consider whether the benefits of the mark-to-market election are great enough to justify taking the risk that the IRS will treat those securities as trading securities.

Part VII
Other Taxes

29

Alternative Minimum Tax

THE ALTERNATIVE MINIMUM TAX affected millions of taxpayers each year before 2018. From that year forward, changes made by the Tax Cuts and Jobs Act are projected to slash that number by more than 90%, to about 200,000 taxpayers. It's unlikely you'll have to pay this tax now, even if you paid it in the past. There's one situation, however, where the types of income covered in this book can invoke AMT: it can apply when you have a large long-term capital gain. (My book *Consider Your Options* addresses AMT in connection with the exercise of incentive stock options.)

Background

The basic idea behind the alternative minimum tax is that people with very high levels of income shouldn't be able to pay little or no income tax while the rest of us pony up each year. Historically, the AMT was a poor reflection of that idea. The pared-down version that took effect in 2018 is more closely focused on high-income individuals who are lightly taxed compared to others at their level.

Whatever its merits or demerits, the AMT is a potential problem if you have a large long-term capital gain. Congress never intended to apply the AMT to people in this situation, but the interaction of different provisions can cause the AMT to apply. In fact, while he was president, Bill Clinton had to pay AMT because of capital gains in his blind trust.

In some circumstances, you get a credit in later years if you pay AMT. For example, people who pay AMT because they exercised incentive stock options usually recover some or all of the tax in a later year, in the form of an *AMT credit.* Unfortunately, if you incur AMT liability because of a long-term capital gain, you aren't eligible for the AMT credit. You won't get this tax back in a later year.

The AMT exemption

Why pay AMT when you have a long-term gain? The major reason is elimination of the *AMT exemption.* This is a special deduction that's designed to prevent the alternative minimum tax from applying at lower income levels. The problem is that the AMT exemption is *phased out* when your income goes above a certain level. Capital gain is income even though it's taxed at a special rate, so it can reduce or eliminate your AMT exemption.

> Effective in 2018, the Tax Cuts and Jobs Act significantly increased both the size of the AMT exemption and the income levels at which it begins to phase out.

When your income is in the range where the exemption is being phased out, each dollar of long-term capital gain adds $1.25 to your AMT income. That means the effective rate of tax on capital gain under the AMT can be much higher than the rate under the regular tax, even though the "official" top AMT rate for long-term capital gain is 20%, the same as under the regular tax.

You don't automatically pay AMT when you have a long-term capital gain. Whether you end up in that situation depends on various factors, including the size of your income, the size of the gain, and the number of items on your return that are affected by the AMT. There are no good rules of thumb, other than to check the AMT calculation if you have a large capital gain.

What you can do

There isn't an awful lot you can do about this situation. I often hear people offer ideas for reducing AMT liability, but most people have limited ability to take advantage of those ideas, and sometimes the ideas are simply unsound. Still, there are a few things you should consider.

Take a close look at deductions that are allowed under the regular tax but not under the AMT. An example would be the deduction for state and local taxes. If you can schedule some of your payments of such taxes so they don't fall in the same year you have an AMT problem, you may get a greater benefit from the deduction.

On the flip side, you may find that you pay a lower rate of tax on income you receive in an AMT year. For example, if you're paying AMT because of a long-term capital gain, you might choose that year to exercise nonqualified stock options. At least some of the income from exercising your options may end up being taxed at the AMT rate (26% to 28%) rather than your regular income tax rate, which may be as high as 37%.

Caution: Your effective AMT rate can be as high as 35% in the range of income where the AMT exemption is being phased out. Also, accelerating income into an AMT year may not be a good idea if you're eligible for the AMT credit (for example, because you exercised an incentive stock option). Make sure you've considered all the consequences before accelerating income into a year you're paying AMT.

30

Net Investment Income Tax

BEGINNING IN 2013, a 3.8% surtax applies to the net investment income of high-income taxpayers. This tax was imposed to pay part of the cost of the Affordable Care Act (the healthcare reform you may know better as Obamacare). It applies to common forms of investment income, including interest, dividends and capital gains—but only if your modified adjusted gross income is above the level specified for your filing status.

Modified AGI

You don't pay this tax unless your modified adjusted gross income exceeds the "threshold amount" for your filing status:

- $250,000 if you are married filing jointly or a surviving widow or widower;
- $200,000 if you are single or a head of household;
- $125,000 if you are married filing separately.

For this purpose, your adjusted gross income is modified only if you took advantage of the foreign earned income exclusion permitted for certain individuals working overseas, or if you directly or indirectly own stock in a controlled foreign corporation or a passive foreign investment corporation. For most taxpayers, modified AGI is simply AGI.

> The threshold amounts set forth above are *not* adjusted for inflation.

Example: If you're single with AGI of $205,000, including $25,000 of net investment income, you pay this tax on $5,000, because that's how much is above the $200,000 threshold. If your AGI is $240,000, the entire $25,000 of net investment income is taxed.

Non-investment income or deductions

For planning purposes, you should be aware that income other than investment income can cause you to pay net investment income tax as a result of pushing your overall income above the threshold amount described above. For example, the exclusion of retirement plan distributions from net investment income does not prevent it from influencing the amount of tax you pay on other income that's included. A distribution from your IRA or 401k account, or income from a Roth conversion, could increase the amount of net investment income tax your pay, or push you into paying the tax when you otherwise would avoid it altogether.

Example: Before taking retirement income into account, your adjusted gross income, including $20,000 in net investment income, is $10,000 below the threshold amount. A $40,000 Roth conversion would not be included in net investment income, but it would push your AGI above the threshold amount so that you now pay net investment income tax on the $20,000 of investment income that otherwise would have escaped the tax.

Deductions can have the opposite effect, but only if they are *above the line* deductions—that is, deductions that are allowed in calculating adjusted gross income. Deductions for contributions to 401k plans or traditional IRA accounts fall into this category.

Net investment income

The rules for determining net investment income for purposes of this tax are quite complicated. Much of that complexity pertains to topics not covered in this book: investment income of trusts and estates, passive activities, special rules for real estate professionals, and dispositions of interests in partnerships and S corporations. Here are some details on items related to owning or selling stocks, bonds and mutual fund shares.

Interest income. As expected, interest income is included in net investment income. Interest on state and local government obligations is exempt from this tax to the same extent it is exempt from regular income tax. Interest received in the ordinary course of a trade or business in which you actively participate (other than as a trader in stocks or other securities) is also excluded.

Dividends. While dividends in general are included, Alaska Permanent Fund Dividends and dividends paid on stock held in an employer retirement plan are excluded.

Annuities. Income from retirement plan annuities is excluded, but income from nonqualified annuities is included. As both types of annuity income are reported on Form 1099-R, it is important to distinguish between the two. Generally income that is included will be indicated on this form with code D in box 7.

Capital gains. Capital gains and losses incurred in typical investment activities of holding and selling stocks, bonds and mutual fund shares are generally calculated the same under this tax as under the regular income tax. In particular, the capital loss allowance of $3,000 per year is allowed, and capital losses that remain unused as a result of this limitation carry forward. Adjustments may apply to certain capital gains and losses, such as those related to passive activities or sales of property used in connection with a trade or business. If you have such adjustments, your capital loss carryover for purposes of this tax may differ from the carryover you use for the regular income tax.

Expenses. Investment expenses that are deductible in figuring regular income tax are also allowed for the net investment income tax. Elimination of the deduction for "2% floor" deductions in the regular tax (as of 2018) means those deductions are no longer available for this tax. Note, however, that if your regular income tax calculation includes a deduction for state or local income tax, an allocable portion of that deduction is allowed in calculating net investment income. The instructions for Form 8960 provide a worksheet for making this allocation.

> Beginning in 2018, far fewer people will itemize due to an increase in the size of the standard deduction and a $10,000 limit on the itemized deduction for state and local tax. As a result, fewer will get the benefit of deducting these taxes under the net investment income tax.

Retirement plan distributions

Retirement plan distributions are excluded from net investment income. The exclusion applies to payouts from 401k and other qualified employer retirement plans as well as from IRAs, both Roth and traditional. It applies as well to amounts that are treated as distributions, such as Roth conversions and situations where a loan to the retirement account owner is treated as a distribution.

Net unrealized appreciation. A special rule permits account owners to receive shares of stock as a distribution from an employer plan, reporting distribution income equal to the original cost of the shares. The amount by which the stock increased in value while held in the retirement account is *net unrealized appreciation*, or *NUA*. The owner can sell the shares after receiving them and report long-term capital gain instead of ordinary income.

Although NUA gets treated as capital gain, it represents part of the value that was held in and distributed from the retirement plan. The regulations say this increment of value is excluded from net investment income. Any additional gain, resulting from an increase in the value of the stock after it was distributed from the retirement plan, is included in net investment income.

> In certain circumstances dividends paid on stock held by an employer retirement plan will be paid out directly to the account owners. These distributions are excluded from net investment income.

Coordination with other taxes

The net investment income tax relies heavily on rules used in the regular income tax for determining such matters as when a capital gain or loss is realized, whether a distribution is taxable as a dividend, and when an investment expense is allowed as a deduction. This tax is paid at the same time as regular income tax and included in the total that must be paid in estimated taxes to avoid a penalty. Yet the net investment income tax doesn't affect your regular income tax or AMT. It doesn't affect the basis of your assets, and you can't use AMT credit to offset this tax. It's a separate tax paid in addition to any other taxes that may apply.

Part VIII
Many Happy Returns

31

Reporting Capital Gains and Losses

OUR PURPOSE HERE IS NOT TO COVER ALL ASPECTS of income tax reporting for capital gains and losses, but to highlight certain areas that may give rise to confusion. We'll look at the six categories of capital gain and loss that go on Form 8949, discuss how to deal with situations where basis information reported by the broker isn't correct, and highlight a friendly rule that makes capital gain reporting easier in some situations.

Six categories of transactions

Back in the dark ages before 2011, taxpayers were asked to divide their capital gain or loss transactions into two categories: short-term and long-term. Now, each of those categories is subdivided into three, producing six different groupings. The first is for all sales or other capital gain events for which the broker reported basis on Form 1099-B. The second is for transactions that have been reported by the broker, but without transmitting basis information to the IRS. The third category is for transactions that are not reported at all by the broker, although you are still required to report them on your income tax return.

The IRS now requires you to report each of these categories separately. Unless an exception applies (see below), your long-term transactions with basis reported by the broker will go on Form 8949 with box D checked at the top. If you also have a long-term sale for which basis was not reported by the broker, your return will include another Form 8949 with box E checked. If your sales are in different categories, your return will have two of these forms, even if there are only two sales.

Avoiding category confusion. Brokers are permitted to provide you with additional information that may be helpful in preparing your income tax return even though it is not reported to the IRS. For example, they may have records indicating the amount you paid for shares you bought before brokers were required to maintain basis records. If you don't read the broker's tax report carefully, you may include these shares in the category where basis is reported to the IRS, when in reality the basis appeared only as additional information provided to you. Similarly, if you use your broker to sell an asset that isn't reported at all to the IRS (the third subcategory), you may receive tax information from the broker that could be construed as belonging in one of the first two categories.

> Beginning with the 2014 tax year (returns filed in 2015), brokers are required to indicate which box should be checked (A through F) on the tax reports they send to customers.

The types of transactions reported to the IRS expanded in 2014 to include certain debt obligations and options. Reporting began for some additional categories of bonds and options in 2016. As a result, the third subcategory, transactions not reported at all by the broker, is shrinking.

The broker isn't always right

Apart from the possibility of errors, there are various reasons the basis or holding period reported by the broker on Form 1099-B may not be accurate. When this happens, you'll have to show on your tax return what the broker reported, and also show the amount of the required adjustment together with a code indicating the nature of the adjustment.

Wash sales. One common source of discrepancies is the wash sale rule. Brokers are required to apply the wash sale rule in determining your basis for covered shares (that is, shares you acquired recently enough to be covered by the basis reporting rules). Yet they don't apply the wash sale rule if you sold shares at a loss in one account and bought replacement shares in a different account. They also don't apply the rule if you sold noncovered shares at a loss, even though the rule will affect the basis and holding period of the covered shares you bought to replace the noncovered shares you sold.

In both of these cases you're required to apply the wash sale rule even though the broker did not. To the extent required by the rule, you have to eliminate the loss on that sale. Furthermore, you have to adjust the basis and holding period for the replacement shares. When you make a later sale of those shares, the broker won't make that basis adjustment, because the broker didn't report the wash sale in the first place. That means the basis shown by the broker will be smaller than your actual basis in those shares. Your holding period may be different as well: the broker may show the shares as short-term when in fact they are long-term due to the adjustment required by the wash sale rule.

You don't need to get the broker to adjust their records or alter the information in their tax reports. The IRS understands that broker tax reporting will include these kinds of discrepancies and provides a way for you to correct them on Form 8949. The onus is on you, however, to maintain accurate records and carefully follow the directions in that form for showing the necessary adjustments.

Equity compensation. If you receive stock or options from the company where you work, you should not assume that the basis information reported by your broker is correct. Due to the way the IRS implemented these rules, it is possible the broker will not report basis information, but *also possible that the broker will report basis information that is too low.*

> **Example:** You exercise a nonqualified stock option, paying $20 per share when the stock is worth $30. The bargain element of $10 per share is included in your wage income for the year you exercise the option, and added to your basis so that the shares have a basis of $30 per share. Later you sell the shares at $32 and the broker reports your basis as $20, the amount you paid for the shares.

This is not the broker's error, just a feature of how the basis reporting rules work. It's your responsibility to adjust the basis by $10 per share when you prepare your tax return. If you fail to do so, you'll end up paying tax on capital gain of $12 per share when your actual gain is only $2 per share. You'll be paying tax twice on the same $10 of income.

Details not required

The IRS previously required you to report details of each individual transaction on Form 8949 or Schedule D, or else provide an attachment that included all the same information you would report on those forms. Beginning with tax returns for 2014, the IRS says you can aggregate certain items and report totals directly on Schedule D. This time-saver is not available for sales of collectibles, and applies only when all of the following are true:

- The transactions were reported on Form 1099-B or a substitute for that form.

- The form indicates basis was reported to the IRS (it will show that the applicable checkbox on Form 8949 is A or D, depending on whether the sale was short-term or long-term).
- The form does not show any adjustment in box 1g (used by the broker to show adjustments necessary for events such as wash sales).
- You don't need to make any adjustments of your own to the figures reported by the broker.

These conditions will be true most of the time when selling covered securities—that is, stocks, mutual fund shares and other investments bought recently enough to be covered by the rules requiring brokers to report basis to the IRS. Taxpayers who engage in a large number of transactions will be able to do less work and file thinner tax returns.

> You'll still need to list each transaction when selling older investments, or when adjustments are required.

32

Estimated Tax Payments

IF YOU'RE AN EMPLOYEE, you may have never had to worry about making estimated tax payments. The amount of income tax withheld from paychecks may be enough to cover the tax you owe and then some, providing a refund. Even if you owe some tax on April 15, estimates aren't required unless you owe more than $1,000.

When you invest in stocks and mutual funds, there's a good chance you'll end up with a tax bill of more than $1,000 in one or more years. In that situation, it's possible that you'll incur a penalty if you don't make quarterly payments of estimated tax.

First things you should know

If you've never had to deal with estimated taxes before, the whole idea can seem foreign and uncomfortable. There are two things you should know right away to put your mind at rest.

- **It's easy.** In most cases, the process of figuring out how much to pay isn't hard at all. And paying the tax is a snap.

- **No jail time.** You won't go to jail if you make a mistake and pay too little. In fact, the penalty isn't exactly a killer. It's just simple interest on the amount you underpaid, and the interest rate isn't terribly high. If you somehow blow it and underpay by $400, and correct the underpayment with your next payment three months later, your penalty will be less than $10. It's better to avoid the penalty, but really, this is nothing to lose sleep over.

General rule: 90%

The general rule is that your estimated tax payments, when added to your withholding and credits, must add up to 90% of the current year's tax liability. If your withholding and credits already add up to 90% of your tax liability, you don't have to make estimated tax payments. Yet in many cases you don't have to make estimated tax payments even if your withholding and credits fall short of the 90% figure, for reasons described below.

> When we talk about the *tax due*, we mean the total amount of tax you owe—including any self-employment tax, net investment income tax, and the dreaded alternative minimum tax (AMT).

Tax due less than $1,000

Here's a rule that makes it easy for many people who have withholding that falls just a bit short to avoid dealing with estimated tax payments. No payment is required if the amount due after subtracting withholding and credits will be less than $1,000.

Example: Suppose you expect your wage withholding to be just enough to cover your income tax liability. Then you have a $4,000 long-term capital gain you didn't plan on. This gain will be taxed at 15%, so the added tax is $600. You can make an estimated tax payment if you feel more comfortable doing so, but there won't be a penalty if you wait until April 15 of next year to send in the payment because it's less than $1,000.

The only problem with this rule is that sometimes it's difficult to know what your tax liability will be. But $1,000 is a reasonable amount of leeway for most taxpayers.

Prior year safe harbor

Most people can avoid paying estimated tax if their withholding and credits equal 100% of the tax shown on the *prior year's* income tax return. I call this the *prior year safe harbor.* This rule often permits taxpayers to avoid making estimated payments if they receive a large sum of income on a one-time basis.

> For purposes of this rule, your prior year tax isn't the amount of the check you sent in, but the total amount of tax you had to pay, including withholding. For example, if your withholding was $12,000 and you had to pay another $250 when you filed your return, your prior year's tax was $12,250—*not* $250.

Example: In a normal year withholding is enough to cover your income tax—in fact, you usually get a small refund. This year you sell stock with a capital gain of $200,000. Despite this huge increase in income, you don't have to make estimated tax payments if your withholding will be at least equal to the tax shown on the prior year's tax return.

Similarly, you normally don't have to make estimated tax payments if you had no tax liability at all for the previous year. Remember, "no tax liability" doesn't just mean your withholding was enough to cover your tax. It means even if you didn't have any withholding at all you wouldn't owe any tax.

Higher income, higher percentage. There's a rule that requires taxpayers with adjusted gross income above $150,000 on the prior year's return ($75,000 if married filing separately) to pay 110% of the prior year's tax (not just 100%) when applying the prior year safe harbor. Congress has been known to tinker with this percentage, so check the form instructions.

Even if the prior year safe harbor doesn't allow you to completely avoid making estimated tax payments, it permits you to determine an amount that will avoid a penalty without making an accurate estimate of the current year's taxes.

> **Example:** Your income tax for last year was $24,000. You expect your withholding for this year to be $21,000. You don't know how much income you'll have for this year, though, because you may sell stock at a gain. Using the prior year safe harbor, you can safely cover your estimated tax requirement by paying $3,000 ($750 per quarter). When added to your $21,000 of withholding, you'll have total payments that equal your prior year's tax.

There are situations where it doesn't make sense to use the prior year safe harbor. You may have a year in which you had an unusually large amount of income. When the next year rolls around, you would be paying estimates that are larger than necessary if you pay based on that banner year. In this case you'll want to estimate the current year's tax and try to pay at least 90% of that number.

> **Example:** Last year you made a killing in an IPO and reported an extra $80,000 of income. This year you won't have that extra income, but still need to make estimated tax payments. If you base the payment amount on last year's tax, you'll pay a lot more than necessary. It makes more sense to use a realistic estimate of your current year's tax.

Estimating your tax

As you've seen above, there are plenty of situations where it isn't actually necessary to do any estimating when you make estimated tax payments. But sometimes you need to make an estimate of the current year's tax. Otherwise you'll either pay way too much, or come up short and end up with a penalty.

Form 1040-ES (the form used to pay estimated tax) comes with a worksheet you can use to estimate how much tax you'll owe for the current year. There's certainly nothing wrong with using this worksheet—but most people don't. The reason is that the worksheet takes you through more detail than may be necessary, but still leaves you with nothing better than an educated guess about your tax liability. You don't file the worksheet with the IRS, and there's no requirement to justify how you came up with the amount of your estimated tax payment. So most people use a somewhat simplified method to figure their estimated tax:

- Look at each number on the prior year's tax return and ask yourself if this year's number is likely to be significantly different. Ignore differences in wages because there will be a corresponding difference in withholding. Use rounded numbers and don't worry about minor changes.
- Add up all the differences to see how much larger or smaller your taxable income will be for the current year.
- Apply the tax rates to see how much difference this will make in your income tax. (If the difference results from a long-term capital gain, apply the capital gain tax rates.) Round the number up or simply tack on an added amount if you want to increase your comfort level about avoiding a penalty.

Many people using this method don't bother looking up the changes in the tax rates that result from inflation adjustments. These changes will decrease your tax slightly, so that's one way of providing a cushion of extra payments.

Voluntary payments

Depending on your situation, the amount of estimated tax you're *required* to pay could be quite a bit less than your true estimate of the amount of tax you'll owe. That's because you're allowed to pay estimates based on the previous year's tax, even if you know this year's tax will be higher. When that happens you have a choice. You can pay the minimum amount required—and pay the rest on April 15. Or you can pay something close to the true estimate so you won't owe a lot on April 15. Which is better depends on your comfort level and money management skills.

Pay now and relax. Some people choose to make estimated payments even when the payments aren't required. The reason? Perhaps they're concerned that the money won't be there when they need it to pay taxes. Perhaps they're simply more comfortable knowing that they won't have a huge tax bill in April. There are a variety of good reasons to make estimated tax payments even if the payments aren't legally required. The biggest one is peace of mind.

Pay later and earn. The main reason *not* to pay more than you have to is that you lose the use of your money between the time you pay the estimate and the time you would have sent payment with your return. You should be able to earn at least a little bit of interest during that time. So there's at least one good reason to pay later, even though there are good reasons to pay sooner.

Which is better. Which approach is better—making voluntary payments, or paying the minimum—depends on your personality and your circumstances. Consider the following example:

> **Example:** You normally don't pay estimates because almost all of your income is from wages subject to withholding. In January of the current year you sell stock and have a capital gain of $40,000. You expect to owe $6,000 of tax, but you don't

have to pay estimates because your withholding this year will be at least equal to your tax for the previous year.

You have several choices, including the following:

- You can put $6,000 aside in an interest bearing account until April 15 of next year when the tax is due. This way you can make a little profit on the money before sending it to the IRS. If you have the discipline to leave the money alone, you come out ahead using this approach. There's a danger, though. If you start with this intention, but end up spending the money on a trip to Aruba, or losing it when you try to cash in on an IPO, you may wake up with a headache on April 15.
- You can send in a single estimated payment of $6,000. This approach is easy, and may seem relatively painless if you do it at a time when you're flush with money from the stock sale. It's also very safe: this approach assures that you won't somehow lose or spend the money before you file your tax return. It doesn't allow you to earn interest on the $6,000, though.
- You can send in four quarterly estimates of $1,500 each. You may prefer this approach if you don't like the idea of writing a single check for $6,000 to the IRS (who does?). And this approach gives you the flexibility to reduce later payments if you have a capital loss or other reduction in taxable income later in the year. There's a little more paperwork involved in this approach though, and more opportunity to lose or spend the money before you file your return.

There's nothing illegal or immoral about any of these approaches. They're all equally acceptable to the IRS. (They won't be upset if they receive a $6,000 payment for one quarter and no payment in later quarters.) If you find yourself in a situation like this, choose the approach that works best for you.

Increasing your withholding

There's a way you may be able to cover your extra tax liability without making estimated tax payments: increase the amount of tax withheld from your paycheck. You get a special benefit with this approach: *extra withholding that comes late in the year is treated the same as if it was spread evenly over the year.* You can use this approach to avoid late payment penalties.

How to do it. To increase the amount of federal income tax withheld from your paycheck, ask your employer for a new Form W-4. You're required to fill out this form when you start working for an employer. You can fill out a new one whenever your circumstances call for a change in the amount of withholding.

This form previously asked you to come up with a number of "allowances" that would determine your rate of withholding. Form W-4 has been revised to provide a more understandable way of providing the necessary information. There's now a line where you can report an amount of additional income that isn't subject to withholding, such as interest or other investment income. Your employer's payroll department will use this information to increase the amount withheld from your paycheck. The hope is that the boost will be about what is needed to cover the tax you'll owe on the additional income.

If you know how much additional withholding you need, there's another way that's more precise. You can simply ask to have an additional dollar amount you specify withheld each pay period. Check with your employer to find out when the change will go into effect. Often there's a time lag between the day you fill out this form and the day it's processed, so you may not see the change in your very next paycheck. Keep an eye on your pay stubs to confirm that the change was properly made, and had the effect you anticipated.

Avoiding late payment penalty. The nice thing about using withholding to cover your estimated tax liability is that it can get you out of a late payment penalty. Withholding is presumed to be received evenly throughout the year.

Example: Suppose you realize in May that you need to pay $6,000 estimated tax for the year, and you've already blown the first $1,500 payment that was due April 15. It won't be a big deal if you send in the payment a few weeks late because the penalty isn't all that terrible. But you can avoid the penalty altogether by increasing your withholding for the rest of the year by $6,000. The IRS will assume the withholding occurred evenly throughout the year, with $1,500 coming in the first quarter. You get the benefit of this assumption even if all of the added withholding comes in December!

Making estimated payments

Estimated payments for any year are due on April 15, June 15 and September 15 of that year, and January 15 of the following year. Whenever one of these dates falls on a legal holiday or on a weekend, the due date is the next day that isn't a holiday or weekend day. Here are some points to keep in mind:

- If you owe money with your tax return, *and* have to make an estimated tax payment, you have *two* payments to make on April 15. Be prepared!
- Although the payments are "quarterly," they aren't three months apart. The second payment sneaks up on you, just two months after the first one.
- Like your tax return, estimated payments are considered "on time" if you *mail* them by the due date. It's faster and more secure to pay online, though (see below).
- Most states that have an income tax require estimated payments on the same schedule as the federal payments. If you itemize deductions, it may be to your advantage to make your fourth quarter state estimated tax payment in December, not January, so you can deduct it a year earlier.

- A small number of individual taxpayers use a fiscal tax year that ends with a month other than December. Their payment schedule is different (but equivalent): the fifteenth day of the fourth, sixth and ninth months of their fiscal year, and the fifteenth day of the first month of the following fiscal year.

How to pay. Nowadays the easiest way to pay is online. Get info and instructions at irs.gov/payments.

When you make estimated tax payments by mail you need to enclose Form 1040-ES, Estimated Tax Voucher. This form comes from the IRS as part of an intimidating package that includes lengthy instructions and detailed worksheets. As mentioned earlier, you don't have to fill out the worksheets unless you think they'll be helpful. And you should *never* send these worksheets to the IRS. The form itself is about as simple as they get. It asks for your name, address and social security number—and just one other item: the amount you're paying.

Other important tips. *Estimated tax payments don't go to the same address as your return!* Don't enclose an estimated tax payment with your Form 1040. Check the instructions for Form 1040-ES for the proper address.

Enclose your check. Write your social security number on the check and a notation of what it's for, like this: 2023 2Q Form 1040-ES. If you're doing this before your first cup of coffee in the morning, double check to see that you *signed* the check.

You don't have to justify your estimated tax payments. In fact, there's no place for a *signature* on the form. When you send it in, you're not promising that this is the correct amount. All you're saying is, "Here's a payment on account."

Be sure to keep an accurate record of your estimated tax payments so you can claim credit for them when you file your return. The IRS is good at tracking these payments and will send you a reminder if you fail to claim it.

Joint payments. If you're married, you can make joint estimated tax payments with your spouse. (There's an exception if either spouse is a nonresident alien.) Paying joint estimated payments does *not* mean you have to file a joint return. But if you end up filing separately, you'll have to sort out who gets credit for what amount.

33

Special Rules for Children

IF YOUR CHILDREN ARE INVESTORS—or you're investing money for them through a custodial account—you need to know a few special rules that apply to children. One requires certain children to pay tax at their parents' rates when investment income exceeds a minimum amount. Another permits a parent to report the child's income on the parent's return in certain circumstances. First, though, let's answer one of the most frequently asked questions about children's income tax.

Who files the return?

If a child has investments, who files the tax return? Here's what the IRS says, in Publication 929:

> Generally, a child is responsible for filing his or her own tax return and for paying any tax, penalties or interest on that return. If a child can't file his or her own return for any reason, such as age, the child's parent, guardian, or other legally responsible person must file it for the child. If the child can't sign his or her return, a parent or guardian must sign

the child's name followed by the words "By (signature), parent (or guardian) for minor child."

Note that the child doesn't have to be of legal age to sign the return. The IRS doesn't tell us when a child is "old enough" to sign. Your five-year-old can sign the return and it would be perfectly legal. If your child is too young to deal with issues that may arise with the IRS, though, you should sign the return, or make sure it shows you as a "third party designee" who can respond if something comes up.

Custodial account information. As explained in Chapter 21, assets in custodial accounts under the Uniform Transfers to Minors Act—*UTMA accounts*—are owned by the child. Income from those assets belongs on the child's return (except as explained later in this chapter for parents who elect to include the child's income on their own return). The Uniform Act requires the custodian to supply relevant information to the child or the person responsible for filing the child's tax return.

Standard deduction

Taxpayers who don't itemize deductions claim the *standard deduction*. This amount is much smaller for a dependent child than it is for an independent taxpayer. For the year 2023, the standard deduction for a minor child is the *greater* of the following two amounts:

- $1,250, or
- The child's earned income plus $400, but not more than the regular standard deduction for a single person ($13,850).

It's frequently said that if you shift investment assets to a child, the first $1,250 of income will be tax-free. That's generally true, but it should be noted that as soon as the child begins earning money, the amount of investment income that escapes taxation shrinks to as little as $400—or zero, if the child earns more than the regular standard deduction amount for a single person. The standard deduction grows as the child earns more money, but the amount that applies against investment income shrinks.

> **Example:** Suppose your child's only income is $2,000 of investment income. The child will have a standard deduction of $1,250 and pay tax on $750. If the child earns $2,000 in addition to the investment income, the standard deduction is $2,400, so only $400 of the investment income is sheltered by the standard deduction.

Kiddie tax

At one time, wealthy families could save a great deal of money by transferring investment assets to minor children. Tens of thousands of dollars in investment income produced by those assets would be taxed to the children at the lower rates that apply to individuals who have relatively little income. Congress decided to limit the tax benefit from shifting investment income to children and young adults, giving us what has come to be known as the *kiddie tax.*

> **Unofficial name.** The rule originally applied to children under 14 years of age, leading many to call it the *kiddie tax.* The name stuck even though subsequent legislation extended it to certain students up to age 24, and now even the IRS uses that term.

There are two ways to handle this tax obligation. The general rule, described in this section, requires filing of a tax return for the child (or young adult) with a special tax calculation using the parents' tax rates on an attached Form 8615. (At one time Congress changed the law to apply rates that apply to income of trusts and estates, but quickly realized this was a mistake and went back to using parents' tax rates.) The section after this one describes an alternative: if certain requirements are met, parents can elect to include the child's investment income on their own return, so the child doesn't have to file a separate return.

Income threshold. You don't have to worry about this rule until your child has investment income greater than a threshold amount, which is two times the amount allowed as a standard deduction for a dependent who has only investment income. For 2023, that amount is $1,250, so the kiddie tax begins to apply when your child has more than $2,500 in investment income.

> **Note:** Your child can still owe regular income tax with less than $2,500 in income. This is merely the threshold amount of investment income for the special kiddie tax.

Children affected by the rule. The application of the kiddie tax depends partly on your child's age as of the end of the year. For this purpose, a child born January 1 is treated as if he or she reached the age of that birthday on December 31 of the previous year. We now have different rules for four different age groups:

- Until the year your child turns 18, the kiddie tax applies automatically if your child has the amount of investment income described above.
- In the year your child turns 18, the kiddie tax applies unless your child's earned income is more than half his or her overall support. Note that "earned income" for this purpose includes money your child earns by working but not investment income.
- For the year your child turns 19 through the year your child turns 23, the kiddie tax applies to a child who is a full-time student during any part of at least five months during the year unless the child's earned income is more than half his or her overall support. In other words, your child has two ways to avoid the kiddie tax: earn enough income or stop being a full-time student.
- Beginning with the year your child turns 24, the kiddie tax doesn't apply at all, even if your child is living off investments and plugging away at that PhD.

Exception: The kiddie tax doesn't apply if your child is married filing jointly.

How it works. If your child has more than $2,500 (as of 2023) in investment income, the tax is figured according to a special calculation. The first $2,500 of income is still taxed at the child's lower rates, but any additional investment income is taxed at the parents' tax rate.

Example: In 2023 your child has $3,500 of interest income and no other income. The first $1,250 of investment income escapes taxation: your child's standard deduction takes care of that. The next $1,250 is taxed at the child's rate of 10%. That leaves $1,000 to be taxed at the parents' tax rates.

Comment: These rules don't entirely eliminate tax savings that may be available when shifting investment income to children. Remember, though, you can't shift this income without shifting the investment *assets* to the child, which may or may not be a wise move for various non-tax reasons. See Chapter 21.

Reporting your child's income on your return

When the kiddie tax applies, you may be able to report the child's investment income on your tax return. This may result in a higher or lower overall tax, but most people think about doing this mainly because of the convenience: you avoid filing a separate tax return for the child. You're never required to do this, so you shouldn't make this election if it will cost you more than the benefit you get from avoiding paperwork.

Not everyone can make this election. Requirements include the following:

- Your child had income only from dividends and interest. For this purpose, dividends include capital gain distributions and Alaska Permanent Fund dividends.

- The dividend and interest income was more than $1,125 (figure for 2023) and less than ten times that amount.
- The child has no credits for withholding or estimated tax, including a prior year overpayment that was applied to estimated tax.
- The child isn't married filing jointly.

The requirement that trips people up most often is the limit on the types of income. Sometimes people make stock investments with their children's assets, and then have a capital loss. They see that the capital loss won't produce any tax benefit on the child's tax return, and wonder if they can benefit from this loss by electing to include the child's investment income on their own tax return. Unfortunately this isn't possible. The only items you can move to your own tax return are dividend and interest income.

Effect of the election. If you elect to include your child's income on your tax return, you still get the benefit of the child's standard deduction. What's more, the child's tax rate still applies up to the same threshold as if the income were reported on the child's tax return. That means most people won't pay much additional tax if they make the election. You can even gain an advantage by making the election, because the child's investment income counts when determining the limit on your investment interest expense deduction (see Chapter 14).

The election can cost you money, though. Certain deductions your child might otherwise claim are not allowed on your return, and a portion of your child's income from qualified dividends or long-term capital gains may end up being taxed at a higher rate than would apply on the child's separate return. For that reason, it's a good idea to take a close look at the return, or perhaps even prepare it both ways, before committing yourself to reporting your child's income on your return. If you're not sure about the election, don't make it. In most cases it isn't that hard to prepare a separate return for the child.

When there's a capital loss in your child's UTMA account, and your child doesn't have enough income to pay any tax, it seems like a shame for the capital loss to be wasted. Yet there's no way to claim the capital loss on the parents' return. The election to include your child's income on your return doesn't apply if your child has capital gains—or capital losses.

Part IX
Planning for Lower Taxes

34

Tax Planning for Capital Gains

ONE NICE THING ABOUT CAPITAL GAINS AND LOSSES is that you have some control over them. You can sell your stock now or later, depending on which choice produces better tax results. You can choose which stock to sell and even choose *which shares* of that stock to sell if you bought shares at different times or different prices. Choose intelligently and you can reduce your tax bite.

Remember, tax considerations shouldn't control your choices. Overall, a sound investment strategy is more important than tax savings. You'll achieve the best results if you let tax planning influence the details of how you operate within your overall strategy.

Three tax planning goals

Most tax planning is aimed at one or more of three goals. Sometimes you can achieve more than one of these goals at the same time. In other situations, you may find that you can achieve one only at the expense of another. The three main goals of tax planning are:

- *Reducing taxable income.* Of course, it's easy to reduce taxable income by earning less. The trick is to have income that isn't *taxable.* For example, interest on municipal bonds is tax exempt, and earnings in a Roth IRA escape tax permanently if you wait long enough before taking distributions.
- *Paying lower tax rates.* If you can't eliminate tax on your income, the next best thing is to reduce the tax rate. The main way to do this is to maximize your use of the lower rates for long-term capital gains and qualified dividends.
- *Deferral.* That's a dull-sounding word for a mundane but powerful concept: other things being equal, it's better to pay taxes later rather than sooner. The principal tax benefit from most retirement savings arrangements comes from deferral. Often it's possible to defer capital gains simply by holding winning stocks for a longer period of time.

The power of tax deferral. If you've never stopped to think about it, you may not realize what a powerful benefit you can achieve by deferring taxes until a later year. There's a tendency to think you haven't really saved much because you're simply paying the same amount at a different time. Yet deferral, especially over long periods of time, can have a significant multiplier effect on your investment return even without any reduction in tax rates.

> **Example:** You put $2,000 in a taxable account, and another $2,000 in a nondeductible IRA. Both investments earn 10% per year, but in the taxable account you pay tax each year. In the IRA, you don't pay any tax until you pull the money out. After 25 years your taxable account has grown to a little over $10,000, assuming you pull money out each year to pay tax at the rate of 33% (federal and state). Your IRA has grown much faster because you haven't pulled tax money out each year. If you pull the money out at the end of 25 years and pay tax at the same 33% rate, you end up with over $15,000.

In this example, you've increased the after-tax money available for your retirement by about 50% without reducing your taxable income or your tax rate. You did it with *tax-free compounding*. That's the power of deferral.

Winners and Losers

The most powerful tax planning techniques for people who buy and sell stocks and mutual funds are also the simplest. They're so simple that it almost seems foolish to mention them. Yet they're so powerful that it would be foolish *not* to mention them. To achieve better tax results in investing—*are you ready?*—you must do two things:

- Hold your winners.
- Sell your losers.

When you're tempted to sell a winner, consider holding it a little longer. Then a little longer still. Then keep holding it. Holding for more than a year allows you to pay tax at the lower rate for long-term capital gains. Holding until January allows you to delay paying tax until the following year. You might find that you can hold on until the *following* January and delay tax for yet another year. If you *never* sell the stock, the basis will be adjusted at your death, and no one will *ever* pay tax on the gain.

Exactly the opposite consideration applies to losses. Sell before you have a long-term loss and you may get a greater benefit from your deduction. Sell before the end of the year and you'll get to claim the loss earlier. If you don't sell during this lifetime, neither you nor anyone else will enjoy the benefit of a deduction for the loss.

What about investment concerns? As I stressed earlier, you shouldn't let tax planning concerns push you into an unsound investment approach. Sometimes there's a very good reason to sell a winner, even if that means paying tax now on a gain that might otherwise be deferred. But consider this:

Studies show that investors tend to sell their winners too soon and hold their losers too long.

There's a natural tendency, when you buy a stock that rises, to think about harvesting that profit. *I'll feel awfully dumb if the stock goes back down before I sell,* you tell yourself. Somehow the possible mistake of losing a profit by selling too late seems more important than the possible mistake of losing *future* profits by selling too soon. Time and again, investors give up future profits by selling winners that still have a lot of wind in their sails. That's bad investment planning *and* bad tax planning.

At the same time, most investors are reluctant to sell losers. They don't want to admit they made a mistake. They hold on, thinking the stock or mutual fund is sure to recover, but often that recovery is a long way down the road. Meanwhile your money is tied up in an investment that isn't going anywhere. If you sell the loser, you can move to a better investment *and* reduce your tax for the year with a loss deduction.

It isn't always right to hold a winner, and it isn't always right to sell a loser. When you find yourself resisting these maxims, though, ask yourself whether you have good reasons. You may find that you're responding to the psychology of investing in a way that increases your tax bill without increasing your wealth.

Build your own tax shelter

Sometimes I hear from people who have saved the maximum in their 401k or IRA and wish they had some other way to shelter their savings from taxation. There's a way to do that, and it's right under your nose: *buy stocks and hold them.*

Not sexy enough for you? Consider the example of the nondeductible IRA earlier in this chapter. Using this method to obtain deferral resulted in a 50% increase in the after-tax profit from investing. Yet if you adopted a buy-and-hold strategy *without* the IRA, you would achieve an even *better* result. Profits from the IRA are taxed as ordinary income even if they come from stocks that increased in value. If you buy and hold in a regular brokerage account, you get the same benefit of tax deferral and tax-free compounding—and when you're done, your profit is taxed as long-term capital gain.

There are some potential speed bumps on this road to riches. If you invest in stocks that pay dividends, you'll pay at least some tax even with a buy-and-hold strategy. It's also possible that you'll have to pay tax because of a forced sale. Often that's a mixed blessing: you received a nice premium on your shares when Bigco swallowed the company, and that can take the sting out of being forced to pay tax you would have preferred to defer.

Despite these potential problems, the buy-and-hold strategy remains as a powerful, do-it-yourself tax shelter. It may seem like a boring way to accumulate wealth, but sometimes boring is good. There are less expensive ways to amuse yourself than paying tax on gains from stocks you didn't have to sell.

Tax Loss Harvesting

These observations lead to an overall tax strategy often called *tax loss harvesting*. In this approach, a portfolio is monitored throughout the year to detect situations where a sale of any holding will produce a tax loss worth harvesting. These sales alter the portfolio's holdings, but the effect on investment performance may be minimized by replacing the item sold with a similar investment, perhaps with the plan of switching back to the original holding after the wash sale period expires. A program of tax loss harvesting may employ guidelines as to the size of loss that will be justified in view of any transaction costs.

The idea behind this strategy is to minimize capital gains tax by maximizing capital losses. Depending on your portfolio's investment performance and your investing style, you may simply reduce your annual capital gains tax, or you may build up a capital loss carryover that will protect you from paying any tax at all on capital gains for many years to come. Computer simulations indicate that a tax loss harvesting strategy can boost after-tax returns over a simple buy-and-hold strategy by a full percentage point or more for a number of years. The benefit diminishes with the passage of time as the portfolio grows to have more built-in gains and fewer loss harvesting opportunities. Yet the effect of having boosted returns in the early years of the program can compound over time into a significantly enhanced result.

When holding periods matter

It's important to know your holding period for shares of stock and other assets you may sell for a capital gain or loss. Specifically, you need to know if the holding period is long-term and, if not, when it will become long-term. Generally speaking, if you have a gain, you want it to be long-term, and if you have a loss you want it to be short-term. Yet there are situations where the holding period doesn't matter.

> **Example 1:** Earlier in the year you had $10,000 of short-term capital gain and $10,000 of long-term capital gain. Now you're ready to sell stock at a $5,000 loss. Assuming no other transactions, you prefer to have a short-term loss, because that will net out against your short-term gain, preserving the $10,000 long-term gain that qualifies for special, lower tax rates.

> **Example 2:** Change the previous example so all your gains earlier in the year were short-term. Now it doesn't matter whether your loss is short-term or long-term. Either way, the loss will apply against your short-term gain. The holding period for the stock you sell at a loss also wouldn't matter if all your earlier gains were long-term.

> **Example 3:** Earlier in the year you had a $10,000 short-term capital loss. Now you're ready to sell stock at a $5,000 gain. Assuming no other transactions, it doesn't matter whether this gain is short-term or long-term. Either way it disappears because of the loss.

These examples show that it's useful to have a current picture of your overall capital gain and loss situation when you do tax planning for capital gains and losses. There's no point doing back flips to make sure your losses are short-term and your gains are long-term if it won't make any difference on your tax return. Of course, you might be in a situation where you don't know how your year is going to turn out, and in that case you want to make reasonable efforts to have your gains and losses fall in the proper categories.

Managing the capital loss limitation

It's important to keep the $3,000 capital loss limitation in mind if you may be reporting large losses. Remember, any unused loss carries forward but you can't carry it back to previous years.

> **Example:** Earlier in the year, you sold stock for a gain of $40,000. Another of your holdings has done poorly, and if you sell now you'll have a loss of $30,000. You don't know if you'll have gains in future years.

In this situation, you should seriously consider taking the $30,000 loss in the same year as the $40,000 gain. If you postpone that loss until a later year, perhaps hoping for the stock to recover, you may find that you end up having to deduct it at the rate of $3,000 per year—a process that will take ten years. If you sell the stock now, you can claim the entire $30,000 loss as a deduction against your $40,000 gain.

Sometimes you have to make a judgment call in a trade-off between the detriment of the $3,000 capital loss limitation and the benefit of the lower tax rate for long-term capital gains.

Example: Earlier in the year you had a long-term capital gain of $5,000. Late in the year you have stock you plan to sell at a $5,000 loss, and you have to choose which year to sell it. If you sell it this year, you'll deduct the entire $5,000 in one year, but it will reduce long-term capital gain, so the benefit will be relatively small. If you wait until next year to sell, you may have to wait two years to get the full tax benefit of this loss, but it may apply against short-term gain or ordinary income, producing a larger overall tax benefit.

Holding for qualified dividends

Before making a short-term sale of shares of stock, check to see whether you can gain tax savings from qualified dividends by holding a little longer. You need to hold the shares at least 61 days (counting the day of sale but not counting the day of purchase) to benefit from this rule.

Example: You bought shares of XYZ and received a dividend. Now you're thinking of selling, after holding the stock 57 days.

If you hold the shares just four more days, your dividend will qualify for the lower tax rate. Sell now and you'll have a nonqualified dividend that's taxed as ordinary income.

35

Tax Planning for Mutual Funds

IF YOU INVEST IN MUTUAL FUNDS, you may be able to improve your after-tax investment return by paying attention to some tax issues specific to this form of investment. In this chapter we'll look at the following:

- Allocation issues
- Investing before the annual dividend
- Tax efficiency in mutual funds

Allocation issues

Mutual fund investors face two allocation issues. One is how to allocate their investments among different types of mutual funds: stock funds, balanced funds, bond funds, money market funds, and all the variations on these themes. The other is how to allocate different types of investments between taxable accounts and retirement accounts.

Tax-advantaged funds. Some funds provide a tax advantage by holding government bonds. Tax-free bond funds may be suitable for people in higher tax brackets (32% and higher) but usually are less attractive for people in lower tax brackets. The reason is that these funds receive a lower rate of interest, relative to the risk involved, than funds that invest in taxable bonds, such as those issued by corporations. To justify this lower rate you should receive a substantial tax benefit, and your benefit is substantial only if you are in one of the higher tax brackets.

To a lesser extent the same consideration applies to funds that invest in federal securities. These funds may be able to pay dividends that are at least partly exempt from state income tax. That means they're more attractive to people who live in states that impose income tax at relatively high rates. For most people this isn't an overwhelming concern as they decide how much to invest in this type of mutual fund, but it's a point worth considering.

Taxable vs. retirement accounts. Another issue is how to allocate investments between your taxable investment account and your retirement account. The tax characteristics of these accounts are very different. You have to pay tax on income earned by the taxable account on an annual basis, even if you don't withdraw the earnings. Earnings in a Roth IRA or Roth 401k will be entirely tax-free if you follow the rules for those accounts. Other retirement accounts aren't taxable until you withdraw them—but when you do, the earnings will be ordinary income, even if they arose from capital gains within the retirement account.

These considerations make it appear that if you have investments that produce ordinary income—nonqualified dividends and interest—the best place for these investments is your retirement account. You get the significant advantage of deferring tax on these investments for an extended period of time or, in the case of Roth accounts, eliminating the tax altogether. Investments that are intended to produce mainly capital gains and qualified dividends would be held in your taxable account. Remember, you can often defer tax on your capital gains simply by continuing to hold an asset that has increased in value. When the time comes to report the capital gain, you'll pay tax at favorable rates.

There have been some studies that suggest a contrary approach. Under certain sets of assumptions, it's better to keep stocks in your retirement account and interest-bearing assets in your taxable account. The reason is that stocks have historically produced a significantly higher investment return than interest-bearing assets, so in the long run, the amount of income you're deferring in your retirement account is greater with this strategy.

I haven't examined these studies, but I'm skeptical of the result. For one thing, I don't know if the studies have been updated with today's capital gains rates. For another, there are reasons to doubt that the stock market will continue to outstrip other investments to the same extent it did in the late 1990's, when these studies took place. You need a crystal ball to know which will work out best, but I'm inclined to believe it's best to keep income-producing assets in the retirement account.

Investing before the annual dividend

As a general rule, it's better to avoid investing in a mutual fund just before it pays its annual dividend. To understand why this is so, you need a few facts about the way mutual fund dividends work.

Many regular stocks pay no dividend at all, or pay dividends quarterly. Mutual funds can pay quarterly dividends, but often pay a large dividend late in the year. The reason is that tax rules require mutual funds to pay out nearly all their earnings as dividends. Many mutual funds don't know how much earnings they have until at or near the end of their year, so that's when they pay their largest dividends (or in some cases, *all* their dividends).

When a mutual fund pays a dividend, cash flows out from the fund. That means the fund's assets are reduced, and the share price goes down. Receiving a dividend from a mutual fund doesn't make you richer. It simply changes the form of your assets.

> **Example:** You own 1,000 shares of XYZ mutual fund with a value of $20 per share. The mutual fund pays a dividend of $2 per share. After the dividend, the shares are worth $18 per share. Instead of $20,000 worth of mutual fund shares, you now have $18,000 worth of mutual fund shares and $2,000 cash.

Most people choose to reinvest their mutual fund dividends. If you made that choice, the dividend still reduces the value of the shares you hold—but is used to buy new shares. In the example above, your old shares would be worth $18,000 and you would have $2,000 worth of new shares. The end result is that you hold $20,000 worth of shares, and there's the rub: your wealth hasn't increased, yet you have to report (and pay tax on) a dividend.

Compare two investors: one who invested just before the dividend and another who invested just afterward. After the dividend, both hold $20,000 worth of shares in the mutual fund. The one who invested before the dividend is worse off, though, because she had to pay tax on the dividend.

It isn't all bad for the earlier investor. As a result of the reinvested dividend, she bought additional shares for $2,000. That means the basis for her investment is $22,000. If both investors now sell for $20,000, the one who bought before the dividend will claim a $2,000 loss. In the end, other things being equal, the two investors should come out the same.

Unfortunately, other things *aren't* equal. For one thing, the dividend may be partly or entirely ordinary income, while the loss will be a capital loss. Often, the tax benefit of a capital loss is smaller than the tax cost of reporting ordinary income. More importantly, you can't claim the tax benefit of the added basis from reinvesting a dividend until you sell your shares in the mutual fund. Normally you buy shares in a mutual fund with the intention of holding that investment for a period of time. Until you sell those shares, you're out of pocket for taxes from the unfortunate timing of buying shares shortly before the dividend.

What about selling? Does this mean you should try to time your sales so they occur just before a dividend? In most cases this isn't necessary. If you sell before the dividend, you avoid having to report the dividend but you have a larger gain (or smaller loss). These two effects will often cancel each other out.

> **Example:** Nine months ago, you invested $10,000 in XYZ mutual fund. Now your shares are worth $12,000 and the mutual fund is about to pay a $750 dividend. If you sell before the dividend, you'll report a short-term capital gain of $2,000. If you wait until after the dividend, you'll report a $750 dividend but your gain will be only $1,250, assuming no change in the mutual fund's value other than the dividend payment.

Although these effects often cancel out, there are times when you get an advantage by selling before the dividend—and other times when you're better off if you wait. In the example above, you might benefit by selling before the dividend if the mutual fund pays an ordinary dividend and you have large capital losses for the year. Because of the large capital losses, you would rather report $2,000 of capital gain, all of which will be absorbed by capital losses, than report $1,250 of capital gain and an ordinary dividend of $750.

On the other hand, it might be better to wait until after the dividend if you don't have capital losses to offset your gain. To the extent the payout consists of qualified dividends and capital gain, you'll pay a lower rate than you would on the corresponding amount of short-term capital gain from the sale.

Tax efficiency in mutual funds

Consider two different mutual funds. One pays dividends equal to 5% of share value and the other pays dividends equal to only 1% of share value. Suppose that after reinvesting the dividends, you get the same amount of growth from both funds. Which is better?

The fund that pays the smaller dividend is better. It's providing you the same amount of growth with a smaller annual tax hit. It's more *tax-efficient.*

We aren't talking here about differences between exempt bond funds and stock funds. The comparison here is between funds in the same category, especially different stock funds. There are wide variations in the tax-efficiency of stock funds based on the buying and selling patterns of the managers.

Mutual fund managers can improve the tax efficiency of their funds in various ways. When they reduce their holdings in a particular stock, they can take care to sell the highest basis shares first. They can try to avoid selling winners until the gains are long-term, or postpone gains until after the end of the year. In short, they can do many of the same things individual investors do to manage their capital gains.

Not all mutual funds pay attention to these issues, though. One reason is that many of their biggest investors are retirement plans and other nontaxable entities. These institutional investors don't care whether the mutual fund is tax-efficient, so a mutual fund manager intent on pleasing these investors won't be concerned about taxes. Another reason the manager may not focus on this issue is that even among taxable investors, most are mainly interested in the overall return of the mutual fund. Anything that can boost that return will be attractive to the manager even if it results in a higher tax bill for investors.

It's useful for you to be aware of the tax efficiency of mutual funds when choosing where to invest. Other things being equal, a more efficient fund will provide a better after-tax investment return. Here are some points to bear in mind:

Index funds. One way to classify mutual funds is to divide them between *actively managed* funds and *index* funds. In an actively managed fund, the manager attempts to choose investments that will achieve superior results. These choices may entail buying and selling activity that results in undesirable dividends. In an index fund, the manager seeks to have the fund perform the same as an index, such as the S&P 500 index. These funds sell stocks less often than actively managed funds, so they're likely to generate smaller dividends.

As a result, one way to improve the tax-efficiency of your mutual fund investments is to invest in index funds. You should be aware, though, that not all index funds are equally tax efficient. Consider what can happen in a *mid-cap fund*—a fund that invests in medium-sized companies based on their total capitalization (the value of all their stock). If one of the companies in the fund becomes highly successful, its stock price will rise and the company may "graduate" from mid-cap to large-cap. This stock will no longer be part of the index, so the mutual fund will have to sell it, creating a large gain, and a dividend for the fund's shareholders. The success of this company lifted the value of the fund, and that's good—but the sale of the shares caused the fund to pay a dividend, and that's bad.

Normally, you can expect excellent tax efficiency from broad-based index funds where the list of stocks that make up the index is relatively stable. Funds based on narrower indexes may be less tax-efficient.

Exchange-traded funds. Exchange-traded index funds, like traditional index funds, seek to match the performance of a stock index. Unlike traditional index funds, their shares trade in the stock market. It's possible that these funds will be more tax-efficient than traditional index funds in some conditions.

The reason is that if investors decide to pull money out of traditional index funds, those funds may be forced to sell shares.

Those sales may produce gains, and therefore produce unwanted dividends for the investors who remain in the fund. In an exchange-traded fund, investors who want to sell their shares don't pull their money out of the fund. Instead, they simply sell their shares in the stock market. The fund itself isn't forced to sell shares, so it won't have to create gains that result in dividends.

There's some question whether this possible advantage over traditional index funds is significant. Some people argue that the only time investors are likely to pull large amounts of money from index funds is when the stock market has performed poorly. If the stock market has declined, the index fund may be able to avoid unwanted capital gains by selling shares purchased when the stock market was at a higher level. For now, it's impossible to know whether exchange-traded funds will turn out to be significantly more tax-efficient than traditional index funds.

Tax-managed funds. Another possibility is to invest in a *tax-managed* fund. These are actively managed funds that have tax efficiency as one of their goals. The managers of these funds take tax considerations into account when deciding whether, or when, to sell shares of stock held by the fund. If you find a tax-managed fund that meets your investment objectives, there's a good chance it will be more tax-efficient than a comparable actively managed fund that isn't tax-managed.

Tax load. Some advisors suggest that you consider the *tax load* of a fund before investing. A fund that holds shares that have gone up in value a great deal has a large tax load. New investors may end up paying tax on those inherent gains when the mutual fund sells the shares. When you think about it though, the way a fund gets to have a high tax load is by investing in stocks that grow and holding those stocks for long periods of time. That's a recipe for tax-efficiency. As mutual funds like to remind their investors, past performance does not guarantee future results, and that holds for tax-efficiency as well as pre-tax returns. Yet I wonder whether a high tax load should be considered a negative in all cases, when you consider that the tax load may indicate tax-efficient operation of the fund in the past.

36

Tax Planning for Traders

Traders have some tax planning concerns—and opportunities—that don't apply to investors. In particular, they face two major strategic decisions: whether to make the mark-to-market election, and whether to conduct their trading through a corporation or other entity.

The Mark-to-Market Election

Chapter 28 explains the mark-to-market election, including potential tax consequences, both good and bad. There's no need to duplicate that material here, so we can be brief. If you aren't dealing with the situation where the mark-to-market election will deprive you of the potential to use a large carryover of capital loss from a prior year, chances are that mark-to-market is a good choice. This is only a rule of thumb, though, so you should consider all the tax consequences in light of your own circumstances. If you're uncertain, find a tax pro who knows trader taxation and discuss your particular situation.

> Be sure to focus on the unusual deadline for this election and allow enough time for consultation and thoughtful consideration.

Corporations and other entities

Traders often wonder if they should form a corporation, partnership or limited liability company (LLC) for their trading business. Doing so may have a positive or negative effect on your tax situation. For most people I don't think the benefits outweigh the costs unless you also have nontax reasons for making this move.

In the discussion that follows I'll focus on corporations. You can't form a partnership with just a single owner, and if you're going into a trading business with a partner you should work with a lawyer to structure your business and not rely on a few words from this book. As for limited liability companies, in most states it's possible to form an LLC with a single member, but the tax law completely disregards single-member LLCs. In other words, if you're the sole owner of an LLC, you're treated the same as if the LLC didn't exist and you directly held the assets of the LLC and carried on its activities.

That's not true of corporations. The tax law doesn't disregard a corporation that has a single owner. If you form a corporation for your trading business, your tax situation is likely to change. The question is whether that change is a good one.

C corporations and S corporations. For tax purposes, corporations come in two different flavors. Both are formed the same way under state law. The difference is simply a matter of filing an election with the IRS. If you file this election, your corporation is an *S corporation*; if not, you have a *C corporation.*

Large corporations with familiar names like Microsoft and McDonald's are always C corporations. Yet even a small corporation owned by a single person can be a C corporation. This type of corporation isn't well suited for a trading business, though. The main reason is that if your trading is very successful, you may end up paying double tax on some of your earnings: the corporation will pay tax at 21%, and you'll pay additional tax on what's left when you receive it as a dividend. There are strategies for avoiding double tax, but no way to completely remove the risk of ending up in that situation. I would be reluctant to recommend a C corporation for a trader.

Some traders may want to consider forming an S corporation, though. This approach has advantages and disadvantages, and on the whole I suspect most people are better off without the expense and paperwork of maintaining a corporation. If you're interested in this approach, here are some of the main points to consider.

Flow-through taxation. For tax purposes, an S corporation is treated as a "flow-through" entity. That means any tax consequences of the corporation end up on your tax return. If the corporation has a short-term capital gain, *you* have a short-term capital gain. As a general rule, the corporation itself doesn't pay federal income tax. This is why the double taxation issue mentioned above for C corporations doesn't apply to S corporations.

Trader status. I've heard the suggestion that it's easier to qualify for trader status if you form a corporation. Forming an entity may show a seriousness of purpose that helps in that regard. In the end, though, your claim to trader status will rest on satisfaction of the trading activity and substantial activity tests described in Chapters 25 and 26.

You are not a trader. If you form a corporation to carry on a trading business, *you* are not a trader. The corporation is a trader. You are the owner of the corporation and also a person (most likely the only person) who works for the company. This fact has important implications as follows.

Because you work for the company you set up, you can be an employee. The company will pay you wages for your services, and those wages can be the basis for contributions to a retirement plan.

This is one of the most important benefits a trader may obtain by setting up a corporation. Normally, a trader can't establish a retirement plan because trading income doesn't qualify for this treatment, even if the trader makes the mark-to-market election.

There's a flip side to this benefit, however. Traders don't have to pay self-employment tax on their trading profits. Yet any amounts your corporation pays as wages for your services will be subject to social security tax. Half of this tax is withheld from your pay and the corporation pays the other half, but you own the corporation so in reality you bear all the cost. The tax is substantial. Depending on the amount of earnings, you may pay $10,000 or more additional tax by reason of operating a corporation that pays you wages.

It gets worse. Generally speaking, if you own an S corporation, you can control the amount of wages you receive from your own company. You can choose to retain some of the profits in the corporation or receive them in the form of *distributions* instead of wages, avoiding social security tax on those amounts. Yet if you "pay yourself" too little, the IRS can challenge that result, saying a corporation with earnings that high should have paid a higher wage to its employee-owner. The IRS sometimes uses this argument to collect more social security tax from S corporations and their owners.

There's an advantage to paying social security tax: the more you pay, the higher the benefit you'll qualify for when you retire. Yet most people given the choice of paying $10,000 less in tax for the current year wouldn't hesitate to pay the lower tax, thank you very much. If you consider whether to form an S corporation for your trading business, you need to consider carefully whether the advantages outweigh the cost of this additional tax.

Mark-to-market. There's one other advantage in operating a trading business through a corporation. An individual can make the mark-to-market election only in the first months of the year. If you begin trading after April 15, you have to wait until the next year to make the election. The main cause for concern here is that your trading may produce a loss in the first year. If you don't have the mark-to-market election in place, that loss will be subject to the $3,000 capital loss limitation.

If you form a corporation for your trading business, the corporation can make the election within two months and fifteen days after the start of its first tax year. In the case of a corporation, the election is not filed with the IRS. You make the election by entering it on the books and records of the corporation. Be sure to document this action in a way that leaves no doubt that you acted within the specified time.

> **Example:** You begin your trading business in August. If you don't form a corporation or other entity, you won't be able to make the mark-to-market election until the following year. Losses you have before January 1 of the next year will be capital losses. If you form a corporation for your trading business, you can make the election effective immediately.

Bear in mind that if you incur losses *before* forming the corporation, those losses will still be capital losses. The mark-to-market election will apply only to assets and transactions of the corporation.

Only you can judge whether the benefits described above justify the cost and paperwork of forming and maintaining a corporation. In my experience, only a small percentage of stock traders want to work through a corporation.

Index

U

W

Printed in Dunstable, United Kingdom

82676335R00188